IFRITAH!

Alma's heart called out the name of her mid-class contract spirit, and a giant lion-shaped beast appeared out of thin air.

Seirei Gensouki: Spirit Chronicles

"AMAKAWA-SENPAI."

"IT'S A LITTLE EMBARRASSING TO BE CALLED THAT."

Liselotte giggled, feeling that their relationship had deepened. Rio felt the same way.

Seirei Gensouki:
Spirit Chronicles

"BYE-BYE, HARUTO."

Aishia smiled gently and chuckled cutely. She wasn't her usually emotionally detached self, but a young woman with a vivid range of emotions.

Seirei Gensouki: Spirit Chronicles

Omnibus 10

Yuri Kitayama
Illustrator • Riv

Seirei Gensouki: Spirit Chronicles Omnibus 10
by Yuri Kitayama

Translated by Mana Z.
Edited by Joi
English Cover by Kai Kyou

Originally published as Seirei Gensouki: Spirit Chronicles Vol. 19 & 20
Copyright © 2021 Yuri Kitayama
Illustrations by Riv

First published in Japan in 2021 by Hobby Japan.
Publication rights for this English edition arranged through Hobby Japan, Tokyo.

Find more books like this one at https://j-novel.club!

Managing Director: Samuel Pinansky
Light Novel Line Manager: Kristine Johnson
Managing Translator: Kristi Iwashiro
Managing Editor: Regan Durand
QA Manager: Hannah N. Carter
Marketing Manager: Stephanie Hii
Project Manager: Nikki Lapshinoff

ISBN: 978-1-7183-2889-1
Printed in Korea
First Printing: October 2023
10 9 8 7 6 5 4 3 2 1

Contents

Seirei Gensouki: Spirit Chronicles

Volume 19

Tachi of Wind

Yuri Kitayama
Illustrator • Riv

Flora Beltrum
Second Princess of the Beltrum Kingdom. Finally reunited with her older sister, Christina.

Christina Beltrum
First Princess of the Beltrum Kingdom. Protected by Rio, together with Flora.

Sendo Takahisa
Aki and Masato's brother from their original world. Currently the hero of the Centostella Kingdom.

Sakata Hiroaki
A hero from another world. Operates with the support of Duke Huguenot.

Shigekura Rui
A high school student from another world. The hero of the Beltrum Kingdom.

Kikuchi Renji
One of the heroes from another world. An adventurer unaffiliated with any kingdom, until...

Liselotte Cretia
Noblewoman from the Galarc Kingdom and president of the Ricca Guild. She was a high school student named Minamoto Rikka in her past life.

Aria Governess
Liselotte's head attendant and an enchanted sword wielder. Has been friends with Celia since their academy days.

Sumeragi Satsuki
Miharu's friend from their original world. Currently the hero of the Galarc Kingdom.

Charlotte Galarc
Second Princess of the Galarc Kingdom. Shows strong affection towards Haruto.

Reiss
A mysterious man pulling the strings behind the scenes. Wary of Rio for always disrupting his plans.

Sakuraba Erika
The woman who caused a revolution in a minor nation. Is hiding her identity as a hero.

Rio (Haruto Amakawa)

The main character of this story; he lives to avenge his mother's murder. Currently traveling as "Haruto" due to his arrest warrant issued in the Beltrum Kingdom. In his previous life, he was a Japanese university student named Amakawa Haruto.

Aishia

Rio's contract spirit who calls him Haruto. A rare humanoid spirit with missing memories.

Celia Claire

Noblewoman from the Beltrum Kingdom. A genius sorcerer and Rio's former academy teacher.

Latifa

A werefox girl from the spirit folk village. In her previous life, she was an elementary school student named Endo Suzune.

Sara

A silver werewolf girl from the spirit folk village. Currently traveling with Rio to study the outside world and broaden her horizons.

Alma

An elder dwarf girl from the spirit folk village. Currently traveling with Rio to study the outside world and broaden her horizons.

Orphia

A high elf girl from the spirit folk village. Currently traveling with Rio to study the outside world and broaden her horizons.

Ayase Miharu

A high school student from another world. Haruto's childhood friend and first love.

Sendo Aki

A middle school student from another world. Feels resentment towards her half-brother Haruto.

Sendo Masato

An elementary school student from another world. Currently under the protection of Rio, along with Miharu and Aki.

CHARACTER INTRODUCTION

Contents

⚜ Prologue ⚜

In front of a thick and overgrown forest, far from human civilization…

Liselotte and Aria had been carried several kilometers away from the capital of the Holy Democratic Republic of Erica by Aishia. The intense battle between Rio and the divine beast was so fierce, they could observe it even this far from the capital.

However, with the naked eye, they could only see the large-scale attacks at this distance. They could just make out Rio evading the light beams when they used a physical ability enhancement to boost their vision, but the larger attacks had stopped a few minutes ago. The sky was a clear blue right now.

Aishia had returned to Rio just a short while ago. While they had succeeded in retrieving Liselotte, the mood in the air was anything but celebratory.

"…"

Liselotte and Aria both gazed at the capital with bated breath; they remained that way for some time.

"It seems they've returned."

"Oh…!"

Aria spotted Aishia first, approaching from afar with Rio in her arms. One beat later, Liselotte saw them as well. She started running to shorten the distance between them as much as possible, with Aria following her.

The distance between them was soon closed, and Aishia landed before the two of them. Rio lay limply in her arms.

"Aishia! Is Sir Haruto okay?!" Liselotte said in a panic, panting for breath as she worried for Rio's well-being. She leaned right into his unconscious face and stared at him.

"He's fine. His life is not in danger," Aishia informed her plainly. "But…"

There were red stains by his mouth, as though he had coughed up blood. He had been injured enough in the battle to render him unconscious—that was more than enough reason for her to remain concerned. He had to be allowed to rest right away. And in order to reassure Liselotte…

"Yeah, I want to let Haruto rest." Aishia's voice was usually monotonous, but she nodded firmly and laid Rio on the ground. She then started pushing her magic essence into the ground, preparing the foundations for the stone house. Small stones on the ground sank into the dirt, and the lumpy terrain flattened in the blink of an eye.

"…"

Aria was familiar with the sight from her travels with Rio, but Liselotte's eyes widened seeing it for the first time. That being said, there were more important matters to address right now, so she merely looked on with apologetic impatience.

Ignoring Liselotte, Aishia picked up Rio's arm. It was the arm with a bracelet; the Time-Space Cache was attached, but it could only be activated by the person with the registered essence wavelength. A maximum of two people could be registered. The armband Rio normally used had Celia's essence wavelength in the other slot, so Aishia wasn't registered, but…

"*Dissolvo.*"

Aishia uttered the spell and activated the Time-Space Cache. It was a feat only possible because Aishia was contracted to Rio and had his magic essence flowing through her. "Come in," she said.

"Okay."

Aishia picked Rio up gently and started walking towards the newly installed stone house. Out of her worry for Rio, Liselotte dashed for the entrance before Aria to open the door for them.

"You two should rest here. I'm going to look after Haruto."

The first thing Aishia did after entering the stone house was, of course, tend to Rio. She gave Liselotte and Aria directions to wait in the living room, then made for the back of the house with the unconscious Rio in her arms. However, the two of them weren't about to sit down obediently.

"U-Umm, is there anything I can help with?" Liselotte asked after Aishia's back, her face filled with regret.

"His clothes are stained with blood, so I'm going to change them and wipe him clean." Aishia stated her intentions as though she was open to receiving help.

"If you're going to wipe him, you'll need to take him to the bathroom. I'll get the tub and towels ready first." Aria had stayed in the house for the entire journey to the Holy Democratic Republic of Erica, so she knew where everything was located. She went first into the changing room that connected to the bathroom.

"You come too, Liselotte."

"Okay!"

Aishia started walking with Liselotte. Aria had already retrieved towels and washing agents from the shelf and was opening the door to the bathroom. There, she fiddled with the magic artifacts attached to the washing area to start filling a tub with warm water.

"I'll support him while you remove his coat and shirt," Aishia said to Liselotte.

"Okay." Liselotte lifted Rio's arms gently and removed his coat first. Next, Aishia held Rio's arms up high while Liselotte took his shirt off too. Rio's upper body entered their view.

As a noblewoman, Liselotte had never seen a naked man in her life—not even her father, Duke Cretia—but now was not the time to worry about that. And yet...

"Uh..."

Liselotte stared at Rio's naked body from up close and swallowed her breath. It wasn't because his body was firmer than she had imagined, but...

"These wounds..."

She stared at the countless small scars he had.

"They're not wounds from the battle with the Saint, so don't worry. They're old scars from his childhood. They're all healed already," Aishia said to reassure her.

"I see..." Liselotte's expression didn't brighten. If wounds were treated with magic before they healed, then no scars would be left behind. The fact these old scars remained meant that Rio hadn't received any magic treatment when he suffered those wounds.

Even then, light wounds would naturally disappear over time, yet Rio's body was covered in clearly distorted scars. An unobservant eye might have dismissed them as battle wounds, but Liselotte's eye was unfortunately observant. She suspected they were scars from some kind of torture or abuse.

"…" Aria squeezed the water out of the towel in her hand and stared closely at Rio's body. But while Liselotte's expression was pained with her grief, Aria had an odd look on her face.

"Is something wrong?" Aishia asked, looking at the two of them curiously.

"No… Please use this towel." Aria shook her head slowly and offered Liselotte the damp towel.

"Right." Liselotte accepted the towel and began to wipe gently at Rio's mouth, which was dirtied with blood and spit.

Sir Haruto… Sir Haruto…

Tears welled in her eyes, but her hand never stopped moving. She was worrying so earnestly for Rio, who had gotten wounded for her sake, that the affectionate movement of her hands appeared to be shaking.

"If we're just removing the blood clots, then there should be no need to remove his pants. I'll wash the dirty coat and shirt."

Aria picked up Rio's coat and shirt and began to wash them.

❖ Chapter 1 ❖
One Act Before Trouble

Some time later, in the mountainous outskirts of the Galarc capital...

Orphia, the high elf girl, stood at a location with a fine view several kilometers from the capital of Galtuuk. There was no one else around her; she was moving separately from Miharu and the others in the royal castle in order to set up a destination point for teleportation sorcery.

The first step was to select a location. Barely anyone ever climbed this mountain, but she still had to use spirit arts to stabilize the terrain and secure the area. She put up a perception-blocking barrier and a field to conceal the disorder of magic essence after teleporting. There were a lot of steps, but she was finally done.

"Okay, the spell circle is stable and the barriers are complete... Now, *Dissolvo.*"

Just like how there were two stone houses, there were two Time-Space Caches. Orphia used hers to take out the teleport crystal she had borrowed from Rio in advance.

The destination registered in the crystal was the spirit folk village. Now that the preparations were complete, she had no need to remain here anymore. She would return to the village to bring Gouki and the others here to Galarc.

With Rio gone to retrieve Liselotte, she wouldn't be able to bring them to the castle immediately, so they'd have to remain in the stone house until his return. But the original plan was to bring Gouki's group over as soon as the preparations in Strahl were complete, so Gouki and the others were still waiting for that to happen.

"*Instans Motus.*" Orphia chanted a spell, activating the teleport crystal. The space around her immediately distorted—a sign of the sorcery activating. Just before she teleported, Orphia glanced over at the capital of Galtuuk. Then, just before the spell completed and moved her to the village, the sight of countless black shapes raining down on the capital caught her eyes.

"Wha…?"

The teleportation completed: what filled Orphia's view now was the sight of the forest and spring near the spirit folk village. The scenery was extremely peaceful, but…

"What…was that…?"

Orphia's face stiffened at the sinister omen she'd just witnessed.

"…"

She had a bad feeling about this. Propelled by her intuition, Orphia hurried towards the village.

At roughly the same time, in the capital of the Beltrum Kingdom, Celia's father, Count Roland Claire, was visiting the royal castle. He had been personally summoned by Duke Arbor himself.

"What matters did you wish to discuss today?" Roland asked after they had exchanged curt greetings with each other in a meeting room.

"Negotiations with the Restoration will be held in the near future. The location will be the Galarc Kingdom. I'd like you to attend, Count Claire," Duke Arbor said, stating his demands simply.

"I see... But why me?" Roland feigned confusion as he sought more information.

After being suspected of assisting Christina out of the castle, he was essentially treated as a spy by Duke Arbor's faction. There was no concrete evidence to convict him, but he had been relieved of his position in the capital and placed under the watch of a dispatch supervisor while managing the affairs of his territory. He had also been cut off from any news of the capital, so Roland wanted to use this chance to gain as much information as he could.

"You should have a lot of contacts with that side, no?" Duke Arbor said with blunt implication behind his words.

"Ha ha... I don't think so." Roland tried to brush off the question with a shrug.

"Your beloved daughter seems to have settled over there." Duke Arbor pointed out how Celia, who was supposed to have been kidnapped from the wedding ceremony with Charles, was now a member of the Restoration.

Naturally, Duke Arbor was aware that Celia's abduction had been arranged by Christina, who felt indebted to her from her academy days and wanted her to join the Restoration. Like the spies in Beltrum working for Duke Huguenot, there were spies in the Restoration working for Duke Arbor and keeping him informed.

"I was also bewildered by that news." Roland sighed to express his lack of knowledge regarding Celia's abduction.

Duke Arbor furrowed his brow at the sly reaction. "There's no mistake that your daughter has settled over there. I have contacts who have seen her in person."

"So it appears. I will not deny that it seems she has joined the Restoration," Roland said, implying that he had objections to other accusations.

Duke Arbor looked at Roland with suspicion, but he knew it was futile to make accusations without any evidence—it had been as such since Christina first escaped Beltrum Castle.

He had no intention of digging further into either that or the connection between Roland and the Restoration. Duke Arbor chose to get on with the discussion. "Fine. In which case, it should be clear why your presence is requested."

"However, I cannot imagine my presence making any difference. Are you saying you want me to attend just for numbers?"

Surely not, Roland implied in his tone as he tried to probe for more information from Duke Arbor.

"That's right." Duke Arbor nodded dismissively, preemptively cutting off any questions Roland could lead him towards.

He probably wanted to avoid giving Roland any unnecessary information, but his attitude could also be interpreted as that of a successful veteran soldier who loathed the bothersome tactics of civil officials. At any rate, probing any further against such an attitude would be like stirring the hornet's nest for Roland.

"I see… I have no reason to refuse, then."

Considering how unbalanced the relations were between Duke Arbor and Roland, there was no choice but to accept. He'd also be able to hear the state of affairs himself if he attended, so Roland obediently accepted without a fight.

"Then it's decided. The negotiations will be held in the near future. I will send a messenger to your territory once the date is confirmed. I doubt I need to say this, but keep your schedule open."

Duke Arbor stood up, indicating the end of their discussion. He made sure to add a snide remark about Roland's lack of duties in the capital as well. Making Roland travel all the way out to the capital for a message like this was also a clear act of harassment, but Roland showed no particular irritation.

"Understood. I shall take my leave after finishing this cup of tea," he said, picking up his teacup and sipping it gracefully.

"Hmph." Duke Arbor snorted in disgust and left the room.

What Duke Arbor fears the most right now is nobles outside of his faction regaining power, but... Roland returned his teacup to its saucer and lost himself in his thoughts.

The Arbor family's power had definitely lessened after Celia's abduction from Charles's wedding and Christina's escape from the castle.

At the same time, there was a definite lack of anyone who could stand up to the Arbor faction in the present capital. Everyone had either been expelled from the capital and joined the Restoration, or had been removed from their positions like Roland and lost power. So while there were signs of the Arbor faction's decline, with no other force that could oppose them in the capital, their position was as strong as ever. The other nobles that pandered to Duke Arbor also received favorable treatment without Duke Huguenot's faction around, so they had no reason to risk their positions by stirring things up.

Considering how he's going to negotiate with the Restoration on equal terms—with me of all people present—he must be rather worried about his son being held hostage. Attending the negotiations is exactly what I wished for. I must use this chance to gain as much information as possible. I may even be able to see my little Celia.

Roland's expression softened.

Celia... It seems she arrived in Rodania safely, but is she really happy over there? Her happiness...

But at the same time, he felt lonely. His expression became gloomy.

Well, I'm sure I can leave her in Princess Christina's hands. And with that boy nearby, she should be well protected...

He recalled Rio, who had escorted Christina and Celia to Rodania. He had been worried half to death when Celia was abducted from the wedding, but those emotions had been replaced with true gratitude when he was told the truth of what had happened.

He understood that Celia trusted Rio. And that Celia had feelings for him.

Guh. There's no doubt that she feels for him...

Now that he had caught on to his beloved daughter's thoughts, he wanted nothing more than to support her happiness. This was the genuine truth, but a father's parental love was complex.

What if in my absence, they...? I won't allow it. I definitely won't allow it... They must marry first with me in attendance, at the very least... No, but there'd be no chance to hold a wedding in this situation... Even so, if he touches her before marriage... Or after marriage... Ah, but I do want to see my grandchildren's faces. Hm. Hmm...

Roland lost himself to a spiral of negative thoughts. The only thing he could say for certain was—

I won't forgive him if he makes Celia cry.

That much was simple.

What should I do if he makes her cry...? A demonstration of our family's secret magic would be required at the very least...

Seriousness aside, Roland cared for Celia more than anyone else. Yet, at this moment, there was no way for him to know about the evil that was approaching his beloved daughter.

✦ Chapter 2 ✦
Ambush

A short while before Orphia returned to the spirit folk village, some important guests were visiting Rio's mansion on the Galarc Castle grounds.

"It's been a while, Princess Christina, Princess Flora."

They were Beltrum Kingdom's First and Second Princess and the current Restoration leaders, Christina and Flora.

"Long time no see, Professor Celia."

"It's so nice to see you again!"

The two of them greeted Celia happily.

"You too. I'm so happy seeing you two again. It must have been a tiring trip here."

"Not at all. Thank you for agreeing to see us on such short notice," Christina said with a bow.

Second Princess Charlotte of the Galarc Kingdom was also there, but in Rio's absence, Celia's relationship with Christina and Flora made her best suited as host. Miharu and the other girls didn't have any experience dealing with the noble class either, so she was the only option other than Charlotte.

Charlotte's knight Louise and Christina's knight Vanessa were waiting with the other guards outside the room.

"Unfortunately, Haruto is absent right now…"

"I would have liked to express my gratitude to Sir Amakawa, but the main purpose of my visit today concerns you, Professor Celia."

Celia looked puzzled. "Me?"

"Yes. I've already informed Princess Charlotte—or rather, the Galarc Kingdom is already aware—but a meeting between the Restoration and the main Beltrum Kingdom will be held in the near future," Christina said with a glance at Charlotte.

"That's..."

"Starting with your wedding ceremony, Duke Arbor has had a string of failures to address. Charles and Alfred were taken prisoner, and I was able to escape and join the Restoration. I'm sure he's quite panicked about it, as he has approached us for negotiations."

"Has the ironclad Arbor family finally started losing its power?"

"It would appear so."

At present, over a thousand of Beltrum Kingdom's nobles had joined the Restoration, including spouses and children. But that was still a minority compared to the number of nobles the Arbor faction controlled in Beltrum. And in noble society politics, the size of the faction meant everything. That was why Duke Huguenot's faction was unable to justify themselves and had lost their place in the capital.

However, power was an uncertain substance in noble society. This was because only a small fraction of the nobles in a faction were invested too deeply to back out—most nobles in the faction were able to switch sides to their convenience as circumstances changed.

In fact, many of the nobles in Duke Huguenot's faction had joined Duke Arbor when his territory was lost to the Proxia Empire.

"We can't let this opportunity slip through our hands, then."

Duke Arbor's failures could be used to regain those drifting nobles. Their distance from the capital made it difficult to physically contact those nobles, but Duke Arbor's power was definitely weakening. If he was the one approaching for negotiations, they'd be able to turn things in their favor.

"We're still in the midst of discussing our agenda for the negotiations, but they've requested the return of Charles and Alfred, as well as Alfred's enchanted sword."

Charles was Duke Arbor's heir, and Alfred was the strongest knight in the country. The sword he used, the Light Blade of Judgment, was also a national treasure.

"They're all powerful cards for negotiation."

"Yes. And they were all given to us by Sir Amakawa. I wanted to thank him once again for his assistance, but... It seems like things are rather serious over here. I heard Sir Amakawa headed out to rescue Lady Liselotte."

Christina was acquainted with Liselotte herself and sometimes kept in contact with her. Her expression clouded with worry.

"Sir Haruto will definitely bring Liselotte back to us," Charlotte stated firmly, her posture upright and confident.

"Yes," Celia agreed.

"That's true. If it's Sir Amakawa..." Christina nodded, biting back her words. She had witnessed his talents and strength up close and personal during the battle with Lucius in the Paladia Kingdom, which was why she believed in Rio as well.

"That's right! Sir Haruto can definitely do it!" Flora said.

"I don't know when he will return, but I will send a message out to you when he does," Celia said cheerfully to Christina, hoping to wipe the gloomy expression from her face.

"Perhaps I can visit again when he returns with Lady Liselotte. We plan on staying in the Galarc Castle for a while."

"Oh, really?"

"Yes. The meeting with the Beltrum Kingdom will almost certainly be held at the Galarc Castle, so the plan is to remain here until then."

"In that case, we should hold a small party once Sir Haruto returns with Liselotte. I'll be sure to invite the two of you," Charlotte suggested after listening to their conversation.

"Oh, that would be lovely. Please do!" Flora immediately leapt at the chance, but—

"Flora." Christina let out an exasperated warning as a reminder to restrain herself in the residence of a foreign noble.

"Oh, but only if it isn't a bother to you…" Flora added with a blush, ashamed of her behavior.

"Neither a sleepover nor a dinner party will be any bother, so please don't feel reserved," Celia said with a giggle, looking at her fondly.

Charlotte agreed with a cheeky but charming grin. "Indeed. I have no right to speak as someone half-living in this house out of everyone's kindness, but please come over."

She had succeeded in accompanying Satsuki to Rio's mansion at every possible occasion until she had practically taken up residence there herself, but she also acted as King Francois's messenger and the main point of contact for any nobles who wanted to get closer to Rio.

Whenever something was required, Charlotte would make the necessary arrangements at the speed of light. She did all her work, sometimes in unseen places, and had won over Rio's trust enough for the residents of the mansion to accept her. There was even a room for her in the mansion.

"Thank you very much. Then, if you don't mind…" Christina bowed, accepting the offer.

"Then it's decided. Everyone will be delighted to have you there. They were wondering how the two of you have been doing," Charlotte said to Christina and Flora.

"If there's still time after this, we can invite them all over here," Celia said.

Miharu and the others were inside the mansion, but had excused themselves from the meeting when they heard the visit was for official business with Celia. Only Orphia was elsewhere outside, but she would have come right away if invited as well.

"We wanted to greet everyone as well, so if you're not too busy... We're almost done with what we wanted from Professor Celia too."

"Is there still something you needed from me?"

"Yes, as a continuation from earlier. If the circumstances suit you, would you be willing to attend the meeting with the Beltrum Kingdom?"

"Me...?" Celia blinked.

"In exchange for returning Charles, I am thinking of demanding several conditions that would benefit Count Claire and the rest of your family."

"Could I ask the reason why...?" Celia asked hesitantly, shocked at the sudden proposal.

"It hasn't been officially announced to the Beltrum Kingdom, but even they've noticed that you joined the Restoration after being abducted from your wedding ceremony. Count Claire was also suspected of having assisted my escape from the capital. As long as we have Charles, they wouldn't dare to touch Count Claire, but..."

If the situation changed, the Claire family could be in danger.

"At any rate, there's no doubt that the Claire family has taken the brunt of all these events. The upper ranks of the Restoration have agreed that it would be proper to compensate him."

That's why there was nothing to worry about, Christina implied.

Celia bowed her head in deep sincerity. "Thank you for considering my family."

"Not at all," Christina said, continuing the discussion. "We're still reviewing what kind of conditions should be requested, but…"

It was at that moment.

Boom.

An explosion roared, shaking the room.

"What was that? Some kind of magic training?"

Celia immediately went to look out the window, followed by the others in the room. The booming sounds continued even as they moved. The source of the sound appeared to be scattered in various directions, some near and some far.

"No, it's too loud to be coming from the training grounds of the castle. I believe the sound is either coming from the castle or somewhere nearby," Charlotte guessed undauntedly, looking out the window.

After a short time, the sounds stopped.

"Excuse us for entering."

Charlotte's head guard Louise and the Beltrum sisters' head guard Vanessa came into the room. They had both been waiting outside the door, so they naturally heard the noises as well. They both wore the same grim expressions.

"Can you tell what's going on?" Charlotte asked Louise.

"No. I haven't received any notice of an event that would create such noises either. The only option I can think of is magic training, but the sound came from too close by for that. I also saw something black fall from the sky through the window. I've sent my subordinates to check on the situation, and they'll be back as soon as they know."

"I see. In that case, shall we remain waiting in this mansion?"

"Yes. I've asked the guards who accompanied us to the mansion to station themselves outside. But please relocate to the safe room just in case."

The safe room was a place for important figures to evacuate to in times of emergency. The level of refuge varied depending on the type of emergency likely to occur, but they were all made to be secure from outside attack.

This mansion was located on castle grounds, so the castle served as the evacuation point in true times of emergency. Thus, the safe room here was only a simple one.

"All right. Let's group up with Lady Satsuki and the others first," Charlotte immediately decided.

"We're coming in, Char."

Just then, with Satsuki in the lead, she, Miharu, Latifa, Sara, and Alma entered the room where they were holding their meeting. They must have heard the unnatural explosions and felt the abnormal air, as they all had worried looks on their faces. Sara and Alma even held their weapons just in case.

"You heard that loud noise earlier?" Satsuki asked.

"Yup. We don't normally hear something like that around here, so we were shocked..." Miharu replied.

"We're not sure of the situation either, but we were going to go to the safe room just in case. The knights have gone to check things out. Will you come with us?"

"I see... And yes, please."

Satsuki exchanged a look with Miharu and nodded. At this point, there was still no clear danger, so there was no real sense of urgency yet, but...

"R-Reporting! A group of monsterlike creatures has descended upon the castle!"

"Wha…?"

One of Charlotte's knights came running in a panic, heightening the tension.

"Calm down. What do you mean by monsterlike creatures? Are they not goblins or orcs?" Louise asked her subordinate calmly. Powerful monsters like minotaurs had been commonplace in the Divine War that took place a thousand years ago, but goblins and orcs were the only monsters left in the modern era. There were some exceptions to that rule, but not even adventurers that worked in monster subjugation encountered them very often. Most of them reached retirement without ever seeing a different kind of monster.

"I only saw the knights fighting from afar, but their movements were much faster than those of a goblin or orc. I've never seen such a monster before. Their shapes were rather humanoid, but the ferocious expressions on their faces were monstrous. Some had gray skin while others had black skin," the knight reported.

"Huh…?" Miharu looked shocked, and Satsuki noticed.

"I see. Any information about their numbers and locations?"

"I'm sorry, I prioritized my return to the mansion… However, they appear to have fallen across the grounds. There are battles taking place everywhere."

Louise didn't seem to have noticed the change in Miharu, so Satsuki waited for the subordinate to finish speaking. "What's wrong, Miharu?" she asked, bringing everyone's attention to her.

"Oh, umm. When I first came to this world, some strange monsters appeared on the outskirts of Amande. Haruto and Ai-chan exterminated them, but they weren't goblins or orcs. Maybe they're the same monsters that appeared here?"

"I remember seeing the same monsters during the attack on Amande. They weren't as strong as minotaurs, but they were fast and powerful," Celia recalled with a frown. "It would take at least a knight with enhanced physical abilities to take them on…"

"I was there too." Flora proceeded to give her account of what she had witnessed when she was kidnapped by Lucius in Amande.

"I see… We can't say for sure, but it's very likely that they're the same monsters. The knights have thankfully intercepted them, but any monsters they miss could slip through to this mansion. We will secure the surroundings, so please head to the safe room immediately, Your Highness," Louise urged.

"I understand," Charlotte said. She then turned to the group. "Princess Christina, Princess Flora, please come with me. Lady Satsuki and everyone else too."

"We will assist the guards outside," Sara offered. At present, she and Alma were the strongest in the mansion, but…

"Oh… That's…" Louise hesitated. She sparred with Sara and Alma on a daily basis so she knew their strength firsthand, but the two of them were still subjects of her guard.

"Alma and I have the role of protecting Miharu and the others in Haruto's absence. There is no need to include us as subjects of protection. It'd be easier for us to move around outside than to have no information locked inside."

"Well, that's how it is. You don't need to worry about Sara and me."

Sara and Alma were both calm, as though they were familiar with such situations.

"…"

Satsuki looked like she was about to say something, but swallowed her words. *I will protect this mansion as well*—those

39

were the words on the tip of her tongue, but she became uneasy. She understood her position as hero and feared her lack of combat experience would make her a hindrance.

Charlotte noticed Satsuki moving her mouth and purposefully gave Louise a push without looking at Satsuki. "Then we shall rely on you. There aren't enough people in this mansion right now, and you two are probably the strongest with your enchanted swords."

"Understood. We shall rely on you." Louise bowed her head at Sara and Alma.

Sara turned around. "Latifa, you stay with Satsuki and Miharu. We're counting on you to protect them if the need arises."

"Okay! Leave it to me!" Latifa nodded firmly in agreement.

"Umm, I'm going to go with the two of them," Celia stated.

"Huh?"

Everyone looked at her in surprise.

"Monsters drop enchanted gems and disappear when defeated, and you need someone on that side to confirm they're the same monsters that appeared in Amande last time. I can cast healing magic if needed, and it would be useful to have a sorcerer in the back line. I've also trained with Sara and Alma in team fighting before," Celia said, explaining herself to convince Christina and Charlotte more than Sara and Alma.

"While we would be most grateful to have a sorcerer of your caliber on the back line... There's no need to expose yourself to danger like that." Charlotte gave Celia a searching look as though to confirm the truth of her thoughts. Nobles who didn't pursue military careers still went through some form of combat training, so she knew that Celia had basic fighting skills.

Because of that, it wasn't unusual for them to join the battlefield when needed—in fact, it was seen as one of the duties of the noble class. However, it depended on the time and place. In the current situation, there was only a slight chance of a monster being missed by the knights. It'd be preferable to keep a count's daughter protected rather than to have her fight.

"I'd like to do what I can in Haruto's absence," Celia replied calmly and clearly. Her intentions were evident on her face—that she wanted to fight, that she didn't always have to be protected, that Haruto could rely on her if he needed to.

"We're familiar with Celia's magic skills, and it would be most reassuring to have her support," Sara added in approval.

"I see... In that case, it would be insensitive of me to stop you," Charlotte accepted in a slightly envious tone, glancing at Christina. Although Celia was currently Rio's assistant, she was still a noble of the Restoration. Christina's opinion also mattered.

"I will leave it to your discretion, Professor," Christina said, nodding.

"Thank you very much. Let's do this, Sara, Alma."

"Right."

Sara and Alma were both warriors. Since they'd started living with Celia, they understood her intentions well—and so they nodded firmly.

Beside them, Louise was discussing how to proceed with Vanessa.

"Please go with the princesses and guard the safe room."

"Understood."

"In that case, everyone should head through this door that's connected to the safe room. I will station several knights in this drawing room just in case."

With the necessary arrangements done, Louise pointed to a different door from the exit. There were three safe rooms in the mansion, and one of them was located in the drawing room for the sake of important guests.

Thus, the residents of the mansion split into those taking refuge in the safe room and those going outside to stand guard.

Around the same time, a man floated in the skies above the capital, looking down at the castle grounds below him. It was the perpetrator behind the release of monsters across the grounds— Reiss himself. Less than an hour ago, he had been observing the fierce battle between Rio and Saint Erica from afar, but he had used a disposable teleport crystal to move to the Galarc Castle in an instant.

At present, the noncombatants of the castle were panicking while the knights fought the revenants throughout the castle grounds.

The first movement after sending out my precious magic-sealing orbs and revenants. Hopefully it'll be enough to smoke someone out… Oh?

Reiss narrowed his eyes. His gaze fixed onto a single point from far above. It was the mansion Rio was gifted by Francois, and Celia, Sara, and Alma had just left through the front door.

It would've been problematic if they had shut themselves away inside the castle, so this is perfect. But it's best not to underestimate those girls when they're outside. I'll hold nothing back.

A jet-black shadow sprung from Reiss's feet, spreading across the blue sky. Five black orbs several meters in diameter appeared.

All five orbs rained down on Rio's mansion like meteorites. Each descent was accompanied by a booming roar, shaking the building.

That's all the revenants I have on hand. But I fear they won't last long against those girls—better call those guys over as quickly as possible.

Once he had watched the orbs land, Reiss took out a new teleport crystal and smirked, rising even higher into the sky.

After exiting the mansion, Sara walked along the outer wall of the building and moved on top of the roof for a better view. She strained her eyes to look over the area, checking that there were no monsters near the mansion.

"There are no monsters approaching the mansion as of yet. Though there are some people fighting here and there…"

She descended to the ground and reported what she saw to Louise and her knights, Celia, and Alma.

"Thank you. Though I would like to send assistance to our allies, we cannot leave our stations. Let us prioritize the protection of this mansion."

As long as there was a chance of monsters reaching the mansion, they couldn't afford to leave the mansion guards shorthanded. It was a shame they could only watch their allies fight from afar, but it was the right tactical decision to make. They considered the option of bringing Miharu and the others to the castle, but it wouldn't be wise to risk the safety of so many noncombatants while on the move.

"I will continue keeping watch from the roof."

"I will assist."

With that, Sara and Alma left to climb the roof. It was at that moment that the black orbs Reiss had released fell down nearby.

Thundering shock waves surged upon them, blowing up a cloud of dirt.

"Wha...?!"

Their vision was suddenly stolen, leaving them speechless. Meanwhile, the dark surfaces of the orbs that had fallen started melting away. There were a total of five orbs, and they were less than a hundred meters away from the mansion. Twelve revenants leaped out of each orb.

"Kshaaah!"

Sixty revenants started running at Sara and the others before the mansion. There were only a few that could defend against such a surprise attack.

"A-Alma and I will stand at the front!"

"Everyone else, focus on protecting Celia and preventing any strays from getting into the mansion!"

The first to respond were Sara and Alma.

"*Duo Magi: Maius Terra Murum*!!!" Meanwhile, Celia cast a spell while touching the ground with both hands. Less than two seconds later, two walls of earth appeared between them and the revenants. The walls were each one meter thick, five meters wide, and ten meters tall. The purpose of setting up the obstacles wasn't to stop the revenants' approach, but to avoid a situation where they were overwhelmed by the enemy's advantage in numbers. The walls Celia created had a one-meter gap in between. This reduced the revenants' options to passing through the gap, going the long way around, or climbing over the tops of the walls.

Restricting the enemy's invasion route meant they could focus their firepower to where it was needed most. Being able to reduce the number of enemies to face at once was a huge benefit as well.

"Sara, Alma!" Celia yelled. "Please assume a formation surrounding me! Alma, you take the right side!"

"Got it!"

Sara and Alma understood Celia's intentions instantly and split up to the left and right. The revenants had chosen not to climb the walls, but to advance through the middle and around the sides. As a result...

"*Tres Magi: Ignis Iecit!*"

"Haaah!"

"Hmph!"

The revenants coming from the middle, left, and right were met with powerful attacks from Celia, Sara, and Alma respectively.

"Grah!"

Three magic circles for sorcery spells appeared before Celia. One of them released a one-meter-wide fireball that blew back several of the revenants coming from the middle. The other two magic circles remained on standby beside her.

A lance of ice shot out of Sara's dagger and pierced through several bodies at once, while Alma's mace mowed down multiple enemies with a swing.

"They're the same monsters I saw in Amande! Their skin is hard and they're very tenacious, so be careful! The black ones move faster than the gray ones!" Celia shouted, warning Sara and the others about their characteristics. As though to prove her words, the enemies at the front staggered back to their feet even though their skin was now half-melted.

Out of the enemies Alma attacked, only the one at the very front died; the others behind it were already getting back up on their feet. The revenants pierced through the abdomen by Sara's ice lance weren't killed by just that attack either, and were squirming to pull the lance out.

"So it seems...!"

45

Sara summoned a long blade of ice to enshroud her dagger, beheading the revenants that were impaled on the ice lance. They finally died after that, the bodies vanishing and leaving behind enchanted gems.

"How troublesome!" Alma brushed aside an enemy that threw itself at her and swung her mace at the new revenants charging. It seemed that a clear hit from her mace was enough to kill them, as the one sent flying soon vanished.

Celia also fired the second and third fireball shots she had on standby from her multicasting, finishing off the revenants she missed the first time.

"…" Louise and the other knights were speechless at how unfazed Celia and the others were at the sudden ambush. They understood one another's fighting styles and trained with each other every day, so there was nothing more reassuring. It was truly splendid.

In particular, Celia's first move with the earth wall was a fine tactic against the revenants. Her ability to cast multiple intermediate spells at a rapid speed and calmly observe the enemy's movements at the spur of the moment was incredibly impressive.

Louise looked at Celia in awe. "Defend Lady Celia so that her magic isn't obstructed! Don't overlook any monsters that run for the mansion!"

She pulled herself together and gave her subordinates orders. Only six or seven enemies had been defeated so far—the revenants were still advancing upon them.

"*Sextus Magi: Ictus Lancea!*" Celia seemed to get an idea from watching Sara's ice lances and used her magic to create thirty-six spears of ice at once. She saw how piercing once wasn't enough to kill and prepared multiple to make up for it.

The role of a sorcerer during group battles was to focus their firepower on the approaching enemies and reduce their numbers. Celia was trying to fulfill that role, but casting thirty-six spells simultaneously was a challenge even for a royal sorcerer. Although it was basic magic, the fact Celia had accomplished such a feat in the midst of battle left the knights around her shocked.

Ignoring the knights' reactions, Celia continuously fired ice spears from the magic circle above her head. She stopped the revenants from approaching through the gap between the walls one after another.

Calm down and observe carefully… A sorcerer on the back line needs to have a broad view of the enemy's movements and the ability to make preemptive moves.

Celia took a deep breath and focused on staying calm. Of course, she was nervous about fighting for real—in fact, she was terrified.

However, Celia knew firsthand what it was like to be a burden on the battlefield. The frustration of being immobilized by fear. She recalled the events leading up to her arrival at the Restoration.

In the many battles that occurred while escorting Christina to Rodania, she had watched on while Rio, Sara, Alma, and Orphia did all the fighting. Despite having the ability to help as a sorcerer, she was more useless on the battlefield than she could have ever imagined.

That's why ever since she joined the Restoration, Celia had begun to learn how to use her magic in real battles. With the assistance of Sara's and Gouki's groups, she began training regularly. The result of that was now blooming before everyone here.

"The people around Sir Amakawa are truly amazing…" Louise muttered in astonishment. The flashy magic spells made Celia's power easy to identify, but Sara's and Alma's efforts were also eye opening.

Sara was fighting both with speed and the number of her hits. She moved swiftly and acrobatically, confusing the revenants with a mix of martial arts and ice-cold dagger swings. The daggers she held in each hand slashed at the revenants' hard bodies faster than the eye could follow.

Meanwhile, Alma fought impressively. It was evident that her physical body enhancement was the source of her strength, but it was hard to believe such a small and delicate body had so much physical power packed within it. She swung her heavy-looking mace, killing a revenant with each hit.

Their battle styles were different, but both Sara and Alma had stable ways of fighting. They were cleanly keeping the revenants on both sides at bay.

Only a third of the enemies had been defeated so far, but at this rate, the extermination would conclude without a hitch. That's what Celia and the others thought as they fought.

The group that had evacuated to the safe room could tell that the battle had started outside. The sixteen-meter-squared room, connected to the drawing room by a single door, had no windows. Miharu, Satsuki, Latifa, Christina, Flora, and Charlotte were inside the safe room, Vanessa was in the corridor leading to the drawing room, and two of Charlotte's knights were in the drawing room.

Once they started hearing the sounds of a fierce battle taking place, they all stopped speaking. The sound of Celia's magic and the revenants' screeches echoed through the mansion walls. It was clear that a life-threatening battle was taking place.

Everyone's fighting outside right now...

Affected by the tension in the air, Satsuki fell silent with a meek look. She was thinking about those fighting outside, and...

I'm taking shelter in a safe room. Even though I'm the hero.

...herself.

Sara and Alma were both younger than her. Celia was older, but she was as delicate as a younger girl. Yet all three were fighting outside while she was taking refuge in the safe room.

Am I really okay with that? Shouldn't I fight as well? Sara, Alma, and Celia are all my precious friends... I'm on good terms with Louise and the knights too...

Right now, Satsuki was regretting how she hadn't offered to stand guard outside with the others. They weren't certain that the monsters had approached earlier, so she thought it would be better to stay by Miharu's side—but that may have been an excuse for her fear.

Ever since coming to this world, she had been working hard at her spear training. She had recently started sparring with Sara and the others, but those matches weren't enough to prepare her for duels to the death. She had merely participated with the same mindset as participating in a sports tournament.

Perhaps it would be more correct to say that the safety of the castle had clouded her view, making it hard for her to feel the imminent danger. Though she understood that war could start at any moment, she had averted her eyes from what that meant, training with a vacant mind.

But at this moment, Satsuki was keenly aware of the lives at risk outside. She wondered if it would have been better for her to fight as well.

My friends are fighting right nearby, yet I'm hiding in a safe refuge... Even though I'm the one with the hero powers. How can I face them all after the fight ends? I have no right to be the hero.

Whether she liked it or not, her close friends were risking their lives beside her. To put it simply, the warlike atmosphere was affecting her emotions.

The last time she had been in a life-threatening situation was when she had reunited with Miharu at the banquet and invaders had attacked the gathering. Rio's assistance had resolved the situation in less than a minute, so although it left a bad aftertaste, she hadn't felt the tense atmosphere for nearly as long as this.

The sounds of fighting outside could still be heard even now.

"Are you okay, Satsuki?"

Miharu had noticed her pale expression. She called out to her worriedly.

"Say, Miharu..." Satsuki started, making up her mind.

"You look like you want to go out there and join the fight."

Charlotte guessed first, beating Satsuki to the punch. She seemed to be opposed to letting Satsuki outside, as she was sighing heavily as she spoke.

It was at that moment that the sounds from outside stopped.

"Have you found out anything new?"

King Francois was in the temporary command post set up in the hanging gardens. With all the monsters invading the castle grounds, the rooftop garden was the best place to look over the situation and give orders.

The hanging gardens were normally off-limits to everyone except the royal family and their personally invited guests, but it was currently packed with a flurry of military personnel. Aerial knights patrolled the skies above on griffins, watching for any kind of aerial attack.

"Only one type of monster descended during the attack. They all possess the strength of a knight with their physical abilities enhanced."

"The number of invading monsters is estimated to be a few hundred."

"Most are in combat with the knights outside, but some have snuck into the castle. The ones that were spotted were eliminated, but we've allocated some people to search the interior to be safe."

A number of knights were giving their status reports to Francois, who was heavily protected by several guards. Francois was nodding along to the reports when five new black orbs fell from the sky, dropping to the ground near Rio's mansion with a booming crash.

"What was that sound?! Don't tell me...!"

Had more monsters appeared? Francois quickly turned in the direction of the sound, but he was unable to see Rio's mansion from his current position.

Shortly after, one of the griffins that had been circling the skies descended to the garden. The aerial knight riding it gave his report in a hurry. "R-Reporting in! A huge number of monsters have appeared near Sir Amakawa's mansion!"

"What? That's not good. Send two platoons of the reserve aerial knights at once. Tell them to provide support from the skies if possible. Protect the important figures inside the mansion! For detailed orders, do as Charlotte says—she's probably over there herself," Francois said, giving hurried orders with a glance at the aerial knights on standby in the hanging gardens.

One platoon consisted of four knights, so two made eight. At present, there were forty aerial knights on standby in the rooftop garden as reserve forces, so a fifth of them would be mobilizing.

"Right away!" The knight that made the report pulled on his reins, directing his griffin towards where the aerial knights were waiting.

Just what is happening right now?

Francois glared at the skies with a grim expression. The clouds in the blue sky appeared as peaceful as ever. The only other objects in the air were the griffins carrying the aerial knights.

The knights in the air had been searching for a while now. The griffins they rode on maintained an altitude of ten to several tens of meters, similar to that of a regular bird seen in everyday life.

If a griffin were to ascend as far as it could by itself, its maximum limit would be around two hundred meters. In modern Earth terms, it would be the height of a sixty-floor building, and the aerial knights searching the skies naturally searched all the way up to there too. However, they were yet to find anything to report on.

All they knew at this point was that the monsters had been sealed in some kind of orb that fell from the sky.

The attack on Amande was also said to have been quite strange, but I've never heard of monsters attacking in this form before. The black orbs that contained the monsters... Could they be some kind of magical artifact?

If so, that would mean there was a human behind this attack. In other words, there was a clear goal behind the black orbs that were sent into the castle grounds.

There's someone either too high up to be seen with the naked eye, or hiding behind the clouds... Or perhaps they fired the magic artifacts into the castle grounds from afar? At any rate, there's nothing that can be done without any proof. How frustrating... Francois thought with a furrowed brow.

"Follow me."

He wanted to see Rio's mansion with his own eyes. The guards surrounding him followed as he marched towards somewhere that could overlook the mansion.

A mere two or three minutes later, beside Rio's mansion...

"Haaah!" Sara created ice lances out of the ground, stopping the revenants in their tracks. She then approached them faster than the eye could follow, kicking them flying and slicing off their necks with her daggers.

"Hmph! Hah!" At the same time, Alma swung her mace with a powerful ease that was unbelievable for her small frame, sending the enemy flying. She moved in light-footed leaps, cleanly eliminating all the revenants that were rushing at her.

Meanwhile, Celia was firing the magic ice lances she had prepared in the air, killing the monsters that slipped past the walls she had put up as an obstruction.

The sixty revenants that originally fell had already been reduced to fewer than ten. The landform Celia had created at the beginning played a big part in that.

"Gaaah!"

The revenants' eyes glinted with an eerie light. There was no sign of any rationality within them as they screeched in anger, enraged by how their attack was being thwarted.

However, no matter how passionately they screamed, their numbers continued dwindling. Their forces were clearly declining by the second.

"I'm almost at the end!"

"I'm on my last enemy now!"

"There are no more monsters between the walls either!"

With no more monsters coming around the sides, Sara, Alma, and Celia each reported on their situations in turn. Things went smoothly after that—Celia finished her group first, followed by Sara and Alma a short moment later.

"That seems like the last of it…" Sara checked behind the wall and reported. She then returned to where Celia and the others were with Alma.

Louise commended them gratefully. "I can't believe the three of you cleaned up so many monsters in such a short time. It was splendid work. I'm sorry we were only able to watch on…"

"No, it was very reassuring having the knights at our backs," Sara replied with a smile.

"I was also able to concentrate on my magic. Oh, by the way, Alma."

Celia called out to Alma like she had just remembered something.

"Yes? What is it?" Alma asked, puzzled.

"Could you break down the dirt walls with your mace?"

Although they had been necessary to block the enemy's advance, they couldn't just leave them standing there like this. Celia looked in the direction where the revenants had come from. The huge dirt walls she put up at the start of the battle towered tall, blocking the castle behind them.

She had used an immense amount of magic essence to make them as sturdy as possible, and now that some time had passed since putting them up, the only way of removing them was to break them. Only with spirit arts could the ground be manipulated freely to lower them.

However, Celia had specifically asked for Alma's mace because of the knights' presence. They didn't know about spirit arts, so the weapon provided the convenient cover of an enchanted-sword-like ability that could control the ground.

"Yes, I can. They ruin the view, so I'll turn it back to how it was now."

"Thanks. Sorry for the trouble."

"Not at all. It made the fight much easier," Alma said, then approached the walls.

"The battle might be ongoing in other areas, so don't let your guards down. I'll scout the area from the rooftop."

"Please do."

Sara leaped up to the rooftop lightly.

The best moment to launch a surprise attack was when the opponent had their guards lowered. In other words, the moment a battle had finished was the easiest time to make a successful ambush. Her actions were made in understanding of this.

However, veteran mercenaries were well aware that experienced soldiers didn't let their guards down easily. That's why they planned the most meticulous and cunning strategies, watching for the best moment to attack and adapting themselves to changing situations.

"Some knights are approaching this way on griffins," Sara called from above, pointing at the sky. The gaze of the party followed her hand.

Two groups of griffin-riding knights scouting the situation from above had been circling the skies above for a while now, but the approaching troops consisted of two small squads, totaling eight people. Their approach in the mansion's direction made them all the more eye-catching.

"They must be the reinforcements. It's about time too," Louise answered loudly enough for Sara to hear, then turned to a female knight beside her. "Hey, go give an update to the princess."

The arrival of reinforcements made their defenses seem adequate, softening the tension that was hanging in the air. But then...

"Umm... Is that squad descending rapidly over there also on our side? There's quite a lot of them, and they're coming in from a rather elevated altitude..."

Sara pointed farther up in the sky with a dubious look. While the aerial knights were flying in from an altitude of several tens of meters or so, the new griffin squad was coming in from several hundred meters up.

However, they appeared to be free-falling with gravity, as their distant figures were rapidly increasing in size. Sara had only spotted them early because she was using physically enhanced vision to watch for more monster orbs falling down.

"How odd…" Louise stared at the distant troops in the sky.

There were fifty griffins, which amounted to three squadrons of the aerial knights—a considerably large force. Why would such a large number of troops be falling at a speed they couldn't land safely at?

"*Augendae Corporis.* That's…"

Louise immediately used magic to enhance her vision, straining her eyes to see them clearly. Then, she spotted the soldiers wearing uniforms clearly different to those of the aerial knights of the Galarc Kingdom.

The unknown soldiers started to chant some kind of spell on their griffins. Magic circles appeared one after another before them.

"They're not allies! Those aerial knights are not from our kingdom!"

"Alma, get ready to defend!"

Louise and Sara both yelled with looks of horror. At the same time, a barrage of light bullets rained down on them.

✤ Chapter 3 ✤
The Heavenly Lions

The Heavenly Lions. A veteran mercenary group once led by the late Lucius Orgueil.

At present, fifty mercenaries wearing the group uniform were flying in towards the Galarc Castle. They descended rapidly until they reached an altitude of two hundred meters, where they started firing bullets of light towards the ground.

Each light bullet was a few centimeters in diameter. They were actually bullets of magic energy, but they could be compared to hard orbs just under one kilogram heavy being fired at a speed of three hundred kilometers per hour. Such an attack was being rapid-fired by fifty people at once.

The light bullets became a rain, closing in on the ground in an instant. Their targets were Sara on the roof, Celia and the others around the mansion, and the two platoons of aerial knights Francois had dispatched. They split into groups proportionate to the number of targets.

"Haaah!"

Sara and Alma both summoned a huge barrier of magic essence, blocking the bullets from reaching them. Sara focused on minimizing the damage to the mansion, while Alma protected the others around her. Their defenses worked successfully, but the aerial knights were helpless against the attacks from above.

"Gah?!"

"Gwargh!"

The knights and griffins let out screams of pain as they were hit by the attack.

The knights that were critically hit lost consciousness, their griffins turning violent from the pain. While they had safety tethers, they started falling out of their saddles one by one. By the time the attacks stopped, there was no one left flying. It was pandemonium.

"Ngh..."

Sara and Alma were unable to do anything but watch on. The attacks were incessant, leaving them no choice but to focus on keeping their barrier up. During that time, the assailants came within landing distance of the ground.

Tch, all the top-priority targets are unharmed. Mister Reiss said there was a high chance they'd block the first attack, but at least one could have gone down and made things easier for us...

One of the mercenaries of the Heavenly Lions, Arein, clicked his tongue in annoyance. But he immediately switched gears.

"Follow the plan! Lucci, your squad takes the outside! Ven, your squad heads inside the mansion! My squad will be the commando unit. We'll stop the castle knights from approaching by foot. Move out!" he ordered his comrades around him.

"Right!"

The mercenaries moved swiftly. Thirty of them continued the attack from above with Arein, while the others split into two groups to descend to the ground. Eleven mercenaries and Lucci landed near the dirt walls Celia had put up earlier, while Ven and the remaining seven closed in on the front door of the mansion.

"Ngh, the enemies are getting inside...!"

The number of assailants firing bullets from above had decreased, but the fierce barrage still continued. Sara had no choice but to continue holding her barrier.

They're completely ignoring me… Are they after the princesses?! This is bad!

Sara guessed at the mercenaries' aim and called out to the others below. "I'm going to support the others inside! Take care of the outside!"

"Go, Sara!" Celia replied immediately. The rain of bullets tried to stop Sara from moving. However…

With their forces split up, the focus on me has lessened. If it's like this…!

While keeping her barrier maintained, Sara summoned several spears of ice around her. Then, she fired them to the sides, sending them to the sky in a curving arc. She controlled their trajectory with spirit arts, aiming for the mercenaries attacking her.

"Tch."

The mercenaries being targeted circled in the air, evading the lances. In doing so, their attack on Sara faltered.

"Now!"

Sara spotted that slim opening and used the chance to jump down to the ground floor, rushing into the mansion through a window.

While Sara was returning to the mansion, the mercenaries under the command of Lucci reached the ground.

"Guh, they're on the other side of my dirt wall…!" Celia cried in frustration.

The moment of landing was a big chance to counterattack, but they had landed out of line of sight of her to avoid her magic. Their knowledge of how to handle the terrain in battle, their carefully planned ambush strategy—it was clear they were a much more formidable enemy than the revenants that had attacked earlier.

"*Quattuor Magi: Magicae Displodo.*"

Celia fixed her gaze on the two walls she had created and chanted an attack spell. Magicae Displodo was a spell that fired a powerful magic cannon, making it extremely lethal. The possibility of casualties flashed through Celia's mind.

...This isn't the time to be holding back!

If she hesitated here, someone among them would definitely die. She manipulated her magic as fast as she could, spending three seconds to create four magic circles before her. However, she didn't fire them immediately.

"*Potentia Incantatio! Superfundo!*" she shouted.

The glow of the magic circles increased in luminosity. The next moment, four powerful bursts of light were fired from the circles like cannonballs.

They were, of course, aimed at the two giant dirt walls Celia had created. The tip of the light collided with a loud explosion. By controlling the trajectory of the spells, she made sure to break the walls down thoroughly. In reality, the enemies on the other side of the wall were buried alive by the rubble.

"Ooh!" the knights cheered.

But immediately after...

Boom.

The fallen rubble was blown away with great force.

"Wh...Wha?!"

A torrent of darkness came from the other side of the wall, swallowing all four of Celia's magic bursts in a violent storm.

"Guh…!"

Everyone recoiled at the shock wave—except for Alma. She moved the barrier she had placed over their heads to her front, blocking the advancing wind. The flying rubble collided with the wall, but it disintegrated on impact.

The wind eventually stopped, leaving a cloud of dust that obstructed their view. The mercenaries wouldn't be able to see them either.

"Ha! Ha! Ha ha!" From the other side of where the wall had stood was a man cackling in gleeful laughter. It was the larger man in the group, Lucci.

"Damn, this sword is great! The commander's memento is amazing!"

He looked down at the black sword in his hand with a smirk, a crazed look in his eyes.

"Ngh… Alma, I'm going to keep the enemy in check and secure a line of sight. Take down the barrier to the front."

"Right!"

"*Vortex.*" Celia used a new spell to clear their vision and keep the enemies in check. A swirling whirlwind was released from the magic spell, blowing away the dust cloud while moving forward. However—

"Just try me!" Another shock wave of darkness blew at them violently. Lucci had swung the sword in his hand, mowing down the whirlwind magic Celia had used.

At the same time, their vision rapidly cleared. All the rubble had landed by then, so the two sides could finally see each other properly. Celia's side was met with the sight of twelve mercenaries in black combat uniforms.

"Wh-What was that…?" Celia trembled uneasily.

"All hands, draw your swords! Enhance your physical abilities!"

Louise drew her sword and immediately assumed combat readiness. She chanted the spell to enchant her physical ability, and her six subordinates followed suit.

It was a bad move to act with no idea of the enemy's position, but now that the view had cleared up, the battle could start at any moment.

"I'll take over the barrier casting, Alma. *Magicae Murum*," Celia chanted in a hurry. Her barrier overlapped with Alma's from the inside, creating a wall against physical and magical attacks.

Maintaining a barrier limited the caster's movements, so it was better for a sorcerer like her to handle the spell over the highly mobile Alma.

The attacks from above had ceased after Sara slipped inside the mansion, but there was no telling when they could start again. She had to keep the barrier up just in case—this was what it meant to have control of the air.

"Please." Alma nodded and canceled her own barrier. She advanced forward while glaring at Lucci and the other mercenaries with their weapons held ready. Yet despite the critically tense atmosphere, Lucci burst into a hearty laughter for no identifiable reason.

"Ha ha ha!"

It was so creepy, Celia and the others frowned in response.

"Celia, have you realized it?" Alma whispered to Celia without moving her gaze.

"Realized what…?"

"That man with the black sword is part of the gang that attacked us on the way to Rodania with the princess." Alma had faced him herself, so she remembered him clearly.

"Ah…!" Celia gasped.

"Ha! Looks like you've finally caught on to us. We even wore our squad uniforms to make it easy for you. Hey, let's continue from where we left off."

Lucci pointed his sword at Alma without any attempt at hiding his identity. Alma had won last time, but his haughty attitude seemed to imply he thought his victory would be certain this time.

What kingdom is that aerial knight uniform of? Could it be a mercenary squad uniform? Either way, why would they attack our castle in clearly identifiable uniforms...?

Without knowing anything about him, Louise came up with her own guess. Like the Galarc Knights, this group of people wore a combat uniform of the same design. But that aside—

"That brat with the mace and the tiny sorcerer casting the barrier are our targets, right, Lucci?" a mercenary beside Lucci asked. There was no one else among them that Alma and Celia recognized the face of.

"Yeah, exactly like the briefing. You guys aim for the sorcerer. Take care of the extras around her as well. The mace-wielding brat would be too much for you, so she's mine."

"Just because you have the commander's sword now..." a disgruntled voice mumbled. The other mercenaries looked at Lucci's black enchanted sword with discontent.

"I was the only one that matched it in compatibility, remember?" Lucci said boastfully. The jet-black enchanted sword that Lucius used was powerful. They had just witnessed its power moments ago. It was understandable for Lucci to be excited about fighting, but—

"Tch... Don't forget that taking just one target hostage is enough to accomplish the mission," one man warned Lucci, reminding him not to forget about fulfilling the assignment in his enthusiasm.

"Of course. Why else are we here?"

Lucci glared at the man with a frown. They were here for revenge on the man who killed their captain.

"Let's finish this before the enemy reinforcements arrive. Follow my lead."

He pulled himself together and returned his gaze to Alma, adopting a battle stance.

"Celia."

Sensing the enemy's movements, Alma called out to Celia while moving to stand in front of her. They planned a strategy using the least amount of words possible.

"I know."

Celia had a barrier held up overhead and to her front, but she removed the one to the front. Alma then walked forward.

Next, Louise and the other knights stood before Celia. Celia adjusted the shape of the barrier to create a dome shape with an opening only to the front of the knights.

Once Alma saw that, she slammed the head of her mace on the ground. A thick wall rose from the ground behind her, stopping at a height of one meter. It partially blocked the section of the barrier Celia had left open before the knights.

"…"

They had already confirmed that both sides could make wide-ranged attacks. It would be reckless to charge forward, so they had no choice but to glare warily at each other.

However, the more time passed, the more of a disadvantage the attackers would be in. The silence would soon be broken.

"Let's go!"

"Come at me!"

Lucci and Alma yelled at the same time. Lucci burst into a run towards Alma, followed by the other mercenaries one beat later.

They're fast...

That kind of speed wasn't achievable with magically enhanced physical abilities alone: they had to be using enchanted swords that could reinforce their physical bodies as well. Lucci's movements in particular were something special; he was considerably faster than the others.

However, Alma had her physical abilities and body enhanced as well, which was why she was able to capture their initial movements accurately.

This formation was the right choice after all.

The knights on their sides could only enhance their physical abilities, so they wouldn't have been able to keep up with that speed. Last time she faced Lucci, Arein, and Ven, the three of them possessed enchanted swords that could enhance their physical bodies. Fearing that the other mercenaries were in possession of similar weapons, she had asked the knights to stand back.

"Hah!" Alma charged straight forward, and in the next moment, Lucci was within her reach.

However, the converse also applied to Lucci. Their weapons clashed together with a screeching ring. Alma tried to push forward with her dwarven strength, but Lucci had more arm strength than she'd expected. In fact, he was clearly stronger than the last time they fought. She could tell he had a powerful physical body enhancement applied through Lucius's enchanted sword.

"Guh..."

"Damn, where does that animal strength come from?!"

Alma's physical strength won by a faint margin, pushing Lucci backwards. It wasn't enough to knock him off-balance, however, as he immediately charged forward once again.

"You're taking too long, Lucci!" While he was pushed back, two mercenaries passed by on each side of him, slashing at Alma.

"Hey, you two! That's my prey!" Lucci growled.

It doesn't matter how many there are of you. No one's getting past me! Alma slammed her mace on the ground, unaffected by the number of opponents. The ground cracked open, sending a shock wave of stones and pebbles flying.

"Gah!"

"Out of my way!"

The two mercenaries stepped back and Lucci charged forward in their place.

"I won't let you!" Alma slammed her mace against the ground before her, using magic essence to create spikes of earth, similar to those of a hedgehog.

"Ooh, how scary." Dreary darkness flowed out of Lucci's sword. In one swing forward, he flattened the spikes of earth, then in another swing back, he swung at Alma, who was no longer obstructed.

"Ha!" Alma raised her mace reflexively, blocking Lucci's sword.

"This brat is my prey! You all attack the others from the sides!" Lucci yelled at the other mercenaries.

"Tch!" There were some mercenaries who frowned unhappily, but they swallowed their pride and prioritized the goal. They split up as ordered, passing by Alma to aim for Celia and the knights.

"Now!"

"*Ignis Iecit!*"

"*Fulgur Sphera!*"

At Louise's order, two of the knights cast attack magic through the gap in the wall before them. They weren't sorcerers, so their magic ability was limited, but they could still use lower-grade spells—

and when it came to battle with humans, lower-grade attack magic was more than enough of a threat.

While the barrier protected them from outside attacks, there was no way of attacking from inside the barrier. That was why Celia had purposefully left the front of the barrier open and Alma had built a low wall to act as an obstruction.

Like this, Alma could stop the enemies from advancing through the middle, while Louise and the knights could stop any enemies trying to go around with orb-style spells. This was the plan Celia had come up with on the spot earlier. However...

"Tch."

Orb-style attack spells had high lethality even at lower grades, but the trade-off for their power was a slower projectile speed. This made it difficult to aim at experienced soldiers with bodies boosted by their enchanted swords. The mercenaries fell back and went around the points of impact, negating the spells.

"*Photon Projectilis!*"

Two other knights aimed for the moment the mercenaries evaded the spells. Photon bullets had less power than orb-style spells, but as bullet-style spells, they had much faster projectile speed. Light-type bullets were the fastest of them all, but...

"How annoying."

"They're not the pushovers I expected. That's some skill."

"Don't underestimate your enemies! They're still elite knights."

The mercenaries continued to evade the magic with ease. They even had the leisure to complain while leaping about.

Meanwhile, Alma's mace collided with Lucci's sword in a life-or-death struggle. "Take that!"

Lucci was evidently stronger than the last time they fought. His basic techniques hadn't improved, but his physical abilities had increased dramatically. Alma had slightly more physical strength, but they were on par in terms of speed. On top of that, Lucci was clearly more experienced in fighting against other people. All his mercenary experience wasn't just for show.

I'm meant to be luring the majority of the enemies too! Alma gritted her teeth, frustrated that she was only able to distract a single enemy. It was times like this where her lack of combat experience left her disadvantaged.

"Ha. I see your friends have focused on going on the defense to buy you time. But they won't hold on for long," Lucci taunted, seeing through the panic in Alma's expression while swinging his sword.

"Guh…"

The situation wasn't looking good. The assailants were all skilled mercenaries from the renowned Heavenly Lions. Though they couldn't advance with the barrier and spell barrage hindering them, they weren't about to retreat quietly.

"*Photon Projectilis.*"

The mercenaries started counterattacking as they evaded. Their target was, of course, the unprotected front of the barrier.

The low wall Alma had built provided good cover from projectiles, but there were gaps for the knights to expose the upper halves of their bodies and cast their magic. The photon bullets slipped through those gaps and rebounded around the inside of the barrier.

"Ngh. Lady Celia, stay down."

"O-Okay." At Louise's order, Celia bent over.

The most important factor of a magic duel was cover. The risk of being hit was reduced by the amount of cover they had while casting.

"Keep your heads low and the spells coming! Cast until you run out of magic essence!"

"Yes, captain!"

The knights crouched down and continued casting spells over the wall, but their accuracy naturally dropped with their heads so low. That made it easier for the mercenaries to move.

"All right, get around them!"

"A barrier of this size has gotta be a burden to hold up!"

"Break it with your attacks!"

Eventually, the mercenaries surrounded them on all sides and began attacking the barrier.

"Ugh…" Panic filled Celia's face as she watched the malicious assailants attack her barrier with their magic and weapons.

There was no doubt her barrier was a powerful defense method capable of blocking all attacks and keeping out intruders, but it also consumed a lot of magic essence. Just having it up consumed essence, but blocking attacks consumed even more. The essence consumption went up exponentially as the area of the barrier increased, and the barrier's strength weakened the less essence there was remaining.

If she wanted to minimize her essence consumption, she had to shrink her barrier while keeping it sturdy enough to withstand the enemy attacks—but doing so was no simple feat. Most people had no choice but to use all their magic essence just to make the barrier big enough. That's why barriers normally consumed a lot more essence than was necessary. It wasn't practical to use the spell on the battlefield unless the attack was unavoidable.

Celia had much more essence than the average sorcerer, but even she would struggle with over ten mercenaries surrounding her barrier. They were basically on board a sinking ship right now—and the moment she ran out of essence, the enemies would wipe them out instantly.

71

I-It's okay... I have the essence in the spirit stone Rio gave me, and they've caused this big of a fuss already. Reinforcements will be here soon. I just have to hold on...!

Rio wasn't here right now... That fact weighed on her heavily. But in order to prove she was fine without him, she had to fight. Celia clutched the spirit stone she received from Rio and frantically told herself that it'd be okay.

Alma could see Celia holding the spirit stone as she fought and came to a decision.

There's no other choice...!

She still had one ace up her sleeve, and she had hoped to keep it hidden—no, her village had ordered her to keep it hidden at all costs. But if she didn't use it here, the situation would become irredeemable.

Ifritah!

Alma yelled the name of her mid-class contract spirit in her heart. A giant lion-shaped beast appeared out of thin air.

Ifritah immediately charged at the mercenaries surrounding the barrier.

Some time before Alma summoned Ifritah...

In the hanging gardens of the castle, King Francois was aware that the newest assailants were humans. In fact, he was irately watching things take place from afar in the very present.

It was clear that the battles on the ground were not going well. Several people had entered the mansion, and the enemy griffin riders were circling the skies, preventing any reinforcements from reaching the area.

"The nerve of these people..."

Francois gritted his teeth to stifle his anger and frustration. Losing his composure wouldn't help the situation, and above all, he had his dignity as the king not to do something as unbecoming as breaking down and shouting before his vassals.

Besides, he had already given orders to deal with the situation. The knights on the ground were still engaged in combat with revenants, but his aerial knights were heading for the mansion.

However, the revenants that preceded the mercenary attack had created much chaos in the castle, and support teams were focused on transporting the injured. One-third of the aerial knights were stationed in the castle, but out of the six hundred knights available, only one hundred could be sent as reinforcements.

Despite that, there was still a considerable number of troops flying towards Rio's mansion at once. Arein and his subordinates had no choice but to intercept them, sparing Celia and the knights on the ground from an aerial assault. But that was the extent of their effect.

There were thirty mercenaries in Arein's group, and a number of them had descended to stop any reinforcements from approaching on foot. In terms of numbers, the Galarc Kingdom side had the overwhelming advantage, but what was most burdensome was the supporting fire that occasionally rained down on the aerial knights from far above.

On top of that, the mercenaries that had descended to the ground had released their griffins back up to the sky to assist the others. Because of that, the Galarc side was yet to assume control of the air.

Sandwiched between fire from above and griffin attacks from below, the aerial knights were forced into combat with Arein and his squad. Francois could see they were struggling to make a proper advance.

"Your Majesty! The assailants have been identified! The emblem on their uniforms is of a mercenary group called the Heavenly Lions."

A soldier ran up to where Francois was being protected by his own knights and sorcerers. Finally, the identity of their enemies had been revealed.

"What?" Francois furrowed his brow.

They were a famous mercenary group, so it wasn't that he hadn't heard of the name before. What had actually caught his attention was their leader, the man who was killed by Rio for being an enemy to his parents. He was also the culprit behind Christina and Flora's recent abduction.

"Hmm…"

Right now, those mercenaries were raiding the mansion of their leader's killer. Inside the mansion were the two princesses that were previously abducted.

Francois thought hard about why the Heavenly Lions would launch an attack like this.

Meanwhile, Ven's squad had just charged into the front door of the mansion. The mercenaries opened each door as they went past, checking the interiors.

"It's Sara! Please open up!"

Sara had the advantage of knowing the mansion's layout, so she went straight for the window of the room connected to the safe room. However, she knew she could be mistaken for an enemy if she charged straight in, so she knocked on the window in a hurry.

The knights inside the room had been watching what was going on outside, so while they were surprised by Sara's sudden appearance, they immediately let her inside.

Standing before the corridor leading to the safe room were Satsuki with her spear-shaped Divine Arms, Latifa with her dagger, and Vanessa. Satsuki and Latifa had been inside the safe room, but decided to join the defense efforts when the battle started.

"Excuse me…"

Fearing the enemies' detection of her location, Sara kept her voice low as she slipped inside. She held a finger up to her lips, signaling to the others to keep quiet.

"Sara."

They could see the battle outside from the window, so they must be aware of the situation already. Satsuki called Sara's name quietly, a fretful look on her face. Just then, Miharu, Christina, Flora, and Charlotte emerged from the safe room.

"There are intruders in the mansion. Not monsters…but people."

"R-Right. What do we do?"

Hearing that their opponents were humans made Satsuki's expression even more uneasy. The others were similarly nervous. The battle had just started outside.

"I will defeat them."

Sara looked between the entrance to the room, the window, and the direction of the safe room. Then, after a moment of hesitation, she steeled herself. "Everyone here will continue to protect this room. I will defeat the enemies in the mansion."

She started for the door leading to the outside corridor.

"I-I'll go too," Satsuki offered in a fluster. However…

"Your spear will be difficult to use in a corridor. If you wish to fight, you should do so in this room. I saw a total of eight intruders. Please stay in this room and fight any that I miss."

The enemy is probably aiming for this room, Sara's words implied.

"I understand…" Satsuki nodded, struggling to swallow.

"There's a chance of being attacked from both ends of the corridor. We will accompany you," one of the two knights under Louise offered, drawing her sword. They were equipped with short swords suitable for fighting indoors, so they would have no trouble in the corridor.

"Please," Sara said, giving a short reply. She looked at the entrance of the safe room. "Latifa, please remain here. If the enemies enter, you and Satsuki will be the final line of defense."

"Okay…"

Latifa nodded with a stiff expression. It was at that moment that the battle outside the mansion commenced. The fierce sound of clashing weapons reached their ears.

"Once we leave the room, lock it and stay back from the door. Be careful of the window too. Now…"

With those parting words to Satsuki, Sara exchanged looks with the two female knights. They all nodded at each other, then went out to the corridor.

The meeting room was at the end of the first-floor corridor. Since the corridor connected to both the entrance hall and the dining hall, it was possible for enemies to come from both directions.

"Let's split into two groups to protect the corridor," Sara suggested.

"There they are!"

"At the back of the first floor!"

Mercenaries appeared out of a room along the corridor towards the entrance. They had been moving in pairs, so they shouted loudly enough for the other intruders in the mansion to hear.

"I'll deal with them. Protect the side leading to the dining hall!"

As soon as she finished speaking, Sara charged towards the two mercenaries.

"It's the silver-haired dagger girl! Be careful!"

"Her enchanted sword gives her the power to control water. Sounds fun!"

The two mercenaries shared information with each other as they drew their swords and stepped forward to meet her. They took a diagonal position to each other as they closed the distance. There was no hesitation in their movements—it was clear they were veteran fighters.

They had probably received an explanation from Arein, Lucci, and Ven, who had previously fought with Sara. She had used water spirit arts to defeat the three of them, so they naturally assumed her enchanted sword could control water.

They know about me? Then…!

Meanwhile, at this point, Sara was still unaware of her opponent's identity. She was confused to hear that they had information about her, but she wasn't about to let that affect her movements. In fact, if they knew of it already, there was no need to hide it.

"Haaah!" A few steps before the two came within reach, she swung one of her daggers to release an opening slash of water. The power was suppressed out of consideration of the mansion interior, but it was strong enough to feel like a whip strike against an unguarded human.

"Whoa, there!" The two mercenaries evaded the water slashes by sliding under them.

So fast!

Sara could tell their reaction speeds were faster than that of a knight with physically enhanced abilities. The intruders inside the mansion were equipped with shorter swords than those outside, but they were most certainly enchanted swords with physical body enchantments.

"Take that!"

One of the mercenaries slashed at Sara's feet while sliding. But instead of using the blade to slice at her feet, he tried to slam the flat side of the blade against it.

"Ngh!" Sara jumped to avoid the attack.

"Gotcha!"

The other mercenary similarly swung the flat side of his blade at Sara while she was in the air. Short of being able to fly freely, jumping always left one defenseless. That was the reasoning behind their improvised strategy, and it was executed perfectly. The only thing Sara could do was block the attack with her dagger. Yet...

"...Huh?"

The man's sword swung through empty space.

Sara had jumped in midair. She proceeded to do a backflip and evade the attack, retreating with nimble steps.

"Haaah!"

She cast slashing spirit arts through both her daggers at the mercenaries who just finished sliding.

"Damn!"

"Whoa!"

The mercenaries were the ones with no choice but to take the attack. They tried to regain their balance and fall back promptly, but they were too late to evade it. Instead, they parried the slash.

One of the attacks Sara unleashed was a slice of water. Slashing it caused the men to feel a dull impact as water sprayed everywhere. The other attack she made was an ice slash.

After landing on the corridor floor and regaining her balance, Sara retreated to glare at the two mercenaries with their swords held ready once more. They were back to square one.

"There's frost as well. One water and one ice dagger, then."

The man who cut down the ice slash had his blade frosted over. He reacted cautiously.

"More importantly, did you see how she jumped midair?"

The other mercenary was surprised at how Sara did a double jump.

For the record, Sara had jumped midair by creating a small wall of magic essence with spirit arts, using it as a foothold. She could run through the air if she used it continuously, but doing so required a lot of skill—it was easier to just use regular flying spirit arts.

Could these people be…?

It was at this moment that Sara finally caught on to who these assailants could be. Lucci and the others she had previously fought with flashed through her head. "Be careful! These two are fast! They both have enchanted swords. The other intruders might be similarly equipped. Use magic to block the corridor with a barrage of spells!" she shouted at the two female knights.

"R-Right!"

No mercenaries had approached from the direction of the dining hall yet. The two knights who had been protecting their end while watching Sara's fight nodded firmly.

Meanwhile…

"..."

At the end of the corridor leading to the entrance foyer, Ven and the other mercenaries were silently watching Sara from the shadows.

Fighting indoors as a group was extremely difficult. Weapons that were tricky to handle had the risk of getting caught on walls and furniture, movements had to be minimized as much as possible, and the layout of the building could be used to gain an advantage. All of these factors had to be considered when fighting strategically. As mercenaries that had fought many battles before, they understood this well.

"There's no need to send everyone here down such a narrow corridor. But they'll suspect us of something if we don't send some reinforcements... Two of you go down the corridor and back them up. The remaining three of you will come with me. We might be able to get in from a window outside," Ven decided immediately.

"Roger that."

"Let's get this party started!"

They quickly decided who would stay and who would go outside, then commenced their plan.

"There they are!"

"This way!"

The corridor team yelled loudly to draw Sara's attention. Then they ran in to help their comrades.

"All right, we should head off too."

Once he confirmed that, Ven led the remaining three mercenaries outside the mansion.

Around the same time, the battle outside the mansion was growing intense.

The trigger was the appearance of Alma's contract spirit, Ifritah. The beast, which was large enough to fit two or three people on its back, had materialized out of nowhere, so those in the dark about its identity were astounded.

"Grr!"

"Whoa!" The mercenary beside Ifritah recoiled at its appearance. Ifritah used that chance to tackle him, sending him flying. It then proceeded to chase after the man at a speed too fast to follow with the naked eye.

"Grrrah!"

"Oof…" The mercenary that had fallen on his back had his stomach stomped on. Although his body was enhanced by an enchanted sword, it wasn't a hit that could be withstood safely. The damage to his internal organs was severe enough to render him unconscious.

"What is that monster?!"

The remaining mercenaries stopped attacking Celia's barrier to focus on Ifritah.

"Grr!"

Ifritah rushed at the next mercenary, but the enemies were more vigilant now that they had lost one of their group. The target of the attack reacted swiftly, distancing himself from Ifritah with quick movements.

"Tch, we've gotta deal with this monster first!"

Thus, the main focus of the mercenaries shifted to Ifritah.

"Wh-What is that beast…?"

"Where did it come from?"

"It seems to be attacking the enemy, but…"

Louise and the other knights inside the barrier were equally confused. Only the mercenaries were being attacked so far, but there was no guarantee they wouldn't be next. It was only natural for them to be wary. The only person other than Alma who knew about Ifritah's identity was Celia.

"Alma…"

The existence of spirits must not be revealed to anyone. If there was a need to inform someone about them, that person had to be extremely trustworthy. Even if someone was trustworthy, they were not to be informed about spirits without necessity.

These were the rules the elders placed on Sara and the spirit folk girls when they left their village. The spirit folk had long held distrust of humans because of the way they were discriminated against and persecuted by them. That was why the spirit folk departed from the Strahl region before the Divine War commenced, relocating to the depths of the Wilderness. They participated in the Divine War when necessary, but they left Strahl again as soon as it ended.

There were also records of the spirits in the Strahl region moving to the Wilderness with the spirit folk. They had also given up on humans. According to the legends left in the spirit folk village, humans had once used forbidden spells to enslave the spirits.

That was why in modern-day Strahl, spirits were even rarer than enchanted swords. There was literature that mentioned spirits existing in the world at some point, involving powerful secret arts, but it was all lost ancient sorcery now.

No human alive had ever seen a spirit—not even royalty. There were some spirits who still lived in Strahl, but those spirits would never approach humans of their own accord. Even if they did show themselves, they were always mistaken for some kind of animal.

Alma had chosen to expose her spirit in front of humans. Humanoid spirits like Aishia would be assumed human when appearing before others, but Ifritah was a mythical lion beast. It was only natural for others to assume it was a monster—Celia was the only person who knew she had summoned it.

"Tch, what a pain… Did you summon that monster here?"

Lucci hadn't realized it was a spirit, but he suspected it was serving Alma in some form. He questioned her out loud while crossing weapons with her.

"…"

"The silent treatment? C'mon, it appeared out of nowhere at a time like this and just started attacking us. There's no way it isn't your pet! We'll dispose of it quickly!"

"Do you think I would let you? Hmph."

Alma swung her mace with all her might, knocking Lucci back bodily. Lucci instantly leaped back, killing his momentum. But Alma was immediately in front of him again, aiming a follow-up strike.

"Tch!"

He clicked his tongue, and darkness flowed out of his black sword.

"Huh?!" Alma was wary of the mysterious darkness coming from the sword. She immediately poured magic essence into her mace, releasing a shock wave of pure light.

"Rah!"

Lucci lunged forward, slamming his sword at Alma's mace. As a result, light and darkness clashed, offsetting each other.

"Ngh…"

The power of darkness overpowered light, swallowing the shock wave and pushing Alma back.

"I wanted to capture you alive if possible… But this is the way it must be."

With a grating sound, her mace met his sword. Now that Ifritah had been summoned into the situation, Lucci had no choice but to change his plans.

"You were trying to capture me alive…?" Alma asked dubiously. His wording made her suspect she was part of their goals.

"Heh… Unfortunately for you, I still haven't got the hang of this sword's abilities. Don't blame me if I hit the wrong spot, yeah?" Lucci grinned, pushing his sword back against her mace.

"What are you…?" Alma frowned in suspicion, when she suddenly felt an ominous flow of magic essence near her stomach. She looked down reflexively.

But it was already too late. She should have jumped aside as soon as she felt the essence. There was no helping it, though—the attack was impossible to avoid without prior knowledge. Rio was the abnormal exception for being able to deal with such a nasty move at first sight.

"Huh…?" Instead of pain, Alma felt a source of heat. She looked down to see a jet-black sword stabbed through her from behind.

"Move it." Lucci kicked her mercilessly.

"Aah!" Alma screamed in pain. The kick came from the front while the sword was stabbed into her from behind, so she had been forced backwards onto the sword.

"Oops, my mistake," Lucci sneered, apologizing mockingly. A moment later, the sword in Alma's stomach disappeared.

"Urgh…" Alma slumped face-first against the ground.

"Tch. The blood loss will be an annoyance, but at least I didn't get the heart." Lucci chose to leave Alma lying there, not bothering to stop her bleeding. Instead, he turned his attention to Celia.

"A-Alma!" Celia shrieked from within the magic barrier.

"Gwaaark!" With its contract master defeated, Ifritah roared furiously. It abandoned the other mercenaries to lunge at Lucci.

"Damn it, leave the monster to me! Bring that barrier down right now!" Now, Lucci had no choice but to face Ifritah.

"Guh…" Alma took that chance to secretly cast healing spirit arts to stop her bleeding.

Meanwhile, inside the mansion, shortly before Alma was stabbed by Lucci…

During times of war, the group holding the castle had to pay particular care to secure their field of view. Holding the castle meant they were protected by the building itself and could hide themselves, but at the same time, it meant their view of any incoming enemies was obstructed.

Defenselessly exposing oneself to incoming enemies by monitoring the outside was a problem, but hiding away out of fear of being discovered wasn't good either. At worst, it was possible for the approaching enemy to invade without notice.

However, short of constructing forts intended for battle, it was difficult to design buildings with securing a field of view or preventing invasion in mind. Rio's mansion was constructed with a focus on aesthetics, so it wasn't suitable for holding during a siege.

Presently, right beside the drawing room where Satsuki and the others were hiding, Ven and his group of mercenaries were sneaking closer. They communicated to each other with hand signs while checking inside each window for their targets.

Then, they hit their jackpot: they could see Miharu and Satsuki inside the room. Farther inside the room was a passage that led to a safe room.

It's here.

One of the mercenaries signaled with a hand sign. There were a total of four men outside the window, including Ven. They decided on their roles and silently began their invasion.

"*Magicae Murum.*"

One of the men activated a spell to set a magic barrier in front of them and started charging towards the window.

"Haaah!" Latifa, who had been hiding in the corner of the ceiling above the window, fired a ball of magic essence at the unguarded mercenary's head.

"Wha?!" Taking an attack to the head was enough for even a physically enhanced body to fall unconscious. The first mercenary who entered collapsed to the floor. However, they had accounted for the possibility of an ambush. Seeing one of their men go down wasn't enough to shake the others outside, and they responded rapidly.

"Above the window!"

"*Photon Projectilis!*"

One of the mercenaries aimed above the window, hoping to eliminate Latifa from the other side of the wall.

"Aah!" Latifa backed away from the window immediately. She spun midair and landed on the floor.

"The enemy's here! Miharu, go back into the room!"

"R-Right!"

At Satsuki's order, Miharu promptly headed for the safe room.

Satsuki's side was naturally aware of the possibility of an outside attack. They could have all hidden in the safe room to remove the risk of being spotted from the window, but there was no way of hiding the passage to the safe room itself. Considering the likelihood of the enemy coming inside to check, they decided to set a trap. Miharu had been placed in the drawing room on purpose, to act as though they were defenseless.

"Next!"

"*Magicae Murum!*"

Another mercenary cast a magic barrier, attempting to enter again.

"I won't let you!"

However, Satsuki was waiting with her Divine Arms. She fired a wind bullet of materialized magic essence from the end of her spear, hitting the barrier of the mercenary at the front.

"Whoa!" The mercenary who received the attack was sent flying several meters back out of the mansion.

"Get inside!" Ven and the remaining mercenary entered the room.

"Haaah!" The first to move was Latifa. With daggers in both hands, she leaped at one of the invading men.

"Tsk. Whoa, there…"

The mercenary immediately lifted his sword to take Latifa's attack. She followed up with several swings of her daggers, but they were all parried away.

"…"

Latifa retreated with a light step, putting one meter of distance between herself and the man. Her expression was stiff, and her hands clutching the daggers were trembling.

"She's fast, but…" The mercenary instantly perceived that she either had little experience when it came to killing another person, or felt some kind of aversion to it.

"Don't let your guards down. She's stronger than the knights outside," Ven warned his men as he faced Satsuki.

"I know. But who's the target?" The man facing Latifa no longer looked like he was underestimating her.

"Any of the ones at the back will do. These ones will just get in the way, so eliminate them."

"Roger that."

Having exchanged the necessary information, Ven and his men prepared for battle.

"Barging into someone's home like this…" Satsuki muttered, her body trembling.

Ven furrowed his brow. "Huh?"

"…means you're willing to be treated as intruders, right? This is justified self-defense!"

"Huh? What are you…? Whoa!"

Satsuki suddenly accelerated, closing in on Ven. She then swung her spear with all her might. Ven reflexively went to block the spear with his sword.

"Haaah!" Satsuki swung her spear through, knocking Ven away bodily. In response to her anger, her Divine Arms boosted her physical body far more than an imitation enchanted sword.

"Ngh…" Ven was blown backwards with great force. He crashed into the window and toppled outside of the mansion.

"Are you serious…? Hey, Ven, you okay?!" the remaining mercenary in the room yelled.

"Y-Yeah!" Ven staggered to his feet and yelled back. He had received some damage, but he was fortunate enough to block most of the attack itself with his sword. As he was rolling backwards, he was able to adjust his landing to fall safely.

"Get out of here already!"

Satsuki charged at the remaining mercenary in the room.

"Tch."

The man seemed to realize there was no good in remaining in the room. He retreated through the window.

"I won't let you get away!" Satsuki chased him out the window.

"W-Wow, Satsuki…"

Latifa was taken aback by the sudden turn of events. But she soon snapped to her senses and rushed over to the window to check on the situation.

Ifritah's out in the open! A-Alma!

She must have realized Ifritah was going wild from the sound of its roars. Latifa watched on as Ifritah lunged at Lucci, while Louise ran with Alma in her arms.

Meanwhile, far above in the skies where no griffin could reach, Reiss manipulated bullets of light to provide support to Arein and the others on the ground as he observed the battle. Although he could control their trajectories, he was quite a distance away from his targets. His accuracy was low, but it was enough to keep the kingdom's aerial knights back.

I knew there was a bird mid-class spirit here, but I hadn't expected any others… They must be demi-humans of the Wilderness after all, Reiss thought, guessing Alma's identity. He had previously seen a bird mid-class spirit patrolling the area when Rio was escorting Christina to Rodania.

Giving that sword to Lucci was the right decision. That sword is great against spirits. It should be able to take on a mid-class one easily. Though he seems to be struggling... And I don't see the other two outside either.

The "other two" that Reiss was thinking of were Sara and Orphia. If Alma was contracted to a mid-class spirit, it made sense that one of the other two was contracted to the bird spirit.

If two of them are contracted to mid-class spirits, then the third is likely to have one as well... I could deal with the bird one if it appeared in the sky, but another mid-class spirit on the ground would be troublesome.

With one of them materialized with no regard for the human witnesses, it wouldn't be strange for the other two to appear at any moment. Reiss hummed in thought as he focused on the movements taking place near the mansion.

The Heavenly Lions were all experienced fighters. They didn't have any secret abilities, but they were all equipped with imitation enchanted swords that could enhance their physical bodies, an effect stronger than magic. They had enough strength to take on a mid-class spirit as a group. Most importantly, they were here to avenge Lucius, making their movements sharper than ever.

However, although the two most dangerous people—Rio and Aishia—weren't here, the people around Rio were formidable as well. A hidden weapon had just appeared outside the mansion in the form of a mid-class spirit, and Ven's group had gone through a window just moments ago, but was promptly chased back out. The situation everywhere was changing by the moment.

There's a spirit's presence outside the capital? This is...the second mid-class spirit? But why is it outside?

Reiss redirected his attention from Rio's mansion below to the edge of the royal capital. Then, he cast his gaze over to the mountainous region a few kilometers away from the capital, where he saw a huge bird several meters in size flying.

Things involving this boy never go according to plan... I'll have no choice but to use my trump card. That, and a number of the revenants remaining on the ground...

Reiss returned his gaze to Arein and the others below, ceasing his support fire to hold his hand at the ground instead. But nothing visible happened. After a few seconds of maintaining that pose, Reiss began to fly towards the outskirts of the capital.

Moments later, the remaining revenants on the ground all started charging for Rio's mansion at once.

✦ Chapter 4 ✦
Back and Forth

Lucci was busy facing Ifritah. No, to be more precise, he was busy chasing after Ifritah, who was circling Celia's magic barrier.

"Stop running around, you pest!" he yelled, aiming a slash of darkness at Ifritah.

"Grrr!"

Although it was a few meters in size, Ifritah was a lion. It could move around speedily with ease and evade attacks by distancing itself in an instant.

However, it wasn't focusing entirely on fleeing. When Lucci tried to ignore Ifritah and attack Celia's barrier, Ifritah breathed fire from its mouth in an attempt to kill Lucci. "Grah!"

"Tch…" Lucci swung his sword, swallowing the fire with his blade's darkness.

"Grrr!" It seemed that Ifritah was especially wary of the darkness Lucci could release from his sword. That's why it focused on running around without facing him properly. When Lucci grew impatient with the game of chase and tried to ignore it, it would come back to interrupt him. It also attacked the mercenaries trying to break the barrier when it had a breath to spare. Because of that, the mercenaries were struggling to make any progress against it.

If I keep battling this thing, I'll run out of magic essence first. Is that its goal? What should I do? Even if I can warp my blade, I can't keep up with its movements right now. I need to get right up close to it the moment it stops moving...

If the battle drew out, Lucci would be the one disadvantaged. His only options were to avoid any combat with Ifritah or eliminate it completely, but he lacked the means to do that.

Thus, while Lucci and the mercenaries struggled to attack through Ifritah's defense...

"Alma..." With a strained expression, Celia thought about how to retrieve Alma from where she lay a short distance away.

"I will go assist her." Louise, who had been standing at the front of the barrier to lead the knights, turned back to whisper in Celia's ear.

"Louise?"

"Now's the time to save her, while the enemy's in disarray."

"But..." Celia hesitated.

Although Ifritah was running around, there were roughly ten mercenaries surrounding them. Even if they enchanted their physical abilities with magic, the knights had little chance of keeping up with their movements. One wrong move and Louise could end up on the ground next.

Although it had been a surprise attack, Lucius's enchanted sword had taken down one of their opponents. With that sword now chasing after Ifritah, the other mercenaries began to feel more confident in themselves. Alma lay collapsed a mere ten meters away from the barrier Celia had set up, but the situation made that distance feel much farther.

"I haven't contributed anything to this fight. Allow me to do this much for the sake of Lady Alma, who has protected us until now. It is a knight's duty to stand in the face of danger," Louise insisted, determination burning in her eyes.

Celia looked uneasy, but eventually nodded. "I understand… Please take care of her."

"I will. Knights, fire your magic at any enemy that tries to approach me after I leave the barrier. I will focus on movement and evasion alone."

Louise gave her orders, chanted the spell to enhance her physical abilities, then activated the magic. She watched the mercenaries' movements carefully.

"Now!" Leaping over the dirt wall Alma had built to provide them cover, Louise leaped out of the front opening of the barrier. She headed straight for where Alma lay. Lucci was the first to notice her.

"Hmm?" He ceased his attacks on Ifritah and focused his magic essence into his blade with the intention of finishing off Louise.

"Grrrah!" Ifritah must have sensed his intentions. In order to protect its contract master, it breathed fire towards Lucci.

"Tch…" Lucci swung his sword, summoning black energy to block the flames. In that time, Louise reached Alma and picked up her wounded body.

"Ugh… Sorry…" Alma apologized in agony. She had stemmed her bleeding with her spirit arts, but the serious wound prevented her from keeping the art activated consistently. She had suffered heavy blood loss and it was clear her mind was getting hazy.

"Kill them!" The other mercenaries joined Lucci in an attempt to attack Louise.

"*Photon Projectilis*!" The knights stationed within the barrier cast their magic to hinder them. They were all united in rescuing Alma.

This monster shows no sign of attacking the knights… In fact, it seems intent on protecting that brute of a girl. Which means…!

Lucci confirmed that Ifritah was clearly acting to protect Alma and started thinking of a way to use that to his advantage.

Immediately after, he chose to close in on Louise, who was running with Alma in her arms. His decision to ignore Ifritah's interference here was proof of his exemplary senses as a mercenary.

He easily outpaced her running speed by more than double. The few meters between them were closed in an instant, and the black sword enshrouded in darkness was raised in attack.

With him this close, Ifritah was unable to breathe fire over him. It could end up burning Louise alongside Lucci.

"Gaaarh!" Ifritah lunged at Lucci.

"Just as I thought!"

Lucci smirked, having predicted that move. He immediately switched directions from Louise to Ifritah. At the same moment, Ifritah opened its mouth to bite at Lucci.

"Take THIS!" Lucci's sword released a shock wave of darkness, engulfing Ifritah's large body.

"Ifritah!" Seeing that made Celia scream—but Ifritah's efforts had accomplished one thing.

"Ngh…!"

"Uhh…"

Louise leaped over the dirt wall before the barrier, tumbling to the ground. Alma fell with her.

"Ifritah will be all right…" Alma muttered to Celia before falling unconscious.

"It's only natural to prioritize the monster's extermination over the wounded brute of a girl," Lucci cackled heartily as he basked in his victory over Ifritah. He then turned to Ven, who was staggering to his feet by the mansion. "Yo, Ven! You having trouble against a single girl? Need help?"

Ven had been hit by Satsuki's attack, which had sent him through the window moments before Lucci defeated Ifritah. A short moment later, his fellow mercenary and a spear-wielding Satsuki jumped out of the window after him.

"Shut up! Stick to your own damn post!" Ven yelled in irritation. One of his men was unconscious after Latifa's attack inside the mansion, but there were still three on their side capable of a fight. The three of them moved to surround Satsuki.

"Everyone…"

Satsuki spotted Celia's magic barrier, the soldiers surrounding it, and the unconscious Alma inside, and fell speechless.

"How…? How could you do such a thing?! Who are you people?! Stop this already!" she yelled at the mercenaries, glaring at them with all her might.

"Ha ha." The mercenaries exchanged looks and smirked as though Satsuki's anger was terribly misplaced.

"A bastard called Haruto killed our commander. That's why we're here! We'll take you hostage to get our revenge on him. We can't let a bastard like that walk free," Ven replied.

"Haruto did what? Wait… Do you mean…? What are you saying?! That was because your commander killed his parents! He also abducted Princess Christina and Princess Flora! Haruto protected the two of them. Your commander was wrong first!" It was unjustified resentment, and Satsuki tried to protest with logic.

"Who cares!" Ven clearly had no intention of listening to such arguments.

"But…"

"We're only accepting the fight that was picked. If you don't want to be hurt, don't resist in the first place. That's all." It was the equivalent of saying that the victim should just endure their pain, that they wouldn't allow an excuse of self-defense. That they could go and cry about it.

"What a horrible way of thinking…" Their senses of values were so different, Satsuki was at a loss for words. She barely managed to utter a comment in response.

"Horrible? He's the same as us. The type to return things in kind. That was why he sought revenge on the commander," Ven said.

Satsuki snapped back. "No. Haruto is not like you people."

"He's exactly the same as us."

"No, he's not! Haruto will throw aside his own happiness to protect the people important to him. He'll never be the same as you."

"He throws aside his own happiness? Spare me the jokes. He's living blissfully in a mansion surrounded by women. His happiness is right there—and we can't forgive that. Seeing you makes us want to mess up his happiness even more." Ven slowly drew near Satsuki as he spoke.

"I won't let you do such a thing!"

"Then in order to protect your own happiness, you'll have to murder us all with your own hands. I don't know if someone as naive as you can kill a human, but I doubt you'll find happiness in doing so!"

"Wh…" Satsuki's anger had reached its peak. She no longer had anything to say, and all expression had fallen from her face. Only her lips trembled as she tightened her grip on her spear. She was completely ready for battle.

Just then, Latifa appeared beside her. "I'll fight too, Satsuki!"

"We'll assist as well." More people came out of the drawing room window—Miharu, Charlotte, Christina, Flora, and Vanessa.

"Latifa, all of you… Why…?"

Why had they left the safe room? It was dangerous—they should return immediately. Those were the unspoken words in Satsuki's confused expression.

"We're here to prove our pride as women. I'm only half-serious, but we overheard you talking. As a princess of the Galarc Kingdom, I cannot allow such low-life rabble to wander freely. That is why we are here," Charlotte explained cheerfully.

"Ha. Those are some harsh words from such a cute-faced brat. But are you sure you should be showing yourselves in front of enemies here to abduct hostages? Those are the princesses of the Beltrum Kingdom with you as well." Ven looked at Christina and Flora and sneered even more coldly.

"Oh? Why do we need to fear cowards who can't even face Sir Haruto without hostages?" Charlotte wasn't about to lose to them in words.

"What did you say?" Ven frowned, having a sore spot pointed out.

"I don't know how you found out, but you came to this kingdom after hearing of Sir Haruto's absence, did you not? A feat that shows no fear of a major nation's power. As expected of a top-class mercenary group—except it also means you *did* fear Sir Haruto's presence. I suppose even cowards are capable of having some good judgment, don't you think?"

Charlotte turned to Satsuki with an alluring giggle. Somehow, that helped her calm down a little.

"Umm, don't ask me… But, I agree. You thought it'd be easier to take on everyone in the castle than Haruto. A rather arrogant view to have." Satsuki smiled more like her usual self.

"Indeed. So, let's show them. Abduct us if you can," Charlotte said, provoking the assailants.

"Ha! Doesn't that sound interesting, Ven?" Lucci walked up to them, ready to face Satsuki.

"I told you to go back to your post, damn it."

"I'm outside the mansion, aren't I? Plus, a bunch of easy targets just came outside to offer themselves. They seem to enjoy talking big, so I should naturally teach them their places, no? The tiny sorcerer can be dealt with by the people I left behind."

Alma had collapsed and Ifritah was gone, so there was no one left to protect Celia's barrier. The only ones left standing were Celia and seven knights that could only enchant their physical abilities with magic.

Three mercenaries with physical body enchantments could easily overwhelm them in no time. Like Lucci had said, there were enough people remaining for that. Meanwhile…

"What should we do? We put on a brave front, but the only ones who can move around and fight are Latifa, Vanessa, and myself. If they push past us, we can't protect you all… We even brought Princess Christina and Princess Flora out here… Is that okay?" Satsuki whispered quietly to Charlotte.

"Flora and I are greatly indebted to Sir Amakawa, and these men were involved in our abduction as well. It is our duty as royalty to stand and fight in times of need. Let us offer what little power we have to the cause."

"Yes! I'll do my best for Sir Haruto!"

"Please don't worry about us," Christina said resolutely. Flora also seemed worked up—possibly because the matter involved Rio—as she was unusually enthusiastic.

"Don't worry. It seems like Lady Miharu and Lady Latifa have a plan," Charlotte said, glancing at Miharu beside her.

"Latifa...and Miharu?"

Satsuki looked at Miharu worriedly. They had been friends for a long time, and she knew Miharu didn't have the personality type for conflict. She couldn't imagine her fighting.

"Yes, please leave it to me." Miharu looked a little nervous, but she nodded with strong determination.

"At my signal, Miharu will take her place and the battle will begin," Latifa explained. "Satsuki and I will be the vanguards, and the princesses will support us with magic. If the enemy comes near, create a barrier with magic. Understood?"

"Yup, got it," Satsuki said. She was still a little concerned for Miharu.

"Yes, leave it to us. I'm starting to get excited." Although it had to be her first time experiencing such a thing, Charlotte looked like she was enjoying the situation.

"I have no objections either."

"Yes!" Christina and Flora also replied.

"Then here goes...!" Latifa took a deep breath. "Now, Hel!" she yelled.

"Grrrah!" Sara's contract spirit, a silver wolf, appeared, with Miharu riding its back.

"Wha?!"

"There's another one of those monsters?!"

For a brief moment, Lucci and Ven froze.

"Go, Hel!" Miharu clung tightly to Hel's back as it charged forward faster than the eye could follow. It weaved its way through the mercenaries until it arrived before the magic barrier Celia had cast.

"Miharu!"

"Celia!"

"H-Help Lady Miharu inside!"

Miharu jumped off of Hel's back and rushed over the dirt wall with the help of the knights. The group over here had originally been planning to take down parts of the barrier for the knights to rush out, but the start of Latifa's strategy had put an end to that idea. With Hel fighting in place of the knights, the situation turned in their favor.

"Wh-What's happening?" Celia asked, bewildered.

"I'm going to help Ifritah materialize once more."

"Y-You can do that?!"

Miharu nodded assuringly. "Yes. As long as I supply the magic essence needed."

Spirits weren't able to be physically harmed in their spirit forms, but their material forms could be damaged. Their physical abilities would decline if they maintained a wounded material form, and their bodies would disperse entirely if they sustained too much damage, but it wouldn't result in their death. They were simply forced back into their spirit form. If the necessary essence was resupplied, they could regain their material form without issue.

The problem, however, was regaining that essence. Whether it was magic or spirit arts, the more unnatural the phenomenon occurring was, the greater the amount of magic essence needed. And it was highly unnatural for a spiritual existence to take a material form. That's why it took a considerable amount of essence for a spirit to materialize. And it would take even more for a wounded spirit to regain an unwounded body.

Because of this, uncontracted spirits would take time naturally storing essence themselves, but a contracted spirit could receive essence from their contract partner and recover in an instant. Furthermore, humanoid spirits like Aishia could freely absorb essence from their contract partner through their connected path.

But that wasn't the case for mid-class spirits like Ifritah. Whenever it needed essence, the contract partner had to be the one to supply it. However, Alma was currently unconscious and unable to prepare any magic essence.

"I'm going to send you magic essence, Ifritah. You're listening, right? Here goes…"

Miharu would form a temporary contract with Ifritah in order to send it the essence it needed. The spirit needed to be the one to accept a temporary contract, but Miharu was well trusted by Alma, so that wouldn't be a problem.

In terms of pure combat power, Miharu was indeed the weakest amongst the residents of the stone house. However, when it came to magic essence, Miharu had more than everyone but Rio. No matter how many times Hel and Ifritah were wounded, she would be able to bring them back without issue.

The main concern was the distance required for a temporary contract partner to supply magic essence—they had to be right beside each other. However…

"Grr!"

Ifritah made a full recovery outside the magic barrier. Hel and Ifritah—with these two mid-class spirits on the battlefield, the battle at Galarc Castle was about to reach its climax.

On one side of the battle were Lucci, who was equipped with the jet-black sword formerly used by Lucius, and thirteen mercenaries including Ven, who were equipped with enchanted sword imitations that, while not as powerful as their genuine counterparts, could still provide physical enhancements superior to ability-boosting magic.

Facing them were Satsuki with her Divine Arms and Latifa with her physical body enhanced by spirit arts. Alma was still unconscious inside Celia's magic barrier.

Vanessa could only use magic to enchant her physical abilities, so it would be difficult for her to hold back the mercenaries alone. Even if she worked together with Charlotte's seven knights inside Celia's barrier, they would only be able to fend off three or so of them.

Celia, Miharu, Christina, Flora, and Charlotte were all rearguard sorcerers—or spirit art casters, in Miharu's case. They had to stay away from the front line of the battle, but there weren't enough frontline fighters for them to maintain such a distance.

That was how Lucci and Ven saw the situation—that is, until Hel and Ifritah joined the fray.

"Whoa?!"

"It's damn fast!"

Hel and Ifritah freely ran around the front of the mansion. The mercenaries might have been able to evade the attacks if there were only one of them. The physical body enhancements of their enchanted swords allowed them to react to the movements in time.

But with two spirits moving at once, they were helpless. If one of them had their attack evaded, the other would just wait for the right timing to make a follow-up attack. The two beasts moved in perfect synchronization, hunting the men down skillfully.

The mercenary men were instantly thrown into disarray. Three of them had already been hit by a charging attack and were now incapable of combat.

Satsuki and Latifa knew they'd just get in the way if they moved too much, and any spells had a risk of hitting Hel and Ifritah, so they left the combat entirely up to them. Instead, they were able to focus on protecting the princesses. However, that didn't mean they were spared from facing Lucci or Ven.

"Be careful of that man with the black sword! That sword can release a wave of dark energy strong enough to swallow up Ifritah's flames! It also has other abilities—the blade of the sword was stabbed into Alma's back while she was facing him. It was as if it teleported!" Celia yelled from the other side of the magic wall, warning Satsuki and Latifa of Lucci's sword.

The blade teleported...? Could it be...?

Unaware of the identities of the spirits, Christina had been greatly confused by Ifritah and Hel's appearance. But after hearing Celia's explanation, she felt a sense of déjà vu from Lucci's sword. It was the same sword that Rio had struggled against when he saved them from Lucius.

Christina gasped. "Th-That black sword is the sword that Lucius used! It was able to slash at us from a fairly long distance away! The blade disappears from the body and reappears wherever the darkness is. The sword's wielder can teleport in the same way, so watch out for any darkness around you!"

She quickly shared all the information she knew about it. Things would take a turn for the worse for them if Lucci used that ability here.

"Wh-What?!"

"That's terrifying!"

"Hmm."

It was quite the troublesome ability. The ones who reacted with the most caution were Latifa, Satsuki, Vanessa, and Louise's knights within the barrier. They looked all around themselves, searching for any darkness. The most likely targets for Lucius's sword weren't the two mid-class spirits moving about, but the groups stuck unable to move. But they didn't find any darkness.

"Tch..." Lucci shot a resentful glare at Celia, then Christina. His enchanted sword's ability had been accurately exposed by the two of them.

An ability like that would have caught one of us by now, but he's barely used it. Why...?

Celia considered the reasons. Perhaps Lucci lacked the magic essence to bring out the sword's ability, or perhaps...

"He hasn't teleported himself during this battle! And he only teleported the blade once, to stab Alma in the back... He might not be able to use the sword's ability very well yet! There have been plenty of opportunities to take, yet he didn't."

That was the more likely reason. And in reality—

Shit...

Lucci frowned at the pinpoint analysis. He was unable to use the enchanted sword as freely as Lucius had been when he was alive.

In fact, he was moving to evade Hel and Ifritah's attacks right now when he could have just teleported away to gain distance. If their goal was to take a hostage, he could have teleported inside Celia's magic barrier or behind Christina and Flora at any time.

"Seems like that's the truth."

"Yes, but it's best not to let our guards down..."

Satsuki and Latifa's expressions relaxed a little. But just then—

"Wraaah!"

Just as Celia's side gained reassuring reinforcements in the form of Hel and Ifritah, Lucci's side gained unexpected reinforcements of their own. It was the remaining revenants on the grounds. There were a few dozen of them left. Without a sideward glance, the revenants charged straight for Hel and Ifritah.

"Wh-What are those things?!"

Satsuki had been inside the safe room earlier, so she was seeing them for the first time. They had humanoid forms, but their shocking appearances were clearly inhuman.

"They're the monsters that fell on the castle! Their movements are quick and they can't be killed without hitting their heads or hearts, so be careful!" Celia called out, providing her with more information. Celia, Sara, and Alma's fine teamwork had rapidly eliminated the revenants around the mansion, but there had still been many remaining in the other areas of the castle.

On top of that, Arein's group was still in the air, bombing them with attacks and dragging out the battle within the castle walls.

Reiss's monsters, huh? Honestly, there's so much that we don't know about him and his monsters, but... Arein thought, definitely grateful for the help right now. Lucci and the others were similarly shocked by the unexpected reinforcements, but they had guessed it was Reiss who had sent them and smirked.

"Ha, perfect timing! The monsters can take it out on each other!"

"Use this chance to capture the hostages!"

Lucci decided to use the opportunity to ignore Hel and Ifritah. Ven and his men responded accordingly right away.

"Grah!"

"Grr!"

Hel and Ifritah tried to mow down the approaching revenants with their breaths of ice and fire, but their hardened skin was resistant to the elements. It was also possible that they couldn't feel the pain. Whether their bodies were frozen or burnt, they advanced without a care.

Meanwhile, the majority of the remaining mercenaries— including Ven—headed towards Satsuki and the others by the mansion. There were ten of them in total.

"Guh..."

Satsuki swung her spear to create a storm wind to push them back. But Ven and his men dispersed to the sides, allowing six of their ten to escape the attack.

"Now's the time! The five of you, go!" Louise shouted from within Celia's barrier.

They had aimed for the exact moment Satsuki activated her Divine Arms. Celia opened a cavity at the rear of the barrier, allowing five of the knights inside to begin charging. She then closed the holes at both ends of the barrier, preventing anyone from entering at all.

"Haaah!"

The knights mercilessly struck their swords at the stomachs of the mercenaries that had been knocked off-balance by Satsuki's wind. A strike in the wrong spot could be fatal, but they spared them from a direct kill in hopes of interrogating any captured men later.

At any rate, four of the mercenaries were taken out in one go. The knights remained calm in the face of their difference in abilities, stubbornly waiting for a chance at victory.

On the other hand, there were still a large number of revenants remaining, clinging to Hel and Ifritah as they tried to shake them off.

"Force your way through! Advance at all costs!"

Ven and the remaining five mercenaries spared no thought for their fallen comrades, moving to surround Satsuki's group. They were met by Satsuki, Latifa, and Vanessa.

They were outnumbered enough for the situation to be grim... Or so they thought.

"I won't let you!" Sara leaped out of the window, slipping past Charlotte to kick away the mercenary that had been approaching her. The other two knights that had been inside the mansion arrived moments later.

"Sara!" Her appearance made Latifa rejoice.

"Sorry I'm late! We've taken care of the enemies inside."

However, the situation was still uncertain. It was easy to have tunnel vision on a battlefield with so many people jumbled together, and ambushes could lie in wait where one least expected it. The ambush in this case was Lucci; he was missing from the mercenaries that attacked Satsuki's group.

"Wait! Where did the man with the black sword go?!"

Satsuki was the one to finally notice his absence, pushing back Ven's sword with her spear and questioning the people around her in a fluster.

"I'm over here!" Lucci called out himself.

There, standing inside of Celia's magic barrier, were Celia, the unconscious Alma, Miharu, Louise, and another knight—and Lucci. He had used his fellow mercenaries and the revenants as a decoy while he headed for the barrier. Celia had sealed all the exits of the dome to make it impossible to infiltrate, yet Lucci was beside them. This meant...

"Ngh, he really can teleport!"

Louise, who had been on guard inside the barrier, was first to slash at Lucci.

"With enough time to prepare and across a short enough distance, that is!" Lucci replied, giving a compact swing of his sword.

"Kgh—Aah!"

Louise was blown back, sword and all. Her body struck the inside of the barrier, and she slumped down on the ground. Lucci's enchanted sword had boosted his physical strength too much for her to handle.

"Captain!"

"Whoa, there."

Only one knight remained. She swung her sword immediately after Lucci was done swinging, but he swiftly blocked the blade.

"Gotta take out the trash first, right?!"

Lucci believed the knight was the only obstacle left and moved to eliminate her first. However...

"I'm sorry!"

Miharu held her palms out at him and released a blast of wind. The way she apologized while doing so was an expression of her personality.

She managed to avoid hitting the knight, but that was because of her current limits in attacking rather than any intentional adjustment.

"Oof..."

The unexpected strike sent Lucci hitting the wall this time.

"*Photon Projectilis*. Nice one, Miharu!"

With her instantaneous judgment, Celia canceled the magic barrier and chanted a magic spell. She was trying to land a rapid-fire follow-up attack on his rolling body.

"That hurt, you little brat!"

"Gah!"

"Urk..."

Lucci was desperate too. Getting hit by someone he had been underestimating angered him greatly, and he yelled while he rolled to evade the bullets of light. At the same time, he swept Celia and the knight off their feet, making them topple off-balance.

"Go to sleep forever!"

"Gwah!"

Getting to his feet, Lucci used his left hand to backfist the knight's face and knock her out.

"You've done it now, haven't you?!"

"Oww..." He stomped on Celia's back with all his might as she tried to get up.

"Celia!"

"Don't move, woman! The rest of you freeze as well, or I'll crush this brat's body."

He must have been especially wary of Miharu, who attacked without chanting her spells. He pointed his sword at her throat while warning Satsuki and the others by the mansion.

"Guh..." Satsuki and Sara pressed their lips together in frustration, grinding their teeth.

"Looks like this battle is over," Ven sneered, distancing himself from Satsuki. The other mercenaries also backed away.

"Tch, what a mess." Lucci checked the status of his unharmed comrades and clicked his tongue.

They had sent a total of twenty mercenaries to the mansion and its surroundings, but only seven were left standing, including Lucci and Ven. Sara had defeated the men inside the building, and most of the men outside were picked off by Hel and Ifritah.

"First, let's have those knights move towards the mansion."

"..."

At Lucci's order, the five knights that had left the barrier reluctantly dragged their feet over to Satsuki and the others.

"And who do the monsters belong to? Let's have them removed promptly."

Lucci made his next demand, glancing at Hel and Ifritah. He didn't know who they served, so he looked around at all their faces.

Hel and Ifritah were currently being clung to by revenants, sealing their movements. Both of them were struggling to shake them off, but the revenants hung on with their teeth and nails, making it extremely difficult to do so.

But conversely, that also meant Hel and Ifritah had suppressed the revenants from any other action. If the two of them disappeared now, dozens of revenants would be released at once.

"Wha—? If we removed them now, those monsters would be freed!" Satsuki shouted.

"I don't care about that," Lucci snorted.

"No, wait. Just leave them like that," said Ven.

"What? Why?"

"That monster reappeared after being defeated. It'd be a pain if that happened again. If we leave them this way, we can at least see their positions."

"I see…" Lucci nodded in acceptance, convinced by Ven's reason.

"But don't try any funny tricks. Order them to be docile, let themselves be attacked, and let the monsters have their way."

"Wh…"

As Hel's contract partner, Sara trembled with rage. Spirits felt pain in their material form just like any other living being. As someone who worshipped spirits, their ability to regenerate their bodies in spirit form didn't mean she was fine with leaving them in pain.

However, Miharu and Celia would be in danger if she didn't comply. Alma and Louise were also unconscious beside them. She had no choice but to endure the situation.

"Fine. This black-haired woman and sorcerer brat should be more than enough. Let's get going. Retreat!" Lucci called Ven and the others back to him.

"W-Wait a minute! We have your comrades held hostage as well!" Satsuki cried, looking at the mercenaries lying on the ground. She probably thought they'd be able to negotiate a hostage exchange.

"Ha. Do what you want with them. We all came here prepared." Lucci was uninterested in the offer. They must have all agreed in advance, as Ven and the other men showed no objection either.

"Why...?" Satsuki muttered in a daze. Weren't they here for revenge on Rio, who killed their commander? If they could feel that much rage at having their comrade killed, they should feel the same rage for their comrades sacrificed here. It was illogical.

In fact, they weren't acting out of logic. One of their own was hurt, so they would repay that pain and then some. If they got hurt in the process, they'd just make sure to add that pain on in the end. That was all it meant to them.

They wouldn't allow themselves to be one-sidedly bested. They couldn't allow it, which was why they had to harass the other side in return. They weren't moving logically, but emotionally.

"You keep an eye on this one." Lucci removed his foot from Celia and grabbed her by the clothes. He then threw her towards Ven and the others, who were approaching gradually.

"Aah!" Celia rolled on the ground helplessly. Then, Lucci's gaze turned to Miharu.

"Too bad for you, eh? Your connection to that bastard is what led to your abduction. You and that sorcerer crawling there are about to experience a world of regret for that connection, but if you're gonna resent someone, make sure to resent him, yeah?" he sneered crudely.

"Eek..." Miharu trembled, but she desperately clenched her fists to suppress her fear.

"W-Wait! I'm the hero! If you're going to take someone, take me!"

"I-I'm his little sister!"

Satsuki and Latifa offered themselves to protect Miharu and Celia. They were followed by Sara and Flora, who were more emotionally driven than not.

"Ha! Who would keep this many liabilities by their side with the threat of retaliation looming over their head? That bastard sure is a fool. But that just proves how it's his fault you're being abducted. We'll give you plenty of reasons to resent him, don't worry," Ven, annoyed by their attitudes, said mockingly, spitting his malice at the girls.

"Ngh…" Satsuki grimaced.

I see… Haruto knew this could happen. That's why he tried to distance himself from Miharu at the banquet…

Her expression turned bitter. She felt terribly panicked at the thought of things going exactly as Rio feared, when—

"Y-You're wrong!" Miharu shouted.

"Huh?"

"Haruto tried to distance himself from me. But I said I wanted to stay with him anyway! That's why it's not his fault!"

Miharu faced Lucci and his men without any fear. In a rare show of both volume and emotion, she tried to stand up for Rio.

"That's right… That's why we have to be the ones to fight. I don't want to have Haruto protect me all the time—I'm not going to be a burden!"

From her position on the ground, Celia used both arms to struggle up weakly. She squeezed out her voice to convey her determination.

"Tch, what a damn drag… So what?! No matter how much you struggle, reality won't change!"

"Hey! Enough already, Lucci." Ven called for Lucci to hold back his raging tantrum.

"What?!"

"Leave the rest for after the abduction. Arein's squad is struggling with their burden. We gotta get going."

Lucci looked up to see Arein's squad holding back the castle's aerial knights even now.

"Fine... But this one attacked me without chanting a spell earlier. It'd be a pain to have her awake while moving, so I'm going to put her to sleep first. It'll also be a thank-you for earlier."

Lucci had nodded reluctantly, but he was fast to change his mind. He removed his sword tip from Miharu's neck and swung the flat side of the blade at her face.

"Eek...!" Miharu squeezed her eyes shut, bracing for the impact. However, what she heard next wasn't the sound of a sword hitting her face...

"My sincere apologies for the delay."

...but the sound of clashing metal and the gentle voice of an older man. Miharu opened her eyes timidly.

"I, Gouki Saga, have arrived to exact justice."

On the other end of Lucci's sword was Gouki, blocking the blade with his own.

⁕ Interlude ⁕
Travel Log

Some time ago, around the same moment Alma was defeated by Lucci…

Orphia had teleported back with Gouki and his people on a mountain a few kilometers from the capital of Galtuuk.

"Let us hurry, Lady Orphia. Please lead the way," Gouki immediately prompted. He had been informed of the situation before they arrived.

Orphia had witnessed ominous black shapes raining down from the sky the moment before she left the capital. There was a high possibility that the castle where Miharu and the others were was in danger, so she had brought them here with great haste.

"Yes, but Ariel is only able to carry eight people at once… No, if we consider the possibility of an aerial battle, it may be best to limit it to five." While Orphia could fly on her own, there were too many of Gouki's people to carry.

There was the representative of their party, Gouki; his wife Kayoko; their daughter Komomo; Sayo, who left her village to chase after Rio; and her brother Shin, who came along out of concern for his little sister. There were also twelve of Gouki's attendants, who had been serving his family for many years.

"In that case, we can split into two groups. Three of my people will come with Kayoko and me," Gouki said, promptly deciding which members would head to the castle. "Aoi, Shin, and Sayo… You remain here with Komomo and the others."

"I will set up the stone house here for them." Orphia quickly set up the stone house nearby for the people staying behind to wait inside. The only basis for the bad feeling she had was the black shapes she saw just before teleporting. If the castle was actually safe, her efforts would be for nothing, but that was fine with her. It was better to hurry just in case. However, on the way to the capital, they discovered that her worries were not unfounded.

"What is that…?" The first person to notice was Orphia, who was flying in the front. She was at a height of roughly five hundred meters above ground, but there were many shapes falling rapidly from even higher before her. They numbered around fifty, and they were approaching them at a rapid speed.

"Th-They may be lower class demi-dragons!" Orphia yelled, identifying the shapes immediately. They closely resembled the winged lizards often spotted throughout the Wilderness.

"So that's a demi-dragon… Hmm." Gouki looked at them curiously, having never seen one before.

"They're most likely winged lizards. But why are they here in such large numbers…?"

Their territory should have been in the Wilderness. The odd individual wandered into the Strahl region from time to time, and there had been kingdoms that tried to catch them for breeding and taming like griffins, but there hadn't been any success. That was what Rio had told her before, so it was strange for them to be by Galarc Castle in such large numbers.

However, there was something about them that was different to the winged lizards Orphia knew. Firstly, their skin color was as dark as a Black Wyvern. Secondly…

"What?!"

When the winged lizard opened its mouth, a breath of fire came rushing out to kill them.

"Haaah!" Orphia flew towards the winged lizard, creating a barrier of wind to protect Ariel and the passengers behind her. The breath was cleanly redirected away.

"Splendid!" Gouki laughed in praise. "These things have appeared to stop us from approaching the castle, it seems. They must be related to the black shapes you saw earlier, Lady Orphia."

There was no basis for his guess, but his senses had been sharpened by many years of combat experience, and that was what his senses were telling him.

"Here they come!" Orphia suddenly warned.

The winged lizards made a rapid approach to bite at Gouki's group.

"Looks like we'll have to eliminate them!" As soon as Gouki shouted that, he leaped from Ariel's back, falling under the force of gravity. "Ha ha! How convenient indeed. As expected of Lord Dominic."

He kicked the air and started running across it. The secret to this feat was in the boots he wore. They were a magic artifact crafted by Dominic, capable of creating tiny magic barriers to serve as footholds for running and leaping through the air.

Sara and Alma could do the same with spirit arts, but it was a technique that required delicate control of essence. If Gouki was to learn the technique from scratch as a human, it would take quite a long time. That's why, although they were a little tricky to use, these boots were designed to support his spirit arts.

I may not be able to fly freely like Sir Rio and Lady Orphia, but at least I can fight in the air now! Gouki rejoiced. This was to be his first battle in the air.

"Hmph!" Gouki charged into a winged lizard from the front, drawing his sword as he passed. The winged lizard's tough body was cleanly sliced in half.

"Ha ha, I couldn't be more grateful to Lord Dominic. What a splendid blade."

The sword he carried was named Kamaitachi. It had been forged by Dominic for Gouki after Gouki had told him about all the weapons and armor in the Yagumo region. The sword had perfect compatibility with its wielder, who had named it—Gouki specialized in wind spirit arts, and this top-class weapon could clad itself in wind arts just like Rio's.

The winged lizards scattered like mist in the air, leaving behind enchanted gems that dropped to the ground below.

Monster gems? They're not winged lizards...?

Orphia was confused by the sight of the gems. She couldn't retrieve the enchanted gems during battle, but an analysis would be necessary.

She used her spirit arts to create several balls of lightning, then fired them at the fake winged lizards at a rapid speed. The lightning orbs struck several of the creatures.

"Gyaaah!" The fake winged lizards merely staggered from the impact and continued to fly.

It seems arts have little effect on them, just like real winged lizards.

Thanks to that, she now knew their strengths and weaknesses. It seemed they were basically winged lizards that could breathe fire.

"Arts that convert magic essence to energy will have little effect. If you're going to attack with spirit arts, create something with physical substance or impact!" Orphia immediately explained to the others.

"I see. Understood. Everyone hear her?" Kayoko asked the three attendants that remained with her on Ariel's back.

"Yes!"

"Then let us go. We didn't come along to be baggage. Let's prove our worth."

With those words, Kayoko jumped from Ariel's back. Her attendants followed. They were elites that had been trained in combat by Gouki and Kayoko from a young age. They ran through the air without any fear.

Incidentally, the weapon Kayoko held in her hand was a kodachi. Even if she was able to run through the air, her weapon reach seemed insufficient to take on the winged lizards. However...

"Grah?!"

A stream of water extended ten meters from the end of her kodachi, wrapping around the body of a winged lizard like a whip. With its moves restricted midair, the winged lizard lost balance.

"Hmm..." Kayoko pulled the winged lizard in towards her, then burst into a run. She then drew one more kodachi from its sheath and stabbed it into the creature's head. The winged lizard died, leaving behind an enchanted gem.

What a wonderful blade indeed. The skin of the creature appeared fairly tough, yet...

The kodachi had pierced the head of the demi-dragon smoothly, like there was no resistance at all. Both of the kodachi in Kayoko's hands were top-class weapons forged by Dominic. They were optimized for water spirit arts, which she specialized in.

If they can be killed with a single strike to the head, then there's no need to restrain them. I should be able to conserve my magic essence. There's no telling how harsh the battle will be once we arrive at the castle.

As she was thinking such things, the next winged lizard drew near to bite her to death. But the moment it opened its mouth—

"If you open your jaw so wide, you'll obstruct your own vision. And it's bad manners," Kayoko muttered. She waited until the last moment before moving. The jaws closed around nothing but air.

"Grr...?!"

Heavy pressure from above caused the winged lizard's body to drop. Kayoko had leaped up, using the momentum of her fall to thrust her kodachi in its skull.

The winged lizard made to scream, but its vision was already black. Its body soon dispersed.

"Right. Let's clean this up quickly!"

The greatest fear of midair combat was the possibility of enemies coming from every direction, but both Gouki and Kayoko handled themselves perfectly in their first midair battle, cutting down every winged lizard that approached. Gouki's three attendants worked as a team to handle their share of the enemies without any issues either.

They're amazing... I can't fight like that, so I'll use my ice...

Orphia was impressed, but quickly activated her spirit arts to join the fray. She figured that simply releasing her essence as cold air wouldn't be enough to freeze them, so she chose to stab them with ice spears instead. If Celia was a master at making fixed forts, then Orphia was a master at making moving ones. She simultaneously cast her flying spirit arts with the ice spear creation, counterattacking all the winged lizards that approached her.

"Kreee!" Orphia's contract spirit, Ariel, manipulated the wind to push the winged lizards back, adjusting how many of them approached at once.

Thus, over thirty winged lizards were defeated in a matter of minutes. At that point, the remaining enemies seemed reluctant to approach just to be killed.

"Gyaaah!"

They stopped their attempts to bite in favor of circling them from a distance.

"Ugh, their movements have changed. Everyone, fall back!" Gouki ordered.

"Please get on Ariel's back. They're about to breathe their fire." At Orphia's suggestion, the humans that couldn't fly returned to Ariel's back.

"Graaah!"

As she expected, the winged lizards began to breathe fire. However, Orphia and Ariel both could control the wind. They didn't allow the flames to reach them.

"Winged lizards normally challenge enemies they have an advantage over…"

The winged lizards here were clearly abnormal. They were monsters that dropped enchanted gems. Orphia frowned, realizing once again that something was odd.

"Hmm. Their movements are strangely unified. I don't see any specific leader of the group… Their only goal seems to be to stall us."

"Although we're able to run through the air now, enemies that can fly freely are still difficult to take on."

"Indeed. There's no telling what's happening at Sir Rio's mansion, so we shouldn't remain here any longer."

Gouki looked around at the winged lizards with suspicion, while Kayoko expressed her annoyance at the battle dragging out. Thus, Orphia came up with a suggestion.

"How about you all go with Ariel to check on the castle first? I can take on the rest of them alone."

"Hmm. Are you sure?"

"Yes. The numbers have been reduced by a lot already. The capital is right before us, and there might be something going on there. Ariel knows where Rio's mansion is located too."

Orphia recalled the black shapes she had seen before teleporting. She wanted to check on things as soon as possible. They were currently one kilometer from the capital. Ariel could make that distance in no time at all.

"Indeed… All right. We will return immediately if everything is fine over there."

Gouki's group specialized in close combat, so they had been disadvantaged from the moment the winged lizards started to keep their distance. Orphia was best suited for long-distance combat with her spirit arts, so it was the most efficient decision to make at the moment.

The winged lizards were breathing fire even at this moment, but Orphia's wind barrier was blocking the attacks perfectly. She should have no issue taking them on alone.

"Yes, and I will follow after you as soon as I'm done. I finished preparing my magic essence while we were talking—I'm going to release a large-scale art. Ariel will take off at my signal."

"Understood," Gouki nodded.

"Go, Ariel!"

"Kreee!"

At Orphia's signal, Ariel started flying for the capital. Until now, Ariel had remained stationary through the use of wind spirit arts, but it accelerated rapidly the moment it flapped its wings.

"Graaah!"

The winged lizards redirected their fire, but Ariel had a wind barrier set up to veer the flames away. Then, once Ariel had made it a certain distance away, Orphia began her attack.

"I am your opponent!" A large tornado appeared around her.

"Grah?!"

The winged lizards were swallowed in the tornado, losing their balance to the point they could no longer fly. However, the tornado itself didn't do any damage to them. Letting them fall to the ground was one way they could be damaged, but Orphia chose to send them higher up into the air instead. Then she took aim at the staggering winged lizards and fired her ice spears.

"Greeeh?!"

An ice lance pierced through the bodies of the winged lizards. Some survived the first spear, but were soon taken out by the follow-up attack.

"All right!"

By the time Orphia cleaned off the remaining winged lizards, Gouki's group had just arrived in the skies above Rio's mansion.

Meanwhile, Reiss was hiding far above the clouds after sending the winged lizards to stall Orphia's group.

A swarm of fifty dark winged lizards was eliminated so easily. I figured demi-dragons would be the best matchup against a caster and her mid-class spirit, but alas...

He had made quite the miscalculation. He hadn't been expecting to defeat her completely, but had thought she would struggle more than this. It should have been enough to fulfill his goal of buying some time.

Winged lizards were the weakest variety of flying demi-dragons, but that didn't make them weak as monsters. Their skin was hard and resistant to magic essence, their teeth were sharp, and they could fly around the air freely. On top of that, the ones Reiss released could breathe fire. They were not weak by any means at all.

What he hadn't accounted for was how skilled Orphia was at spirit arts, even for a high elf.

The spirit art used to fly in the air was highly advanced. That was why most spirit folk were unable to cast large-scale arts while flying at the same time—but it seemed Orphia was an exception to this.

Furthermore, she's brought along some powerful reinforcements. Where are all these troublesome people appearing from, honestly…?

Reiss chuckled to himself. Even he didn't know why he was laughing at a situation one would normally be angered at.

It seems I was completely preoccupied with the Black Knight and his contract spirit.

He had underestimated the people gathered around Rio without realizing it himself. He knew they had some decent skills, but he figured they were fine to leave alone.

However, when all these skilled people gathered together, they formed a formidable force equal to a major nation.

There's no mistaking the fact the Black Knight is the most troublesome, though. We must obtain insurance against him. But if we're unable to secure a hostage, then… At worst, we should consider reducing the forces around him. The attack this time is assumed to be the work of the Heavenly Lions, after all.

If they couldn't secure a hostage, then they'd stop worrying about capturing them alive.

If we do this, they'll be convinced that I'm still alive, but…

But it was worth doing anyway, he decided.

Chapter 5

Hero Killing

Riding on Ariel's back, Gouki's group arrived at the castle to the sight of knights fighting assailants everywhere. They were currently 150 meters above the castle. At the hundred-meter point, the aerial knights were fighting griffin-riding mercenaries, firing magic at each other.

"This is much worse than I expected... Ariel knows the way to Sir Rio's mansion, right? Ah, is it below us?" Gouki asked, spotting Rio's mansion—or rather, the people around it.

"I can see everyone. The situation is rather bad. Everyone, be prepared."

Miharu, Celia, and everyone else were down below. Lucci had just taken the two of them hostage, so it was easy to read the situation immediately. There was no need to hesitate.

"These crooks... Let's go, Kayoko."

"Understood," Kayoko replied.

Without missing a beat, Gouki jumped down from where Ariel was stopped 150 meters above the ground.

"You three wait for Ariel to descend. This is our first battle for Sir Rio. Let us not shame his name," Kayoko said to the remaining attendants, then jumped after Gouki. Thus, the strongest married couple of the Karasuki Kingdom joined the battle.

By creating elastic footholds in the air, the two of them descended to the ground running. Air resistance was no obstacle for them, and they arrived in a matter of seconds. Their attendants were still incapable of such a feat.

"…" Gouki reached the ground first, having jumped off Ariel before Kayoko. He created a foothold right before landing, absorbing the impact and silencing his footsteps. Right beside him, Lucci was about to swing his sword at Miharu's face.

"I'm going to put her to sleep first. It'll also be a thank-you for earlier."

Perhaps it was because of her glossy, long, black hair. The sight of Miharu overlapped with Rio's mother Ayame in Gouki's eyes.

I must protect her no matter what. Now that I have arrived, he will not harm a hair on her head.

Gouki prioritized defending against Lucci's attack. He slipped between Miharu and Lucci, stopping the black sword with his own blade.

"My sincere apologies for the delay. I, Gouki Saga, have arrived to exact justice," he declared solemnly.

"Wh-Who the hell are you?!" Lucci raged, trying to push Gouki's sword back with his physical strength.

"Silence, you fiend!"

"What?!"

However, the one who did the pushing was Gouki. He hadn't sent any of his strength into his sword. All he did was step forward, and that was enough for Lucci's body to be pushed back.

He took another step forward, then vanished. Moments later, he reappeared right before Lucci.

"Lucci!" Ven yelled. He had started running towards Gouki the moment Lucci was pushed back to cover for him, and he made it just in time. If he had started running one moment later, Lucci would have been cut down.

"Hmph…!" Gouki smoothly evaded the sword Ven stabbed from his side, falling back to where Miharu was.

"I have secured Lady Celia." Kayoko joined him, having retrieved Celia from where she lay beside the mercenaries.

"Good," Gouki nodded.

"Wha…? When did she—?!"

"Who is this old man? And this hag?!"

Lucci, Ven, and the five mercenaries still able to fight were dumbfounded as they gathered together in one group.

Kayoko's eyes were ice cold. "Hag? Such disrespectful fools. I'm only just over forty."

"Kreeeh!"

Ariel had also descended to ten-odd meters above ground, allowing Gouki's three attendants to leap off its back. The three of them moved to surround Alma and Louise on the ground as soon as they landed.

"They seemed like rather mobile fiends, so I waited until our defenses had gathered first. Now I can punish them without holding back. Is that fine with you, Lady Miharu? The situation was rather evident, even without the need for words."

Despite glaring at Lucci and his men with seething rage, Gouki's assessment of the situation was extremely calm.

"Y-Yes. Thank you very much…"

Miharu must have been extremely tense, as she staggered just from nodding. However, she was certain they would be fine now, and she was able to get back on her feet right away.

"Understood. Now, I don't know who you people are, but you've raised your hands towards people who are important to my master. Don't think you'll be getting out of this." Gouki's eyes glinted as he glared at the men.

"Uhh..." Sensing danger, the mercenaries all started backing away. The instincts that they had developed through all their combat experience were warning them of Gouki's formidable strength.

"Gouki! These men are the subordinates of the man who killed Rio's mom and dad! Be careful of the man with the black sword! It can release a strong shock wave of darkness, and the sword has the ability to warp the blade and the user!" Latifa yelled, sharing information about Lucci and the others.

"Oh?" Gouki's attention was drawn to the identities of the men more than the sword's abilities. A fire ignited in his eyes.

To think I would be given such an opportunity here...

He shuddered with excitement. Before he knew it, his mouth was moving of its own accord. "Finally... Finally, I can prove my devotion to him," he muttered.

"Huh?" Lucci replied. However, it seemed his words were only audible to Kayoko, who was beside him.

"I will go with you. You three will be able to protect Lady Miharu and Lady Celia, right?"

She entrusted Celia to one of her subordinates, then stood beside Gouki. With a flowing movement, she drew her kodachi and shot Lucci a cold glare.

"We have even more reason to put a stop to you now. There's no need to confirm the situation any further," she said. The two of them held their respective weapons ready.

"I am Gouki Saga."

"And I, Kayoko Saga."

"For the sake of our master!"

"We challenge you to a duel!"

The strongest married couple and pride of the Karasuki Kingdom yelled together, then closed the five-meter distance to their opponents in a single bound.

"They're fast!" The seven mercenaries tried to retreat immediately, but Gouki and Kayoko split up and cornered the scattering men, preventing their escape.

"Shit!" The men they approached readied their swords, but they only lasted a few strikes before they were disarmed and made powerless.

"You've gotta be kidding me!" There were five mercenaries remaining. The two nearest mercenaries to the disarmed men charged at Gouki and Kayoko, swinging their swords. But Gouki and Kayoko vanished before their eyes, evading the swings. All they did was crouch down on the spot, but to the men, it was like they had disappeared.

"Guh!" The men went flying through the air. Gouki and Kayoko swung the bladeless sides of their kodachi to strike the men in the jaw. They were concussed midair and knocked unconscious. There were only three mercenaries remaining, including Lucci and Ven.

"H-Hey now!"

"This old man and hag are bad news!"

The remaining three were extremely shaken and barely able to keep their distance from the couple. But even as they ran around, Gouki and Kayoko were closing in from the sides.

"F-Fall back!" Lucci desperately gathered magic essence in his sword, scattering his shock wave of darkness to hit his opponents.

"Too slow!"

However, Gouki and Kayoko both leaped up, evading the shock wave.

In normal circumstances of war, unnecessarily large jumps during battle opened one to attacks. Humans couldn't control their movements midair, so the time between landing and adjusting their stance was the biggest moment of vulnerability. The only options were to attack while falling or to prepare oneself to block the incoming attack.

"Dumbasses!" The experienced veterans knew this and reflexively went for that opening. Ven and the other mercenary charged at their falling opponents.

However, they should have been more wary of the two that had made such a sudden and grand entrance. Both Gouki and Kayoko crouched midair and leaped again.

"Wha?!" Before the mercenaries knew it, the couple was on the ground. They stood behind Ven and the other mercenary with their backs facing them.

"Wh…at…?" Ven and the other mercenary had dazed looks in their eyes as they collapsed. Gouki and Kayoko had landed two strikes to their jaws as they landed on the ground.

"Guys! Damn it, you've done it now!" Lucci howled, trembling from head to toe.

"Rest assured, we have no intention of leaving the enemies of our master alone. We just held ourselves back for now," Gouki said.

"The young ladies don't need to be exposed to the blood and death of such filth over a situation of this level," said Kayoko.

"We also need to interrogate you on anything else you may be plotting. The punishments can wait until after that," Gouki added.

"That's not what I meant! Don't think you can mess with me!"

"You're the ones messing about. I assume you're here for your unjustified resentment over the death of that man Lucius, but…"

I will be the one to deal with him—Gouki signaled that to Kayoko with his eyes as he replied to Lucci. He then slowly inched his way closer.

"W-Wow. Who are those people…?"

Latifa was familiar with Gouki's group, but Satsuki, Charlotte, Christina, and Flora had no idea who they were. They had watched the one-sided fight take place in astonishment.

"Don't worry! They're on our side!" Latifa informed them happily.

"That just leaves those monsters, then…" Six of the mercenaries had been defeated in an instant, leaving only Lucci standing. But Sara was more focused on watching the revenants swarming near the mansion with a grim look.

Hel and Ifritah were still being held down by dozens of revenants. Their flesh was being torn off and bitten into, leaving them unable to move. They were probably on the verge of losing their material forms.

They were holding on so desperately because of the dozens of revenants that would be released if they turned into their spirit forms. However, now that the tables had turned on the battlefield, they were finally able to do something about it.

"Hel, Ifritah! Thank you, you can disappear now!" a voice cried from overhead. It was Orphia, bow held ready in her hand.

"Orphia!" Sara shouted with joy as Hel and Ifritah disappeared in relief.

With nobody to cling on to, the revenants started to scatter. They didn't seem sure of their next target, but it was clear that they saw Sara and the others as their enemies. But before they could make their next move, Orphia shot a single arrow of light. The thick arrow would have taken quite some time to charge up, but she had been able to stay undetected in the skies and do just that. The powerful light arrow split into two and rained down over the spot where Hel and Ifritah had just disappeared.

"Graaah?!" Two dense masses of pure energy crushed the revenants to death, leaving behind two craters that were ten meters in diameter. The monsters vanished, leaving a large number of enchanted gems behind.

"That should do it." Orphia descended to where Alma lay unconscious. In the one or two minutes since Gouki's group arrived, the situation had been completely turned on its head.

"Ha ha, how wonderful. As expected of Lady Orphia." Gouki chuckled heartily at the sight of Orphia's grand method of eliminating the monsters. He then turned back to Lucci, the last remaining enemy. "Now, shall we put an end to this?"

"Eat shit!" Lucci yelled, making a dash towards Gouki. Gouki also launched himself forward. The two were soon within reach of each other and swinging their weapons.

Swords crossed faster than the eye could see, during which Gouki started a conversation. "Hmph! I just don't understand!" he shouted.

"Understand what?!" Lucci yelled back

"Why are you so mad? What reason do you have to be so emotional?"

"One of my comrades was killed!"

"While it sounds like you have perfectly reasonable values, your actions are completely contradictory! How can you value your own comrades while stealing the lives of others?"

"It's survival of the fittest! Anyone who isn't a comrade is of no concern to me! There's no contradiction anywhere!"

"That isn't much of an answer!"

It was at this point that Gouki's katana sent Lucci flying with his sword. Lucci's body had a more powerful physical enhancement thanks to Lucius's enchanted sword, but Gouki's body was enhanced with spirit arts. They were equally powerful enchantments, but their base strength was different.

"Shit!" Lucci backed away furiously. There was no leisure in his expression at all. He was unable to keep up with Gouki's attacks, and shallow cuts began to accumulate over his body.

"Let me change the question, then. If you believe in both survival of the fittest and valuing your comrades, why do you direct your resentment to Sir Haruto, who's stronger than all of you? Explain that contradiction. Sir Haruto is the one who defeated your leader. Survival of the fittest means you either surrender or hide yourselves once your leader is dead."

Gouki temporarily put some distance between them and pointed the end of his sword at Lucci to ask his question. Why challenge Haruto if that was the case?

"What…? Ngh!" Lucci was about to let his emotions snap, but found himself stumbling over his words instead. He was unable to come up with a logical reason.

"Hmph, no answer again. You're a child with no sense of reason."

"I'd rather die than answer such a pathetic question!" Lucci yelled. His pride wouldn't allow such a thing.

"Then die! If there's someone you refuse to surrender to while believing in survival of the fittest, your only options as a warrior are to die challenging them or to quietly kill yourself somewhere out of sight," Gouki rebuked him sharply. That was what it meant to truly believe in the concept of "survival of the fittest."

"Ngh…!"

"You can't even do that, so you harass him behind his back. How laughable! You only claim survival of the fittest when it's convenient to you. Those are the actions of nothing more than a vain coward!"

"Sh-Shut up! We came to take hostages so he wouldn't run away! That's how mercenaries work!" Lucci howled like a cornered dog.

"Hmm… The same mercenary that's seeking revenge for his leader and comrades? I thought mercenaries were all about fighting for money. How pitiful."

You don't even know your own reason for being here right now, Gouki implied with a look that bordered on mercy instead of contempt.

"Grr…"

"But I can understand you a little more now. There's no justice in your revenge—you have no reason at all. You just want to resent someone. If you value your comrades, you shouldn't have laid your hands on other people's comrades. I hope you can understand this one day…" Gouki trailed off, readjusting his katana's position. Perhaps he had started this conversation in order to vent his feelings for the man who killed Ayame and Zen. Or perhaps he wouldn't feel content without getting the last word in against the fiends who tried to harm his master.

"And regret it deeply for the rest of your life!" Gouki started running, closing the distance between them once more.

"Gah! Ugh— Argh, shit!"

The difference in their physical abilities was minimal, yet Lucci couldn't keep up with Gouki's sword movements. The more Gouki swung his sword, the slower Lucci's reaction speed was.

Sh-Shit, I barely have any essence left as is.

It was all he could do to maintain his physical body enhancement. At this rate, he would lose.

On top of losing the logical argument, he was about to lose in sword mastery. With nothing but complete defeat on the horizon, Lucci began to panic.

"Hmph. Your agitation is showing in your sword. You're full of openings!" Gouki saw through that panic and used that delayed reaction to slide right up to Lucci. He then swung his katana up from left to right.

"Wha—?!" Lucci tried to respond by defending, but his black sword sailed through the air.

"Fuck…" The hand that held the sword was also knocked upwards, causing the upper half of Lucci's body to bend back.

"Justice!" Gouki flipped his blade at the end of the first swing and stepped forward, striking Lucci with the back of the sword before sliding past his side.

"Gah…" Lucci groaned, collapsing to the ground.

"It's over." With his back to the fallen man, Gouki moved with elegance, sheathing his katana with a clink.

"Gouki!" Latifa called Gouki's name happily, waving her hand.

"Good day, Lady Latifa." Gouki's expression, having been sharp throughout the entire battle, immediately softened as he walked over to her.

"Thank you for saving us!"

"It is my duty to protect everyone. Lady Orphia told us of the ominous shapes she saw falling over the castle, so we rushed over here. It was lucky we did so."

"Lady Latifa, may I ask who this is? He seemed to refer to Sir Haruto as his master during the battle, but…"

Charlotte had just finished ordering the knights to restrain the intruders and carry the wounded to the mansion. She questioned Latifa about the curious information her sharp ears had picked up on during the battle.

"My name is Gouki Saga. I served Sir Haruto's late mother while she was alive." Gouki introduced himself respectfully in the Karasuki manner. He seemed to have determined Charlotte's high status from her clothes and demeanor.

"Oh my, is that so…?" Charlotte recalled how Rio's parents were immigrants as she observed Gouki's appearance carefully. His slightly strong accent was probably because he was an immigrant as well. The one thing she was most curious about was how he appeared to be of important status too. His refined movements were clearly ingrained deeply into him, and above all, the sword mastery he showed in the earlier battle was indisputably top class.

How interesting. The mystery around Sir Haruto grows again.

Charlotte smiled in delight, having taken a newfound interest in Gouki's group.

Incidentally, the reason why Gouki and his people were able to speak the Strahl common tongue was because the Strahl region and Yagumo region once had a select few nations that kept in touch with each other.

Rio also learned this for the first time after meeting Gouki in the Karasuki Kingdom, but there were some nations that used the Strahl common tongue as a second or third official language because of this history, and the Karasuki Kingdom was one such nation.

As it was only considered a second or third official language, it was mostly royals and civil officials that bothered to learn it. Their pronunciation was also rather accented when compared to the standard in Strahl, but Gouki and his people had been studying the language since the moment they decided to follow Rio to Strahl. The heavy accent had greatly improved during their stay in the spirit folk village, but there were still some traces of it.

"Oh, pardon me. My name is Charlotte Galarc, Second Princess of the Galarc Kingdom. Thank you for saving us from the earlier predicament. On behalf of the kingdom, I wish to express my warmest gratitudes." Charlotte picked up her skirt by the hem and curtsied elegantly.

"Ah, so you're Princess Charlotte. I've heard a lot about you from Sir Haruto."

"Why, I'm so pleased to hear that. Oh, and allow me to introduce you. This is First Princess Christina and Second Princess Flora from the neighboring kingdom of Beltrum."

"Hello, I'm Christina. Thank you very much for saving us earlier."

"I'm her little sister Flora. It's nice to meet you."

He must be a soldier who used to serve Sir Amakawa's mother. From what he showed of his strength, he would have been one of the strongest in the country...

Someone just like the King's Sword of Beltrum, Alfred Emerle. Since Christina knew that Rio's mother was royalty, she was able to guess his background more accurately than Charlotte. For someone of such strength to leave Yagumo and come this far, he was probably incredibly loyal to Rio.

Memories of her days at the Royal Academy flashed through her head, making her frown. Feelings of guilt surged within her. Rio had told her not to worry about it, but these feelings would probably never disappear completely.

"And this is the hero, Lady Satsuki."

"I'm Sumeragi Satsuki... Ah, that would be Satsuki Sumeragi in this world. It's very nice to meet you, Gouki."

Satsuki seemed quite interested in Gouki's appearance, as he closely resembled a Japanese person, but first gave a simple self-introduction.

"I've heard many stories about all of you. It's very nice to finally be meeting you," Gouki said, bowing deeply.

"Dear, I'd like to move Lady Alma and Lady Celia to somewhere they can rest."

Kayoko came up to them with the wounded Alma in her arms. Miharu, Orphia, and Celia were with her.

Celia had been treated terribly by Lucci earlier, but she hadn't sustained any major wounds or fallen unconscious. Miharu and Orphia had offered to lend her a shoulder to lean on, but she wanted to walk by herself. The only thing she did was cast healing magic on herself just in case.

"In that case, please take her inside the mansion…" Charlotte had just suggested, when—

"A signal flare?" Its light shot across the sky above the castle.

"It isn't a signal flare from our kingdom," a nearby knight observed. There were different signal patterns for each kingdom, but she didn't recognize that one.

"It must belong to the attackers. Their griffin squad must be fleeing," Charlotte guessed. She could see the mercenaries that had been fighting the aerial knights flying away from the castle.

"I guess they gave up on the mansion…?" Satsuki muttered.

"Everyone has their own post in the battlefield," Charlotte explained. "Their goal may have been to raid this place, but with the squad in charge wiped out, there's nothing left for them to do."

"So they'd abandon their comrades?"

Perhaps she found them heartless, or perhaps she was worried they would return. Either way, it was a question only a novice at war would ask. Her question was answered by Gouki, who was an actual veteran.

"Of course, there's a possibility they may return, but the role of the enemies in the sky was to secure a path of retreat and prevent reinforcements from arriving. Rushing over here would be the same as abandoning that role. Unless they had a plan that would allow them to rescue their comrades without a path of retreat, they wouldn't come over here. It'd be the same as an honorable suicide."

Whether it was in enemy territory or on the front lines, rescuing a comrade was a high-risk action. The rescuing side could end up needing to be rescued themselves, and anyone who left their post could cause the front line to collapse, causing even more damage.

They had to look at the bigger picture. If someone insisted on saving their comrade in spite of that, then they had to make sure there was no issue in leaving their post and keep a path of retreat secured.

It was easy for the side being rescued to unhappily think, "Why didn't you come to save me?! You've gotta be kidding me! Some comrade you are!" but the comrades that had to weigh the risks of rescue were just as easily susceptible to stress and guilt over abandoning their allies. But it was something both sides mutually understood when participating in war. There were even psychological tactics to leave captured enemies alive but powerless on purpose because of this. That was what happened in war.

"I see…" Satsuki looked somber, but seemed to understand.

"If the mercenaries in the sky have begun to flee, then it means there's no way for them to retrieve their allies. We can leave the rest to the castle guards," Charlotte stated.

Just then, something roared.

"WROOOOOOH!"

Shortly before the signal flare went up in the sky, somewhere in the rooftop garden.

Splendid work. Thank goodness everyone seems to be safe…

King Francois had just witnessed the fight take place outside Rio's mansion with bated breath. In fact, he was still watching them now. The enemies' movements had made it clear that their target was Rio's mansion, but there was another reason he had been so intently focused on the mansion during the entire ordeal.

It began with Celia, Sara, and Alma taking on dozens of monsters by themselves, followed by the fierce attack of the mercenaries that were faster than what the knights with magically enhanced physical abilities could keep up with, followed by the appearance of a huge beast that started to fight the mercenaries for them, followed by Alma getting stabbed, followed by the hero Satsuki coming out of the mansion…

Who was then followed by the princesses stepping out into the garden, followed by the return of the beast that disappeared, followed by the monsters across the castle gathering before the mansion, followed by Celia and Miharu nearly being taken hostage, followed by the arrival of an outrageously strong man and woman from the skies who began overpowering the mercenaries, followed by more people riding a giant bird…

The situation changed more than just once or twice. There was no way he could look away. Even the reports from his subordinates began to get on his nerves, so he left the command of other areas to them from partway through.

I can't believe they survived an attack of such a scale without any injuries…

There were many things he wanted to confirm as the leader of a nation, but for now, he rejoiced openly.

Those helpers who appeared from the sky are most likely related to Haruto. I can ask the details from him in person when he returns, but I would like to speak to them privately under the pretext of expressing gratitude. Perhaps Charlotte can handle the negotiations.

At that moment, a knight ran up to Francois in a fluster. "The enemy has begun their retreat, Your Majesty! What would you like to do? Shall we pursue them?"

"Go after them, but don't pursue them too far. Make sure the city is not damaged in the pursuit. Some of the enemies must have been captured already—they will suffice for interrogation. What we should prioritize now is assessing the damages and treating the wounded."

"Understood. In terms of casualties, there have been a significant number of wounded, but no deaths."

"Oh? So our military is quite capable after all." He was tempted to compare them to the people of Rio's mansion… But regardless of that, he looked pleased.

"The squad in the sky was mostly moving to buy the others time, so things played out well there."

In addition to that, the castle had many people who were capable of using healing magic. As long as no one was instantly killed in one hit, there were many people available to heal them.

"I see."

"Also, regarding the matter of their swift movement speed—the secret seems to lie in the swords they had."

The knight reporting was about to explain the abilities of the enchanted swords the mercenaries were equipped with, when—

"WROOOOOOH!"

It was at that moment that something roared.

Everyone on the rooftop garden flinched in surprise. It almost sounded like the voice was coming from the sky.

"What?!"

Most people looked up reflexively.

"What…is that…?"

What Francois saw was an embodiment of despair.

Hero Killer.

It all started over a thousand years ago.

During the era of the Divine War, there was a being that was crowned with the name of Hero Killer for slaughtering countless heroes of the war.

The name of the being that even enchanted-sword-wielding heroes feared was Draugul.

"WROOOOOOOH!"

A voice thundered through the capital. It almost sounded like the wailing cry of a man.

The one making the noise wasn't a revenant left behind on the castle grounds. It wasn't a griffin in the sky either. Nor was it Ariel, Orphia's contract spirit that was still in the air. Hel and Ifritah were still in their spirit forms after being wounded earlier. In the first place, it wasn't a volume of sound that could be made by creatures of their sizes.

"WROOOOOOOH!"

The owner of the voice was the Hero Killer, Draugul.

Meanwhile, in the courtyard before Rio's mansion…

"Hmm. This is a rather strange sight…" Gouki furrowed his brow, looking up at the sky.

"Wh-What is that…?" Satsuki asked, trembling. No one there knew that it was the apparition of the legend. However, if Aishia had been there, she would have been able to associate his presence with Reiss, even if she didn't know about the Hero Killer Draugul. She had actually fought him once before.

It all took place in Rodania. While Rio was traveling through the Proxia Empire and Paladia Kingdom for information about Lucius, in the middle of Christina and Flora's abduction taking place elsewhere, Reiss had appeared before Celia. Aishia, who had been guarding her in spirit form, materialized to pursue Reiss, who in turn summoned a large number of monsters and undead knights to fight her.

The Hero Killer was the most powerful of the undead knights Aishia had fought at the time. Unlike the other monsters, he didn't leave an enchanted gem upon defeat. Reiss had disguised himself as Draugul to fake his death when she defeated him. At the time, the Hero Killer had been deterred by her overwhelming power, but the Hero Killer wasn't weak by any means.

The era of the Divine War gave birth to many fierce warriors; there was no way someone with a nickname as exaggerated as Hero Killer could be weak. He had earned the title by continuously sending experienced warriors equipped with enchanted swords to their graves. The nickname of Hero Killer was given because it would take the effort of multiple heroes for him to have any chance of defeat.

Minotaurs were dwarfed by the size of his ten-meter-tall body. He wielded a several-meter-long one-handed sword and sturdy-looking shield, on top of being dressed in full body armor. Two wings grew from his back like a devil or fallen angel.

The undead knight glared down from his position a hundred meters in the sky, eyes glinting with ominous hatred. The people inside the capital perceived his presence.

"If the mercenaries in the sky have begun to flee, then it means there's no way for them to retrieve their allies. We can leave the rest to the castle guards," Charlotte said.

"Can we leave that to the castle guards too, Char...?" A tense wind blew. Satsuki looked up at the overwhelming presence of Draugul above her head as she nervously questioned Charlotte, but Satsuki hadn't asked with the intention of mocking the situation.

Her expression showed how much she wanted to leave it to the guards if possible.

"Probably not…" Charlotte would have loved nothing more than to agree, but she knew things wouldn't end well that way. She would have to borrow the strength of the people here to defeat that monster.

"It's clearly glaring this way. How interesting." Gouki stared back at the Hero Killer in the sky with a smirk.

"N-No, no it's not! It isn't interesting at all!" Satsuki shouted in protest.

"Leave this to me. Since we don't know how it will move, it would be best for everyone here to focus on defending with barriers."

"It sounds like you're planning on charging in alone, but I'm going to fight too, dear." Kayoko lined up alongside Gouki, who was raring to fight.

Gouki looked at his wife and grinned. "Hmm… Fine. But don't think your excitement is being hidden right now."

"Of course not. This is the perfect situation to test our worth in Sir Haruto's absence. It's only natural to feel spirited, wouldn't you agree?"

"It is indeed. We will express our devotion for Sir Haruto by protecting everyone here. It truly feels like I'm swinging my sword for him. Bring the monster on! I couldn't have asked for a more worthy opponent!"

Gouki pointed his katana at the sky and yelled fiercely.

While the fearsome roar and sinister aura of the being had clutched everyone else's hearts with despair, Gouki and Kayoko showed no hesitation at all. In fact, their unfazed attitudes spurred on the others around them.

"I will fight too!" Sara stated first.

"As will I."

"And me, of course."

Celia and Orphia added.

"No no, you should all focus on defending yourselves. Sir Haruto isn't here right now," Gouki said, hurriedly encouraging them to retract their offers.

"That's exactly why!"

"Yup!"

Sara and Orphia were unyielding.

"Hrmm…"

"It's precisely because Haruto is absent right now that we have to work together to overcome this dilemma. If I let someone else protect me here, I'll become someone who always needs to be protected by Haruto… I want to prove that I don't need to be protected. I don't want Haruto to distance himself because of my own weakness!" Celia said. She conveyed the same feelings she had before Lucci and the mercenaries here, in front of the Hero Killer.

"Lady Aishia is the only one who can truly fight together with him, after all. Even if the two of them were here right now, Haruto would leave Lady Aishia behind to protect us and fight alone. But that's so lonely for him, and somewhat frustrating for us."

"We know he's acting for our sakes, but we want him to rely on us a little more."

"Yes!"

Sara and Orphia confessed their true thoughts as though to encourage themselves. At any rate, they had presented their motives for fighting. There was no need for further discussion.

Just like how Gouki and Kayoko saw the situation as a chance to prove their loyalty to Rio, the girls wanted to put up a proper fight in Rio and Aishia's absence.

"The elderly shouldn't dismiss the hearts of young ladies so lightly, dear."

"Hmm... I'm reminded of all the times Lady Ayame made such ridiculous requests." The feelings of the three girls had affected him.

"Either way, Ariel's presence will be indispensable in an aerial battle against that thing. Let us borrow their strength gratefully," Kayoko advised.

"All right, I understand. Let us defeat him together."

Thus, they all found their resolution.

"Protection of the ground will be handled by Miharu, Ifritah, and Hel. The two spirits will put up essence barriers, so could you supply them with magic essence? Offense isn't the only means of fighting. It's an important role only you can fill."

If they were going to fight the Hero Killer Draugul, they couldn't just focus on attacking. Sara nominated Miharu as the key to their defense for her ample amounts of magic essence.

"Sure, leave it to me."

Miharu couldn't imagine herself fighting the enemy that had appeared in the sky. She'd just be helpless and get in the way of others. The somewhat lonely expression on her face was because of how keenly she felt her current limits. However, that didn't mean she had nodded weakly. She wanted to do what she was capable of, so she spoke up with a firm voice.

"The mercenaries might use this chance to attack again. Latifa and Satsuki will be in charge of suppressing them! Please guard the others, you two!" Sara said, leaving an order for Latifa and Satsuki as well.

"Okay!"

"Got it...!"

The two of them braced themselves and nodded.

"..." Meanwhile, the Hero Killer was still looking down at the ground brazenly.

"Why doesn't it come down to the ground...?" Flora wondered out loud. Indeed, it could descend if it wanted to.

"Like the monsters that appeared earlier, it's clearly there to support the mercenaries. I don't know how it's possible, but someone in the Heavenly Lions is clearly controlling these monsters from the shadows. In which case, they might not want to hit their comrades on the ground," Christina guessed, looking around at her surroundings. There hadn't been enough time to gather all the unconscious mercenaries in one spot, so they were scattered about everywhere. If the Hero Killer descended right now, they would be affected by the battle, and she assumed he didn't want that to happen.

At any rate, it was impossible to predict how the apparition would move. There was no telling how long this silence would continue for. They didn't know how he would attack, and they didn't know if there was another reason why he wasn't attacking. They had an overwhelming lack of information.

But they had to make a choice.

"We wouldn't want it to fight beside Sir Haruto's mansion and destroy it either. I'd like to make the first move against it..." Gouki said, presenting his first choice.

"Right. Orphia, please lend us Ariel."

"Go ahead! And Celia, use this to recover your magic essence."

The whole party climbed onto the giant bird's back, including Orphia herself. While doing so, she handed a spirit stone to Celia. Celia recognized what it was right away. "Thank you!"

After keeping up a barrier for so long in the earlier battle, Celia was completely out of essence. Partway through the battle, she had started to draw essence from the spirit stone Rio had previously given her, but she appreciated the extra boost to her recovery.

"All right, here we go!"

With Gouki's shout, Ariel rose into the sky. Then, as though it had been waiting for that moment—

"WRRROOOOOOH!"

Like a fallen angel hovering in the sky, the undead knight howled loud enough to shake the air over the capital.

"Orphia and I will use long-ranged attacks to watch how it reacts first," Celia offered, exchanging looks with Orphia.

"Understood. Kayoko and I will handle the close-range combat, along with Lady Sara."

It was their specialty style of fighting, after all. The division of roles was decided swiftly.

"For now, I'll use intermediate-level magic to gain the advantage in attack numbers. Orphia will watch the opponent while preparing a big attack!"

"Okay!"

"Septet Magi: Magicae Displodo!"

Seven magic circles appeared above Ariel's head. One beat later, seven beams of light fired out of them. Each cannon shot that was fired like a greeting had enough force to knock out a warrior physically enhanced with an enchanted sword.

He's not moving out of the way?

The Hero Killer made no move to evade.

"…"

He calmly raised his shield at the incoming barrage.

"Wha—? You've gotta be kidding me…" Celia was dumbfounded as the fifth, then sixth shot met its target. He staggered a little in the air, but he was continuously taking intermediate-level cannon fire from in front without issue.

Eventually, Celia's seventh shot met its mark.

"I'm ready!" Orphia fired a single arrow of light from Ariel's back. All the magic essence she would have used on flying was able to be refined for her attack, making her arrow much more powerful that Celia's cannon fire.

"Wruuuh!" Instead of raising his shield to block the attack, the Hero Killer swung his shield to knock the arrow down. As a result, he didn't sustain any damage.

"I see... He seems to be rather confident in his defense. But the attack just now had enough force to require him to knock it away with the shield instead," Gouki said, analyzing his movements.

Orphia's one attack had the same amount of force as advanced-level magic. If I want to damage him, I'll have to use advanced-level offensive magic too.

Celia immediately began to consider the candidates for her next attack spell.

"In that case, that shield and armor will be quite the nuisance," Kayoko said, sighing in annoyance.

"Yes. Anything fired from afar will be blocked by that shield. And I'm sure he can evade if he needs to as well."

Sara also realized the high difficulty of defeating him from afar and frowned. During that time, Ariel rose until it was higher than the Hero Killer.

"At any rate, we've now obtained information about his defenses. He's also shown how he responds to long-range attacks. Which leaves the matter of close-range combat! Now, it's my turn to test his reactions!" Gouki leaped down from Ariel's back and ran through the air towards the Hero Killer. His opponent sensed his approach and made eye contact with him.

"..."

"Ha ha! He's even bigger up close!" The Hero Killer was easily ten times Gouki's size, but Gouki just laughed heartily as he charged forward.

The first one to swing their weapon was the Hero Killer. The one-handed sword was several meters long, so its reach was on a different level to Gouki's. However, Gouki understood that clearly as he continued charging.

Good reaction speed, and precise aim! His speed is also impressive, but...

Gouki jumped midair and evaded the attack. The Hero Killer's sword swung under him, missing. The wind pressure pushed his body upwards.

"Let's see how sturdy those weak points of your defense are!"

Gouki weaved through the gap between helmet and armor, aiming for the Hero Killer's neck. However, his opponent wasn't about to allow that so easily. The Hero Killer swung his shield upwards in an attempt to knock Gouki back.

"Whoa! That shield really is a nuisance!"

Gouki used his comparatively smaller frame to his advantage and evaded the attack. He then made a temporary retreat to where Ariel was.

"His reaction speed and movement speed aren't impossible to keep up with, but that giant body and equipment are a huge problem. His defenses are too strong. If we were to bring him down with long-range attacks, I could run around and distract him from lifting his shield. That may be the best way of getting a powerful hit in," he said to the others.

"An alternative would be for Orphia and I to blow away that shield so that you can all get a hit in where the body is uncovered by armor," Celia suggested.

"Ha ha, that sounds equally exhilarating. The thought of cutting down such a huge and solid body makes my heart dance. However, he's yet to show a true weakness. We'll need to observe him while fighting a little more to find his weak points!" Gouki said, then ran off to challenge the Hero Killer again.

"I'll go too."

"I'm going as well!"

Kayoko and Sara jumped off Ariel and followed him. Thus, the battle between five fierce warriors and the Hero Killer commenced for real.

✤ Chapter 6 ✤
Tachi of Wind

Shortly before the Hero Killer appeared in the sky, Arein's aerial stalling squad had just begun to retreat from the castle at the signal flare.

"Run for it! No one's saving you if you get caught!" Arein shouted, hurrying his comrades from the rear of the group.

Shit… We sacrificed so much, and yet…

They were being forced to retreat without capturing any hostages. With no results to show for the price they paid, this was an utter defeat.

The raid on the Galarc Castle had started with fifty people, but there were less than half of them able to retreat. They had lost over twenty-five of their capable comrades, along with all the fake enchanted swords they had been equipped with. It was a huge loss for the Heavenly Lions. Unable to do anything about it, Arein scowled.

If we could at least retrieve the guys in the mansion…

There was no guarantee they were still alive, but he had witnessed the knights capturing their comrades just before they began their retreat.

However, there was no doubt retrieval would be difficult. Their initial surprise attack had succeeded thanks to the use of monsters that sent the castle security into disarray. Reiss had also provided assistance from the air for a while. But the more time that passed since the attack began, the more of the Galarc Castle's army was dispatched for battle. Even if they charged back with their entire group, they'd just be surrounded and beat up one-sidedly.

In fact, the aerial knights of the Galarc Kingdom were pursuing them right this moment, from a distance of several dozens of meters away.

There's no choice but to abandon them... Arein repeated to convince himself.

But just then—

"WROOOOOOH!"

The air across the capital trembled.

"Whoa! Whoa, there!"

Arein flinched in shock, as did the griffin he was riding. It lost its balance in midair and wavered.

"Wh...What is that...?"

At that moment, both the fleeing mercenaries and pursuing aerial knights completely forgot about each other. They were all distracted by the undead knight that appeared above their heads.

"Is that Reiss's work as well? He didn't mention anything about such a huge monster in the strategy meeting before the attack..."

The undead knight in the sky, the Hero Killer, was an irregular being for Arein and the mercenary squad as well. But they already knew who was controlling the monsters in this attack.

"I don't get it, but our pursuers are faltering. This is our chance to get away!" Arein recovered immediately and focused on their escape. Fortunately, the army dispatched by the castle stopped pursuing them there, fearing further damage to the castle.

Thus, they completed their escape from the capital a few minutes later. They descended at a spring in the forest on the outskirts of the capital—the same place they had agreed on gathering after the operation. The moment they alighted from their griffins, exhaustion swept over them. They sat down in silence and sighed tiredly.

"Hmm. Your numbers have decreased a lot." Reiss descended beside them, looking around at their numbers and commenting out loud.

"Mister Reiss…"

"I am aware you were unable to accomplish the goal."

"…" The first thing that came to Arein's mind was an excuse, which he swallowed with a bitter expression. The others around them had similar faces as they looked on in silence.

"I have no intention of criticizing you. You, your squad, and the squads in charge of the mansion all worked well. There were a total of fifty mercenaries equipped with enchanted swords. Of this number, twenty-five were sent to the mansion, which is quite a considerable force. Enough to launch an effective surprise attack on the royal castle of a major power. That's why I thought there was enough power on our side, but my judgment was incorrect. The strength of those at the mansion caught me by surprise. As did the reinforcements."

Reiss lifted his palms and shrugged as though to say he was at a loss for what to do.

"Because of that, I had no choice but to bring that thing out."

He looked in the direction of the royal capital. Gouki's group was fighting the Hero Killer in the sky.

"So that was your doing as well?"

"Yes," Reiss said, nodding.

"…" He was unable to voice any criticisms, but Arein's expression was clearly protesting why Reiss didn't bring out a powerful monster earlier if he had such a strong card up his sleeve from the beginning. Reiss must have read that question from his face, as he began to explain.

"It wasn't my intention to let that thing fight here. I have suffered a considerable loss by bringing it out as well."

163

Namely, giving Rio the ability to determine that Reiss was still alive.

Reiss had already informed Arein and his men that he had faked his death before Rio and Aishia, but he hadn't explained that it was done by making Aishia think he was the Hero Killer and having her defeat him. That's why he didn't specify what it was he had lost in this situation.

"So why did you...?" Arein asked.

"The raid this time has taught me something important—that the Black Knight has surrounded himself with capable people. If we cannot secure a hostage, then we should at least remove some of those annoyances. The other reason is because I have a favor to ask of you."

"A favor?"

"The enchanted sword Lucci wielded was an important memento of your commander. I'm sure you would want to retrieve it as well, no? And so, we're going to retrieve both Lucci and his sword right now."

Reiss revealed the details of his favor.

"N-No way. I mean, I'd love to do so if I could, but going back now is just asking for the people in the castle to snipe us down! Even with that monster in the air, they're going to be on the watch for a second attack!"

They would be heading straight for their deaths, Arein argued back.

"I'm not asking you to charge in headfirst. Take this..." Reiss took out a sparkling gemstone from his breast pocket.

"This is..."

"You should be familiar with its use, no? It's a single-use teleport crystal. It will take you right beside the mansion. And this one is for your escape."

"When did you...?"

"Lucci was being pushed into a rather disadvantageous position, so I snuck through the chaos and set up the teleport coordinates as a backup."

"I see. Nothing gets past you," Arein muttered in awe.

"I've ordered that thing to focus on fighting in the air, so all their main forces will be directed to the sky right now. The mansion should be shorthanded right about now," Reiss said with a smirk.

"Can I save the others inside as well...?"

"As you know, the maximum number of people that can be moved by single-use teleport crystals is six. It will be impossible to retrieve everyone. As long as you keep that in mind, I don't mind what you do. However, the highest priority is Lucci and Lucius's sword. If you let your greed get the best of you, this teleport crystal will not only be wasted, it'll fall into enemy hands and be abused for their benefit. Please understand that."

Reiss placed emphasis on his warning, not wanting the plan to fail.

"I understand... I'll do it. I have no reason not to. I'll form an assault squad immediately."

Sure enough, Arein accepted the teleport crystal from him.

Meanwhile, in the skies above the capital, Gouki and the others were locked in a cutthroat battle with Draugul. Gouki, Kayoko, and Sara were using the sky as the front line, surrounding the Hero Killer. He specialized in close combat, and his power, speed, and abilities as a swordsman were exceptionally high across the board.

"He has a high degree of skill as a swordsman. His use of the shield to defend is also top class. Above all, he has a solid build.

Breaking through from the front is near impossible. It may be better to focus on merely distracting him," said Gouki, who was challenging Draugul from the front. The Hero Killer engaged them in large-scale melee combat, making good use of his sword and shield while staying faithful to the basic fighting forms. He didn't seem to have any means of long-range attack, but by simply swinging his shield, he was able to create a violent storm.

"Raaargh!" His sword swings also disturbed the wind with its aftermath.

"Hah!" Gouki made several jumps in midair, evading the areas with wild winds. It was at that moment that Sara made a move, having snuck around to the Hero Killer's side.

"Haaah!"

Her dagger was within reach of the Hero Killer's helmet. The next moment, his head had frozen over, turned into a giant block of ice. However...

"Rah...!" However, the Hero Killer didn't falter. He didn't stop moving. He shot his arm up to swipe Sara away from his face. Sara leaped on the spur of the moment and distanced herself. But the Hero Killer's frozen head didn't seem to change his field of view. That was how much precision was packed into the swing that chased her.

"Ugh... Where are the eyes on that thing? Jeez!" This time, Sara leaped vertically to evade the strike. She rode the wind created by the huge sword passing under her and spun in the air, shouting.

"Take that!"

Orphia, who was now flying by herself, successively fired thick arrows of light. Each one had the force of an intermediate-level offensive spell, but they all had a homing effect that focused on the frozen head of Draugul. However, he was an iron wall that didn't even flinch over a spell of intermediate level. The Hero Killer twisted his huge body and swung his shield, mowing down the light arrows over an extensive range. But the arrows weren't the main point.

"*Magnus Magicae Displodo*!" Riding on Ariel's back, Celia fired the extra-large magic essence cannon she had prepared at Draugul's frozen head. It was a simple but powerful advanced-level spell that had the same force as all the arrows Orphia just fired added together.

However, her opponent was still able to see every attack. He bent his upper body to easily evade the shot.

"In that case…!" Kayoko used the kodachi she held in both hands to release a water whip, wrapping around the Hero Killer's neck. She then yanked on them with all her might, pulling him off balance ever so slightly.

"Gouki!"

"On it! Hidden Skill, Second Blade, *Aura Mico*!"

Gouki had made his way behind the enemy in the blink of an eye, closing the thirty-meter distance to slash at the Hero Killer's back.

The cuts of wind his secret art created were packed with power, and the slashes caused the Hero Killer's body to fall forward. The armor on his back cracked faintly, which didn't escape Gouki's notice.

"I will provide support!"

The moment where Draugul lost his balance was their biggest chance. Orphia immediately began rapid-firing additional light arrows, this time hitting his head with all of them.

"Haaaaaah!"

Sara had also sent magic essence to turn her dagger into a two-meter-long blade of ice, slamming it down on his head from above. The Hero Killer's head jerked downwards.

"This time it'll work! *Magnus Magicae Displodo*!" Celia had gone around to the front to directly land the second shot of her extra-large essence cannon. Cracks spread across the entire armor as Draugul was knocked back from his forward-bending position.

"Yay!"

Everyone cheered, thinking they had landed an effective hit on him.

"Raaagh!" However, the Hero Killer used the momentum of the knock-back to flap his wings and rise.

"What?!" Gouki shouted, shocked by how vigorously he moved. Everyone was dumbfounded by his impressive show of endurance.

"But I saw there were cracks in the helmet and armor! If we can hit him one more time with an attack like just now...!" Sara said hopefully.

"Great idea, but it seems he's wary of us now!" Gouki warned with a grim look.

Now that he knew that they had attacks that could break through his defenses, the Hero Killer was flying around at a distance to them. His flying speed was fairly fast—too fast for them to keep up unless they were able to fly freely like Orphia or Ariel.

"It's hard to land our attacks when he's moving that fast. And he's too dangerous to approach recklessly..."

Orphia's arrows of light were being evaded with ease.

"H-His helmet and armor... It's repairing itself!" Sara shouted in shock.

Orphia nodded nervously. "Yeah, you're right."

Like Sara said, the equipment on the Hero Killer was rapidly repairing itself in front of her eyes. It wasn't instant, but it was happening fast enough for it to be fully repaired in less than a minute.

They probably had to damage the skeleton body in order to defeat him, but now they had to start from cracking the sturdy armor and helmet all over again. On top of that, he was constantly keeping his distance from them, giving his armor time to repair.

"Something that big, solid, and fast can regenerate itself? That's not fair…"

What could they do about it? Despair and panic filled Celia's face. It was only natural for her to be at a loss—no one there was aware, but many heroes had fallen to this regenerative iron wall in the Divine War.

"He's more troublesome than I imagined…" Kayoko muttered, glaring at the Hero Killer circling in the air with great force.

"RAAAAAAH!"

The Hero Killer changed trajectories and charged towards Celia. His helmet and armor had fully repaired itself, and he was armed with his shield that was far sturdier than the armor.

"Ngh!"

Gouki, Kayoko, Sara, Orphia, and Ariel, with Celia on its back, all scattered in different directions. The Hero Killer focused on Gouki, chasing after him without a second look at the others.

There was no human that could survive a tackle by such a large being, physically enhanced body or not.

"Whoa! This is quite the predicament!" Gouki waited until the last moment before successfully evading the charge. He watched his retreating back with a grim look.

"Everyone, let's all group up with Ariel for now! The situation will only get worse like this! Save your essence and stamina!" Orphia shouted at Gouki, Kayoko, and Sara. "Ariel, get everyone!"

Ariel moved towards Kayoko, Sara, then Gouki, to retrieve them in that order. Finally, Orphia climbed onto its back.

"The enemy has a huge frame on top of all that speed. It may be difficult to attack him from every direction like before…" Gouki glared at the Hero Killer as it circled.

"I don't suppose he'll just fly away like that, will he…?" Celia murmured with a despairing look.

"He's clearly aiming for us, after all. Fortunately, he's shown no sign of heading for the ground, but there's no guarantee this will continue forever. We need to defeat him as soon as possible, but he's quite the formidable enemy. This is bad."

In contrast to his words, Gouki had a fierce grin on his face, watching the Hero Killer.

"You don't look very troubled…" Sara muttered with a sigh.

"He's just a war nut, so don't worry about him. He'll come up with a ridiculous plan sooner or later, so give him a minute."

Kayoko reassured the others, completely used to his behavior. At the same time, she showed deep trust in the strategies Gouki came up with.

Hmm. His body is covered in sturdy armor, and he constantly has his shield up. In order to defeat him, we have to destroy those and smash his skeleton body, but we haven't been able to scratch the shield so far. The helmet and armor seem breakable, but they repair over time. Which means we have to deal even more damage than before, outpace the repair speed of the helmet and armor, then break his body… But he flies so fast, it'll be a real challenge.

In reality, the strategy for defeating the Hero Killer was extremely simple. What Aishia had previously done was close in on the Hero Killer at a faster speed than he could fly around, then use one heavy attack to break everything before it could repair.

But that simplicity was what was most difficult.

If I use my secret arts in succession, I should be able to do enough damage to break the armor and body. In order to do that, his movements have to be stopped. Hmm...

The problem was how to stop the nimble movements of such a monster so that the secret arts could hit their target. Gouki considered the possibilities.

The best time to attack would be when he attacks us... But he's especially confident in his use of the shield to defend his front. He'd ignore any superficial attacks to charge straight for us. Wait, no. I see. He charges forward when...

It was at that point that Gouki had a light bulb moment.

"I have an idea," he proposed with a grin.

Miharu and the others on the ground watched the fight taking place from in front of the mansion. They were protected by Hel and Ifritah, who had set up a two-layered barrier around them.

The Hero Killer had shown no sign of wanting to descend to the ground, so the group appeared to be safe within the barrier. The commander of Charlotte's knights, Louise, looked around at her surroundings and reached the same conclusion.

"Princess Charlotte, I believe now would be a good time to restrain the mercenaries lying around," Louise suggested.

The Hero Killer had appeared shortly after the mercenaries were defeated, so there were still a number of them lying around without any restraints. They hadn't even finished retrieving the enchanted swords that were in the mercenaries' possession. While some of the mercenaries had received fatal wounds, there were others who were merely passed out. If they regained consciousness and started attacking again, things could get dicey.

"Indeed. Can you handle that yourself?" But just as Charlotte nodded in agreement, a dozen or so of the castle's knights approached the mansion.

"Princess Charlotte!"

"They're finally here," Charlotte muttered weakly, watching the approaching knights.

"This is…"

The knights that came running to them took one look around at the surroundings and fell speechless. The aftermath of a fierce battle spread around them—unconscious mercenaries lying on the desolate ground, enchanted gems left behind from the revenants, and a crater caused by Orphia's attack.

At the center of the disastrous spectacle was Charlotte's group, protected by a barrier of light. Two huge beasts in the shape of Hel and Ifritah stood beside them, so it was only natural they'd fall speechless at such a sight.

"Perfect timing. Cooperate with them. Lady Satsuki and Lady Latifa will protect us, as will these two here." Charlotte looked up at Hel and Ifritah to confirm that it wouldn't be a problem, then gave Louise her orders. Louise immediately replied with an affirmative.

"Hel, Ifritah. Can you make a hole in the barrier for the knights to leave?" Miharu asked the two mid-class spirits.

"Gruuuh!" Her words seemed to have reached them, as a hole large enough to fit two or three people opened at the front of the barrier.

"I'll be going, then…"

Louise gave Hel and Ifritah a curious glance before heading out of the barrier. She then went around with the knights to restrain the mercenaries and prepare for them to be sent to the castle dungeons. No one noticed the group of people watching them from the shadows nearby.

Meanwhile, in the skies overhead…

"I have an idea," Gouki began.

"Wow, Kayoko was right."

"Indeed."

Sara and Orphia commented in admiration.

"So what's the plan, Gouki?" Celia asked hopefully. She seemed to find Gouki's unshakable personality very reliable in a situation such as this, as she had the mindset to let out a small giggle.

"About that. Do you have an attack spell that would be effective against him, Lady Celia?" Gouki asked. "If you have a powerful spell up your sleeve, I'd like you to drive it into him and weaken him…"

There was one spell that came to Celia's mind. "I do. It's stronger than the cannon fire magic I cast earlier, and it's the strongest spell in my arsenal. But I only have enough essence to cast it once. Whether I can hit him when he moves around like that is…"

She wasn't confident.

"You only need to hit him once. As long as we can make sure that one spell hits, it won't be a problem."

"R-Right. But how can we make sure…?"

The opponent they were up against was no pushover, but Celia nodded first and waited for the rest of Gouki's idea.

"If it's just for a brief moment, then I have a means of moving fast enough to match his speed. I'll first aim an attack directly at his front, reducing his speed. That should make it easier to hit him with magic. If you use that chance to hit him, you can buy us some time."

"I understand…"

"Lady Sara, Lady Orphia, and Kayoko's cooperation will also be essential. Lady Sara and Lady Orphia, are you able to create water whips like Kayoko's in order to restrain him?"

"It might be difficult if he's moving around. I'm not too sure about it. If the three of us release whips at the same time, we might be able to restrain him, but I don't think it'd take much for him to break free with his strength…"

Sara and Orphia exchanged expressions of uncertainty.

"You'll be restraining him after Lady Celia casts her magic, so his movements should be slowed somewhat. If the three of you could use that opening to restrain him enough to prevent him from flying away, that would be great."

"Right, that should be manageable," Sara said, nodding with more confidence.

"Then the next step is to pass him and make him face a different direction. Lady Orphia, can you ask Ariel to adjust its flight path?"

"I can. Ariel," Orphia called. Ariel began to circle around.

"Now then, I will be the vanguard, so I'm counting on you all to activate your techniques at the right time."

"Roger that!"

They had no intention of losing. They wouldn't have come up to the sky in the first place if they had. That's why the group all nodded firmly at Gouki's instructions.

Thus, the five heroes resumed their battle with the Hero Killer.

"I'm going to prepare the spell. Wait one moment."

First, Celia began her preparations to cast the spell for the plan. The Claire family had a secret attack spell that was passed down through the generations. This secret spell was the magic Celia was about to use.

In terms of modern magic, the spell would be categorized in the highest grade. It was a super spell that could only be cast by those of Claire blood with exceptional magical talent.

"*Aperio: Caelestis Magicus*," Celia murmured, creating a magic circle that wrapped around her. "*Verifico: Celia Claire*."

The magic circle wrapping around her glowed brighter.

"*Salvatio Initium*."

The magic circle condensed around her right arm.

"*Impetus…*"

She then cast an extra spell to provide the necessary magic essence for activation. In response, all the magic essence within her began to gather in her right arm. Magic essence was normally unable to be seen by anyone who couldn't cast spirit arts, but the essence had condensed so much, destructive energy was visibly flowing from her arm before being activated.

Gouki's eyes widened at the sight of Celia's right arm. "That looks like quite the tremendous spell you're preparing," he commented

Celia nodded with a strained expression. "I believe I'll be able to meet your expectations—as long as it hits, that is."

"That's amazing…" Orphia muttered, staring at Celia's arm.

"Yes… I wouldn't want to handle essence this close to exploding. In fact, I can't," Sara agreed, forehead breaking into a cold sweat.

"It's taking all I have to control the essence. Every other task is entrusted to the spell formula…"

All Celia was doing right now was controlling the magic essence. The majority of the other tasks required to activate the magic were left to the spell formula so that all her processing ability could focus on essence control. A spirit arts user would have had to perform all those tasks by themselves, so entrusting such things to the spell formula was something that could only be done with magic.

Thus, after a few long seconds...

"*Mora*... I'm done preparing. All that's left is to chant the spell and the magic will activate. Whenever you're ready," Celia said, having finally completed her preparation to activate the magic.

"Thank you. Seeing your spell has helped me refocus my mind," Gouki said to Celia, then glanced at Orphia. "Now, if you would do the honors, Lady Orphia."

"We just need to charge straight at him, right?"

"Indeed! Please do!"

"Got it. Ariel!"

"Kreeeh!" At Orphia's signal, Ariel changed direction. Until now, it had been flying in circles around the Hero Killer to maintain a distance, but it now backed away in order to make a direct approach.

Ten-odd seconds later, Ariel was glaring at the Hero Killer from a distance of a hundred meters.

"Wruuuh!" The Hero Killer seemed to have sensed Ariel's incoming charge. With full confidence in his own defenses, he lifted his shield and accelerated towards them as though to accept their challenge. At this point, there were only a few dozen meters left between them.

"Kreeeh!" Meanwhile, Ariel was normally surrounded by a wind barrier to keep its passengers from feeling any wind resistance during flight. Under such conditions, Gouki was able to stand and draw his katana.

"Now, here I go!" Gouki said with a light leap. A strong wind blew softly at his back—and the next moment, Gouki was accelerating through the sky, leaving Ariel behind him.

"So fast!" Sara was shocked.

"Is that Haruto's technique for moving at high speeds?" Orphia asked, guessing at the theory behind his high-speed movement with wide eyes. High-speed movement with wind spirit arts was Rio's specialty.

My acceleration isn't as skillful as Sir Rio's, but yes. All I can do is charge forward in a straight line, thanks to Lord Dominic forging Kamaitachi for me!

That's right—by equipping his beloved blade Kamaitachi, Gouki was able to obtain the technique for accelerating in one go.

His technique was still rough compared to Rio's, but he was still able to imitate him. Perhaps it was because he had fallen in love at first sight with the technique after Rio used it against him, and had continuously imagined himself using it ever since. Or perhaps it was the result of all his loyalty towards Rio.

"Hidden Skill, First Blade, *Aura Vulnus*!"

Gouki was already within a dozen meters of the Hero Killer, sending a slashing attack of wind diagonally upwards to the right. His might was far beyond what he had demonstrated to Rio in the Karasuki Kingdom.

"AAAAARH!"

The huge frame of the Hero Killer that was protected by his shield decelerated dramatically. It still wasn't enough to damage him.

"Hidden Skill, Second Blade, *Aura Mico*!"

At that moment, Gouki turned his katana and stepped even closer to the undead knight. He charged into his decelerated opponent and aimed another attack at the shield, this time making direct contact with the surface. The Hero Killer decelerated further.

"This mass sure is a struggle to overpower! I cannot even crack the shield… But he's slowed down a good amount. Now, Lady Celia!" Gouki yelled at Celia behind him. Ariel flew forwards, approaching the Hero Killer. As it passed by, Celia swung her right arm with the magic circle around it like a sword.

"*Durandal*!"

This was the secret spell of the Count Claire family. The condensed magic essence was released as pure destructive energy, attempting to mow down the enemy before them.

"RAAAAAH!" The Hero Killer must have sensed the threat of Celia's magic, as he desperately tried to brace his shield for the attack.

"TAKE THAT!" Celia roared.

"WRAAAAAAAAH!"

The shield that hadn't even chipped until now shattered into pieces. In fact, half of the body that had been holding the shield was gone, armor and all.

The highest grade of attack magic normally focused on expanding the area of its attack range as much as possible, but Celia's Durandal magic focused on condensing the power into as small of a range as possible. As a result, the iron wall of the Hero Killer, which had withstood numerous attacks from heroes during the Divine War, was blown away.

"A-Amazing! That's incredible, Celia!"

"Yeah!"

Sara and Orphia cheered in spite of themselves.

"Th-That's all...I've got..." Celia weakly collapsed against Ariel's back.

"As expected of Sir Rio's teacher. Splendid work, Lady Celia. I doubt there's even a need for us anymore, but a job is a job." Kayoko released the water whip from her kodachi.

"Wait, it's our turn, Sara!"

"R-Right!"

Sara and Orphia created water whips in their hands and used them to grasp the Hero Killer's body.

"RAAAAAH!" With half his body gone and the rest of his body restrained, the Hero Killer toppled off-balance midair, exactly as they planned.

"Ha ha, well done indeed! You've made my job much easier now. However, that would be discourteous to this warrior, no matter how much of a monster he may be. I shall assist in putting him out of his misery with my hidden skill!" Gouki made a huge leap midair, rushing at the Hero Killer once more with his katana held over his head. By imitating Rio's movement techniques, he accelerated as he approached.

"Hidden Skill, First Blade, *Aura Vulnus*!"

A diagonal slashing attack flew towards the undead knight. In his unbalanced state, the Hero Killer was unable to swing his sword fast enough and took the hit directly to his breastplate.

"Hidden Skill, Second Blade, *Aura Mico*!"

Then, Gouki accelerated even further, swinging his katana to release a diagonal slashing attack in the opposite direction. When the two attacks overlapped with each other, the undead knight's armor completely shattered, causing him to roar in pain.

"GRAAAH!"

But he had still yet to die.

"Then take this! Hidden Skill, Third Blade, *Aura Vacuo*!" With his katana swung the whole way through, Gouki made a following horizontal slash, dividing the Hero Killer's rib cage into two.

"…" Not even the Hero Killer could survive that. Both his body and the sword in his hand disintegrated into the air.

"Looks like the Fourth Blade wasn't needed." Gouki sheathed his katana cleanly, then returned to Ariel's back.

Not long after, cheers shook the Galarc Kingdom's capital. It was the voices of the citizens who had watched the battle take place in the sky. A hymn of victory.

⚜ Chapter 7 ⚜
Signs of More Trouble

Cheers echoed across the capital. However, far in the skies above…

I went as far as using the Hero Killer Draugul, yet their numbers haven't been reduced at all. An unsatisfactory result indeed…

Reiss watched on as Gouki and the others descended to the ground on Ariel's back.

Celia Claire… I knew she wasn't an average sorcerer, but to think she could use celestial magic… So the descendants of the divine sorcerers created by the Seven Wise Gods became the Claire family. She must have inherited a large amount of that talent. Considering her youthful appearance, it might be a case of atavism.

Reiss was especially focused on Celia.

In her present state, she's unable to cast the magic without the incantation, and she didn't have the strength to manage Draugul on her own. But there's no telling how much she'll grow from here… She must be removed with highest priority after the Black Knight and the humanoid spirit girl.

The large number of revenants he sent had been subjugated, the mercenaries had the tables turned on them, and the secret Hero Killer had been defeated.

I am unable to summon Draugul successively at present. I have no cards left up my sleeve either.

In a rare show of frustration, Reiss resigned himself to giving up.

That aside, the descendant of a divine sorcerer and three talented girls, most likely demi-humans, each with a mid-class contract spirit. Then there's the formidable man and woman who probably came from the Yagumo region, and the Galarc Kingdom's hero, though still unawakened. Leading them all is the Black Knight, who's strong enough to rival a divine beast controlled by an awakened hero, and his powerful humanoid spirit. In terms of combat power, he's as much of a threat as that awakened Saint. Although she'll probably be the bigger problem with her active hostility.

Now that he had failed to secure a hostage against the Black Knight and reduce the fighting strength at his side, Reiss was unsure how to proceed.

It won't be enough to just have the Hero Killer and Evil Black Wyvern as my primary forces when I execute the plan. If the Black Knight learns of the Saint's survival, his attention might be able to be directed at her. For the time being, it'd be best to have the two of them fight it out while I secure new forces. All that's left is…

If his opponent's forces were greater than he had expected, he had no choice but to replenish his own. Doing so was no easy task, but Reiss had no choice but to work out a solution.

It's about time Duke Arbor took action against Rodania.

He contemplated the other plan he had brewing behind closed doors.

Oh, it seems they succeeded in retrieving Lucci and Lucius's enchanted sword.

Reiss spotted Arein's small squad that had infiltrated the castle and smirked. The operation this time had been a failure, but they had managed the bare minimum of a recovery at the very last moment.

And finally, to silence the survivors...

Reiss took out a small pouch filled with small, gemlike crystals and crushed them in his fist. He emptied the powdered fragments from the bag, watching them fall.

It's time for me to retreat as well.

He then flew away from the Galarc Castle.

Some time after Ariel brought Celia and the others back to the ground, King Francois received a visitor in the rooftop garden, where he was leading the cleanup efforts.

"Your Majesty!"

It was Clement Gregory, the head of a duke family on par with Duke Cretia.

"What is it, Clement?" Francois replied in an annoyed tone.

"I heard that the enemy's target was Sir Amakawa's mansion."

The duke cut to the chase. Anyone observing the commotion would have noticed that the fighting was focused around Rio's mansion. The aerial knights could still be seen circling the skies from their current position in the garden. Ground forces were running to and from the mansion with Francois's instructions, so Duke Gregory may have heard the news from someone along the chain.

"News sure travels fast. That is the most likely assumption for this situation, but there's no way of telling whether it's true."

"At any rate, Sir Amakawa must be questioned immediately."

"Unfortunately, that won't be possible. Haruto is not in the capital right now," Francois said with an annoyed shrug.

"What? At a time like this? Wait, I recall something about a message transmitted from Baudrier's territory not too long ago..." Duke Gregory muttered, searching through his memories.

During his pursuit of the Saint, Rio had used a magic transmission artifact from Margrave Baudrier's territory to send a report to Francois. Messages sent from transmission artifacts could be viewed by anyone within the transmission range, so it wasn't too strange for Duke Gregory to know about it.

"You sure hear things fast, don't you?" Francois sighed in half disgust, half awe.

"First Cretia's daughter, now this. The young ones these days have no respect for their position. The way they wander around rashly without settling down just shows how little awareness they have of themselves as nobility." Duke Gregory shook his head in disapproval.

"Haruto is currently moving on my orders, though," Francois said with a challenging look.

"Ah, is that so? Do forgive me. I am curious as to why he's moving at the direct order of Your Majesty, though…" Duke Gregory's eyes glinted with curiosity as he searched Francois's expression. Only a select few people knew of Rio's mission to rescue Liselotte—not even Duke Gregory was aware.

If he viewed the message from the transmission artifact, he should have guessed that Haruto is moving on my orders already… This old fox never changes.

Duke Gregory was probably using this chance to investigate what he had guessed. There was no need to come probing the moment the enemies had withdrawn, but his intentions were evident—he couldn't pass up this opportunity to fulfill it.

This was because for generations, the two great noble families of the Galarc Kingdom were Duke Cretia's and Duke Gregory's respective families, but the rise of Liselotte's Ricca Guild had caused the Cretia house's power to increase dramatically.

With the recent appearance of Haruto Amakawa, a new noble with many achievements to his name, Duke Cretia's connections were only growing stronger.

At this rate, the gap between Duke Gregory's and Duke Cretia's families would widen greatly in Clement's generation.

Thus, Clement Gregory wanted to find whatever faults he could. If there was anything he could bring Duke Cretia down for, he would take the opportunity to do so just to make his presence felt. He had been vigilantly watching for such opportunities, so this situation where he could pick faults with the newcomer noble Haruto Amakawa—who was on friendly terms with Liselotte—was the perfect chance.

"I plan on releasing the information in regards to what Haruto is doing once he returns. Wait until then."

"Understood." Clement bowed his head respectfully. "However, the residents of the mansion should be questioned about this incident. I know that Your Majesty is extremely busy, so if you delegate the task to me, I can commence the questioning immediately..."

He immediately changed his approach by offering to investigate those around Rio.

"No need. I've left the mansion in Charlotte's hands." Francois dismissed the matter by bringing up Charlotte's name.

"Oh, is that so? Of course, that makes sense. I understand." Clement backed down surprisingly easily.

"However... I've heard many curious witness accounts on my way here. As a newcomer to these parts, Sir Amakawa is surrounded in mystery already. I understand the need to be careful, what with the hero being on familiar terms with him, but there are a great number of people who wish to know what caused the attack..."

Clement said while staring at Francois's face, hinting at his desire to have the details of the attack released publicly.

I see, so his goal was to have me pledge a commitment here...

In other words, it was a roundabout way of exercising control.

A lot of the information regarding Rio and the people around him was kept confidential at Francois's order. This in itself was common knowledge, and not even the great nobles like Clement could easily object to the direct order of the king.

However, it was a different matter when they had a justified reason.

For example, in this situation where Rio's mansion had clearly been the target of the attack, if the matter of the castle and its personnel being harmed was emphasized, Francois would have a difficult time refusing to release the information.

"Of course, the essential details of the attack will be shared. On a later date, that is."

Francois nodded in agreement, adding a clause for only the essential details. With that, the matter became easier for Clement to bring up in the future.

"I am relieved to hear that. In that case, I shall take my leave now." Clement bowed deeply and left with a spring in his step.

Depending on the goal and circumstances of the mercenaries, things could get rather troublesome. Goodness...

Francois sighed heavily to expel his exhaustion, looking over at Rio's mansion as though to see the troubles looming in the future.

The day after Gouki and the others repelled the Hero Killer, in the Holy Democratic Republic of Erica. A unanimous vote had just been passed by the congress.

"Then it's decided," Erica, the first head of state, announced solemnly.

"..."

The congress hall was filled with members representing the people, but it was oddly silent for having just passed a vote.

Everyone was holding their breath for Erica's declaration of the vote.

"Our nation will now invade the Galarc Kingdom."

It was a declaration of war.

"Oooooh!"

The congress hall burst into cheer. Everyone in the room was crazed for war. A tiny nation at the outskirts of Strahl was challenging one of the leading powers of the continent.

It wasn't a sane decision by any means, yet everyone believed.

They believed in their victory.

And they believed that Saint Erica would lead them to that victory.

"Saint Erica!"

"Saint Erica!"

"Saint Erica!"

"Saint Erica!"

"Saint Erica!"

"Saint Erica!"

"Saint Erica!"

The congress members yelled her name with all their heart and soul.

Watching them, Erica smirked softly. "Heh heh."

Her lips twisted, and the corners of her mouth tugged upwards.

As though she were a saint.

As though she were a witch.

Not a single person in the room knew of the future she envisioned, but they believed in her.

They believed that she would lead them to victory.

But the day they would learn of the future that awaited them was much closer than they thought.

⚜ Epilogue ⚜

Three days after the attack by the Heavenly Lions, in the afternoon, King Francois of Galarc was visiting Rio's mansion for the first time since the attack.

Part of the reason was to hear the testimonies of the residents, but he had already received an advance report of that from Charlotte, who gathered the necessary information immediately after the attack. The biggest reason for his visit was to thank those who contributed the most to repelling the insurgents and meet Gouki's group for the first time.

The reason for the wait was related to the reason why Francois was visiting the mansion in person instead of summoning them to the castle.

The battle with the Hero Killer Draugul had been witnessed across the capital, including by those in the castle. It was clear that summoning them to the castle immediately after the fight would result in meddling nobles attempting to make contact.

However, much of the information in Charlotte's report was better kept confidential. Releasing the information carelessly could result in provoking antipathy from Satsuki or Rio, which was undesirable for Francois as well. There were also some matters he wanted to obtain Rio's consent for when releasing the information. Waiting before the visit also allowed him to buy time before Rio's return, which was why Francois was only visiting after three days.

Incidentally, Sara and Gouki had not revealed all their secrets to the Galarc Kingdom. For example, they had explained the existence of spirit arts and how Hel, Ifritah, and Ariel were spirits, but the fact that Sara's group were demi-humans—as the humans would call them—was kept hidden. Gouki's group had introduced themselves as people connected to Rio's parents, but they had refrained from explaining the details of Rio's birth without his permission.

But that aside, they had just finished exchanging the necessary greetings with each other.

"And so, I welcome you to the Galarc Kingdom," Francois said to Gouki and Kayoko.

"We are extremely grateful for your forgiveness over how we entered your castle uninvited." Gouki bowed his head, expressing his respect for the foreign king through his demeanor.

They were currently in the dining hall of the mansion. Although it was comparatively minor, Rio's mansion had been damaged in the mercenary attack. The window in the drawing room was still broken, so they were gathered in the dining hall instead. They were also to be served lunch after this.

Present in the hall were Francois, Gouki, Kayoko, as well as Charlotte, Satsuki, Miharu, Celia, Sara, and Orphia. Alma was fully healed but resting just to be safe, and Latifa was keeping her company.

"Come to think of it, your people entered the castle grounds from the skies. Ha ha, it's fine, it doesn't bother me," Francois said with a hearty smile. He then turned to Gouki. "We can save the details for Haruto's return, but I would like to confirm your intentions from here. Would it be right to consider your people as Haruto's private army—or rather, vassals? Your relationship to him seems somewhat different to that of Sara and the other girls. I am prepared to offer you a befitting status as a reward for your contribution to repelling the insurgents, if you so desire."

"That's another complicated matter to address... For the time being, you can think of us as cooperators instead of vassals. Sir Haruto is rather against the notion of seeing us below him," Gouki answered with a somewhat troubled smile.

"I see... That tends to be a troubling aspect of his personality," Francois said, returning the smile. "But I understand. Perhaps it would be best to leave this discussion until his return after all."

"I'm sure he'll be back in no time at all if he can fly. He may even drop by out of the blue today," Charlotte added.

"The spirit arts you mentioned, was it? The existence of spirits is rather hard to believe, but that was how the Saint was tracked, you said."

Francois's words were uttered with the knowledge of Aishia's identity as a humanoid spirit. This wasn't something that Sara and the others had told him intentionally—the reveal of their spirits had allowed Charlotte to guess that Rio had one as well, which then led to the guess that Aishia tracked the Saint by being in spirit form.

"Umm... Haruto may have returned just now," Sara interrupted, raising her hand.

"Why, I will go meet him at the front gate immediately." Charlotte shot to her feet in delight.

"Wouldn't he be surprised to see you knowingly waiting for him?" Satsuki asked, pointing out how he wasn't aware that she knew about spirits now.

"That's what makes it interesting," Charlotte replied with a thrilled look.

Satsuki was drawn into grinning along. "In that case, I might as well tag along."

And so, it was decided that a group of them would go out to meet Rio.

Charlotte, Satsuki, Miharu, and Celia had gone out to meet Rio at the front gate of the castle.

They watched as Rio and the others walked towards them from the noble district with Liselotte.

"He really brought her back... Amazing..." Satsuki muttered. Her tone was more hopeful and awed than exasperated. He was much more of a hero than her, she thought.

"It's Sir Haruto, after all." Charlotte nodded with a triumphant expression, as though it was only natural.

"It's amazing how convincing those words can be."

"Right?"

Satsuki and Miharu exchanged strained smiles.

"Just as we expected, he looks surprised to see us. Shall we go to him?" Celia looked at Rio's rounded eyes from afar and giggled with a dimpled smile.

"Yes, let's go. Hey, Haruto!" Satsuki waved her arms while breaking into a jog. Charlotte followed behind her. They eventually got close enough to speak to him.

"Welcome back, Haruto! Liselotte, Aishia, and Aria too!" Satsuki said, beaming.

"Hello... We've returned." Rio was still confused.

"Hee hee. A lot happened while you were away, Sir Haruto." Delighted by his confusion, Charlotte walked up to Rio and entangled herself around his arm. She then tugged on it once before turning to speak to Liselotte. "I'm so glad you're safe, Liselotte. Welcome back."

"Thank you, Princess Charlotte."

Like Rio, Liselotte looked bewildered.

"I've completed your entry procedures, so please tell me everything that happened. Gouki and the others are also waiting at the mansion," Charlotte said teasingly, peering at Rio's face.

"..."

Rio was at a loss for words. He was clearly wondering what in the world had happened while he was gone.

"Stop that, Char. These two still haven't given their greetings yet," Satsuki said, scolding Charlotte for trying to monopolize Rio's attention. "I have a lot I want to say too, but Celia and Miharu worked really hard while Haruto was gone, remember? So let them talk to him too. Go on, you two."

She pushed the hesitant Miharu and Celia towards Rio.

"Erm..."

They exchanged slightly embarrassed looks with each other.

"Welcome back."

They celebrated Rio's return with gentle smiles.

Afterword

Hello everyone, this is Yuri Kitayama. Thank you for reading *Seirei Gensouki: Spirit Chronicles Volume 19—Tachi of Wind*.

So, volume 19 has been released! I believe most of you are reading this afterword after the story, but I've also heard that some people like to read from the afterword, so I'll try to refrain from giving too many spoilers.

Now, to start, Rio has a tendency to fight alone too much. Part of the reason is because he has too much power, but his personality that prevents him from getting others involved also plays a big part.

The people who normally spend their time around him naturally understand that, but I hoped to depict how they accepted that, how they wanted to live with that, and what kind of growth they go through!

In the upcoming volume 20, there'll be plenty of action around Rio and Aishia based on the developments of volume 19.

Just like how volume 10 was a big turning point for the story, volume 20 will also bring about big developments...or so I hope, so please look forward to the release!

As always, there's a preview of the next volume at the end of this book, so check that out. The subtitle will be *Her Crusade*.

Next, information about the anime series has started being released bit by bit. The latest news can be found on the official website, *Seirei Gensouki*'s official Twitter, and occasionally on my own Twitter. Please follow them if you're interested!

There are still many things I can't tell you, but I believe the anime of *Seirei Gensouki* will be wonderful.

As the author, I'm cooperating with the production wherever I can, and I can keenly feel the professionalism of everyone every day.

And so, I hope you'll look forward to both volume 20 of the novel and the anime series! Let's enjoy the show together once it broadcasts!

Finally, I extend my deepest gratitude to the readers and everyone involved! Let us meet again in volume 20!

Yuri Kitayama
March 2021

Seirei Gensouki: Spirit Chronicles

Volume 20

Her Crusade

Yuri Kitayama
Illustrator • Riv

Flora Beltrum

Second Princess of the Beltrum Kingdom. Finally reunited with her older sister, Christina.

Christina Beltrum

First Princess of the Beltrum Kingdom. Protected by Rio, together with Flora.

Sendo Takahisa

Aki and Masato's brother from their original world. Currently the hero of the Centostella Kingdom.

Sakata Hiroaki

A hero from another world. Operates with the support of Duke Huguenot.

Shigekura Rui

A high school student from another world. The hero of the Beltrum Kingdom.

Kikuchi Renji

One of the heroes from another world. An adventurer unaffiliated with any kingdom, until...

Liselotte Cretia

Noblewoman from the Galarc Kingdom and president of the Ricca Guild. She was a high school student named Minamoto Rikka in her past life.

Aria Governess

Liselotte's head attendant and an enchanted sword wielder. Has been friends with Celia since their academy days.

Sumeragi Satsuki

Miharu's friend from their original world. Currently the hero of the Galarc Kingdom.

Charlotte Galarc

Second Princess of the Galarc Kingdom. Shows strong affection towards Haruto.

Reiss

A mysterious man pulling the strings behind the scenes. Wary of Rio for always disrupting his plans.

Sakuraba Erika

The woman who caused a revolution in a minor nation. Is hiding her identity as a hero.

Rio (Haruto Amakawa)

The main character of this story; he lives to avenge his mother's murder. Currently traveling as "Haruto" due to his arrest warrant issued in the Beltrum Kingdom. In his previous life, he was a Japanese university student named Amakawa Haruto.

Aishia

Rio's contract spirit who calls him Haruto. A rare humanoid spirit with missing memories.

Celia Claire

Noblewoman from the Beltrum Kingdom. A genius sorcerer and Rio's former academy teacher.

Latifa

A werefox girl from the spirit folk village. In her previous life, she was an elementary school student named Endo Suzune.

Sara

A silver werewolf girl from the spirit folk village. Currently traveling with Rio to study the outside world and broaden her horizons.

Alma

An elder dwarf girl from the spirit folk village. Currently traveling with Rio to study the outside world and broaden her horizons.

Orphia

A high elf girl from the spirit folk village. Currently traveling with Rio to study the outside world and broaden her horizons.

Ayase Miharu

A high school student from another world. Haruto's childhood friend and first love.

Sendo Aki

A middle school student from another world. Feels resentment towards her half-brother Haruto.

Sendo Masato

An elementary school student from another world. Currently under the protection of Rio, along with Miharu and Aki.

CHARACTER INTRODUCTION

Contents

❖ Prologue ❖
Wish

I detest this world.

It sickens me to my stomach.

That is why I will start a crusade.

A resistance against the foolish humans running rampant.

The crusade begins soon.

I think I'll look back on the things that happened since I wandered into this world.

What went wrong.

Who was wrong.

Whether I was wrong.

Whether I've lost my mind.

In order to ascertain that…

I was a lecturer at an urban university when one day, I wandered into this world with my beloved fiancé.

He was an associate professor in his early thirties and an extremely capable person. However, I didn't fall for him because he was capable. His kindness, sincerity, and dedication were what attracted me to him. I loved him from the bottom of my heart.

The two of us first arrived in this world in the middle of the mountains. We were in the university research lab one moment, then surrounded by nature the next. There was a waterfall nearby.

At first, we thought we were in the countryside of Japan. Perhaps we had been caught in a warp, teleport, or rift in space. We had just encountered such an unrealistic event, but we still believed we were on Earth.

However, we were wrong.

This wasn't Earth—it was a different world. We realized this after spending several hours descending the mountain.

There was a human settlement at the foot of the mountain. The village showed no signs of modern civilization. All the people living there had such ragged clothes; we were shocked. But they were the first people we had met since coming here. We had to talk to them.

Judging from their faces, they clearly weren't Japanese people. According to my fiancé, their faces resembled Russian or European people. He then tried to speak Russian, English, and German to them, but they didn't understand him.

But for some reason, I was able to understand them. In fact, their words sounded like Japanese to me. The villagers looked puzzled at my fiancé's Japanese, but they understood every word of my Japanese.

After that, my fiancé and I were allowed to stay in an empty house in the village. We were exhausted from descending the mountain, so we slept like the dead that day.

The night after we wandered into this world, I had a dream. Apparently, I was a hero.

Someone appeared in my dream and told me that. I was dubious at first, but when I woke up in the morning, I had the same power as that I saw in my dream. I could summon a strange staff and control earth with a kind of paranormal power.

I told my fiancé of what I'd seen in my dream. In all probability, he was only in this world because he had been with me. I had dragged my beloved into this mess. Perhaps there was no way of returning to Earth. When I realized this, I paled.

But he just smiled and said, "I'm glad it was you who brought me here. I'm glad you didn't have to come to this world alone."

With that, I was saved.

He saved me.

Even though I couldn't save him…

We wanted to return to Earth if we could, so we tried to search for a means of doing so.

However, I didn't know anything other than the fact I was a hero, and that I had obtained a special power. We had no hints on how to return. If something was hidden, it would probably be at the mountain where we first arrived in this world.

My fiancé and I continued to live in the village. As payment, my fiancé gave the village chief his long winter coat.

Living in the village was the best option until we became familiar with living here.

It was the best option—or so we thought.

After coming to this world, time flew by in the blink of an eye.

Was that unexpected, or was it only natural? At any rate, there was lots for us to do in the village.

The villagers were far too unintelligent. Their lack of knowledge meant that they were living in an extremely inefficient way.

We used our modern knowledge to improve the standard of living in the village. At the same time, I hid my hero powers. I couldn't see anyone else in the village that could use a magic-like power. Only nobility and other special people could use magic. That was why I used the power of my Divine Arms to plow the fields and enrich the soil in secret.

My fiancé studied this world's language bit by bit, and eventually became capable of simple communication with the villagers.

We could feel our work getting easier and life getting better day by day. That was a fulfilling sensation. Of course, it was still inconvenient compared to living in Japan, but...

"Home is where you make it, as the saying goes."

My fiancé would repeat those words like a catchphrase. Every time he did, I would reply with an embarrassed "Yeah."

What truly mattered was who you were with. To me, home was wherever he was.

I was too shy to say that to him directly, but...

I was happy.

More time passed.

My staff apparently had the power to heal people. I became aware of this when my fiancé was cut doing farmwork.

I didn't know why, but for some reason, I thought I would be able to heal him if I put the magic power into my staff. I brought the end of the staff near the wounded area and it started to glow, healing his cut.

I told the villagers that I used a medicine I had on hand, but they were shocked by how his wound had healed in a day.

After that, a rumor that I was a doctor started to circulate, and I was visited by injured and sick people. I had to pretend I was a doctor and heal them while hiding my power. I had never studied medicine, but there was no one else in the village that could be called a doctor.

Meanwhile, my fiancé worked on improving farm tools, creating fertilizer, building waterwheels and waterways, and improving the hygiene standards of the village.

Before we knew it, my fiancé and I had become central figures of the village. Whenever anyone had a problem, they would come to us for advice. I even witnessed the birth of a new life.

I explained to the couple that I had no experience in midwifery, but they insisted that I be there. I was completely absorbed in the experience. There was little I could do other than emphasize the importance of hygiene to the midwife and help prepare clean cloths that were sterilized with boiling water.

It was a terribly difficult delivery. With a conflicted face, the midwife let slip that the mother and child were both in danger. Seeing the pained look on the mother's face, I decided to use my healing power, which I had kept hidden until then.

The villagers had told me about the existence of magic artifacts that had the power of magic within them. I used that as an explanation for my staff and activated its healing effect. Light glowed, and a miracle happened.

The baby was born safely, and the couple was very grateful.

"I will be indebted to you for the rest of my life."

The father's gratitude was so excessive, I was a little troubled. But he definitely didn't seem to be exaggerating.

I held the newborn in my arms and felt the value of life. I wanted to give birth to a cute child like this with my fiancé one day.

I wished that from the bottom of my heart.

We were completely accustomed to living in this world when we decided to visit the mountain where we first arrived once again. Our goal was to search for any hints as to how we might return to Earth.

It took some time before we were able to make the trip, but we had originally chosen to stay in this village for that exact purpose. We had grown attached to the village, but our desire to return to Japan was greater.

The reason why we were still unmarried also had to do with our lingering desire to return to Japan. We had decided that if we were to marry in this world, we would do so with the intention of being buried in this world.

There were two problems. The first was that we couldn't specify the exact location we appeared at. We only knew that it was in the mountains and within a few hours' walk of the village. We had no choice but to rely on our memories. We also knew there was a waterfall nearby.

The other problem was who would go to investigate. We were fortunate enough to descend the mountain safely the first time, but there were many dangerous beasts in the mountains.

Walking into the mountains unarmed was a suicidal act. That's why I wanted to go alone, but my fiancé was worried.

"I'm much stronger than you now," I said jokingly, but he just fell silent with a frown…because my power made that statement true.

If I wished for it, my hero power would enhance my physical abilities to a terrifying degree. My body would get sturdier as well.

In comparison, my fiancé had no such ability. He was a regular human. He had gained stamina from the daily farmwork, but his life would still be in danger against a savage beast, even if he was armed.

Although I was strong, I had never fought in a real battle before. Fighting was scary. I wasn't confident in my ability to remain calm and protect him if we were attacked. That's why I believed it was less dangerous to go alone.

"Even if I run into an animal, I'll focus on running away. I'll avoid fighting."

My persistence eventually won him over. Thus, I was to head into the mountains alone.

Early in the morning, I departed for the mountains.

A little past noon, I found a waterfall that looked like the one we first arrived beside. Then, I found the spot where we had appeared.

There was a waterfall nearby. That was the only memory I had left of this scenery. It was hard to describe in words, but this place was oddly open for being so deep in the mountains.

There was no mistaking it. My fiancé and I definitely stood here when we first came to this world. However, although I had expected as much, there were no clues on how to return to our world.

I probably knew it from the moment we arrived. But we had been so confused at the time, we didn't conduct a proper investigation.

I investigated the area carefully. Both above the soil and underneath the ground. Fortunately, I was able to control the earth with my staff, so it was easy to dig around.

There was nothing to be gained no matter where I dug, but I couldn't give up on going back to Earth after a single attempt. I would come back again later. After deciding that, I returned to the village.

One week had passed since I began investigating the mountains. In the end, we hadn't discovered anything on how to return to Earth.

There was no point in investigating any further than this. With that thought, my fiancé and I began to gather information outside of the village. Was there any literature about heroes in this world? We set out to find the answer.

One day after that, apparently, the village didn't have enough to pay the upcoming taxes. The villagers came to us for any ideas.

Villages paid taxes to the country, in the form of either money or harvested crops. However, there was rarely ever the need to use currency in the village. Thus, the village had no cash savings and usually paid the tax with crops.

It wasn't impossible for them to pay the upcoming taxes, but doing so would cause a large number of people to starve to death.

The modern knowledge we brought to the village had greatly improved their agriculture, but the results wouldn't show until the next harvest. The new crops wouldn't grow in time for the tax payment.

I asked them if it was possible to delay the tax payment, but apparently there was no precedent for such an exception.

I then asked what the consequences were of being unable to pay the tax. Apparently, they would have to gather anything of value and sell it off for cash. If they couldn't manage the tax with that, the country would punish them with compulsory dispossession.

However, none of the families in the village possessed any valuable items. If they did, they wouldn't be struggling to pay the tax in the first place. In cases like this, it was apparently most common to sell someone off as a slave.

When my fiancé heard that, he was the first to strongly oppose the idea. I was also against the thought of selling someone into slavery. My fiancé then offered to try and sell our valuables in the city instead.

Fortunately, we were in possession of a few valuable items— the items we'd brought from the modern world. Clothing and accessories could sell for especially high prices. When my fiancé stated his willingness to sell our possessions, the villagers clearly let out a collective sigh of relief.

They were items that had lost their use as soon as we arrived in this world anyway. There was no point in holding onto them forever. I wasn't opposed to the idea either.

The father of the child whose birth I had witnessed mentioned he had relatives with a store in the capital, so we decided to sell our items there.

We immediately departed for the capital. I wondered why the capital was within walking distance of the mountains, but it turned out this was an extremely minor nation. From how the villagers described it, it was only the size of a few Japanese cities gathered together. The village was by the mountains at the border of the

213

country, but if we left with the sunrise, we would arrive at the capital by morning the next day.

The group heading to the capital consisted of a few men armed with farm tools, and my fiancé and I who owned the items to be sold. The father joined us. He was born in the capital and would lead us to his relatives' store.

We arrived at the capital without any issue. Although it was the capital, it was just the capital of a minor nation. It wasn't even the size of a small city in Japan. From what I could see of the townscape, the civilization level was that of Earth's Middle Ages.

We didn't have the money for an extended stay in the capital, so we immediately went to do our business. We made our way to the aforementioned store and began negotiations.

However, we didn't bring out every item at once. We showed our items in small amounts and watched their reactions. Because our items didn't exist in this world, the price depended on how much the store was willing to pay. We didn't know how much funds the store had, and bringing out all our items at once would reduce their novelty. We feared that would result in a cheaper price.

Negotiations were done by my fiancé and me. As a result, we were able to secure the tax funds after selling just one set of clothes. I'm sure the novelty played a part in it, but it also reflected just how high quality the clothes from Earth were.

We were first given a cheap price, but when I said I was willing to give up on the sale because I was attached to the item, they immediately raised their offer. They asked if we had any other items, but we brushed them off without showing them anything else. We decided it would be better to save them for the future. Thus, the sale concluded.

The purchase price was more than they had on hand, so it was decided that we would receive half up-front and half once the clothes had been resold. Since they were relatives, the baby's father took on the role of staying back for the remaining amount.

The next morning, our group left the capital with one fewer member and returned to the village with half the payment. The return trip was uneventful, and we were back at the village by the morning after we departed.

One week had passed since we returned to the village...

I was visiting the mountains once again; it was my first visit since returning from the capital. My purpose wasn't to investigate—I had already searched the surrounding area extensively. So why was I suddenly here again? The truth was that yesterday, my fiancé proposed again to me.

"What do you think about getting married?"

We had been engaged since before we wandered into this world, but we had put off marriage because we hadn't given up on returning to Earth.

There were no means of contraception in this village. Getting married would inevitably result in having a child, and once we had one, we naturally wouldn't be able to move around freely for a while.

In other words, this marriage proposal symbolized giving up on our search for a way to return to Earth.

Honestly, my answer was pretty much set. However...

"Can you give me just one day to think?"

I've always been like this... Since I was a child, even. My feelings were all but solidified, but I was hesitant to answer on impulse.

That's why I visited the place where we first arrived in this world. If I came here, I would find out whether I still had the desire to return to Earth, or whether I was willing to be buried in this world.

I received my answer. I came here and looked back on my life on Earth, and found I had no lingering attachments.

My fiancé was here with me. As long as he was here, I could live anywhere. My feelings were completely solidified.

I would give him my answer as soon as I returned to the village. With that decided, I made haste back.

The body and physical abilities of a hero were amazing. It had taken us hours to descend the mountain when we first arrived in this world, but now I could make the trip in a mere ten minutes. And once I did...

"Ah... Ah... Ah... Ah..."

I couldn't speak.

I could barely believe my eyes.

His dead body was displayed in the center of the village. Beside the body dressed in familiar clothes was his severed head. The ground was wet with blood. The villagers we should have been close with were throwing stones at his body while yelling with rage.

"They were suspicious from the start!"

"How dare they steal from a noble!"

They weren't making any sense.

Steal from a noble?

Who did?

As I stood frozen, watching the sight of his corpse from afar, I met eyes with the father of the baby whose birth I witnessed. He was the one who said he'd be indebted to me forever for saving his wife and child.

"Th-There she is! That's the woman!" The father pointed at me with a pale face. He was surrounded by his merchant relative from the capital, a well-dressed man, and several knightlike men with swords and maces. For some reason, all our items from Earth had been brought out.

"Bring her here," the well-dressed man ordered.

Three of the five knights around him moved.

"Aaah… Aaah…"

I materialized my staff and approached the men myself.

To be more precise, I approached my fiancé's dead body. Slowly, step by step.

"Hey!"

"Stop! Wha—?!"

"Wh-What is this woman's ridiculous strength?!"

The knights tried to apprehend me, but I pushed forward. My footsteps grew faster and I shook off the knights grabbing at me. I had no memory of any words spoken from that moment onwards.

The well-dressed man was yelling something with a grimace. I ignored the knights that were positioned to protect him.

All I wanted to do was reach my fiancé. I ran towards his corpse without a glance at anyone else. They must have been surprised by me.

"No… No… Don't die…"

I picked up his severed head and activated my healing power on his body. I carefully tried to connect his neck and body, bringing the glow of the staff near the wound.

"No… No…"

As I mumbled to myself like a broken record, someone struck me from behind with all their might. It was the knight with the mace.

I was blown aside while carrying his severed head. The knights surrounded my fallen body, stabbing me with their swords and the pointed tips of the maces.

"Ah... Ah..."

My consciousness faded.

On that day, at that moment...

I was killed.

I was definitely killed.

And yet...

I saw a dream.

Apparently, I had awakened.

Someone appeared in my dream and bestowed even greater power on me.

They taught me how to use it...

But I didn't care about any of it.

What I wanted wasn't power.

Not power...

I woke up.

It was pitch-black.

My body was being crushed.

It was so suffocating. I struggled with all my strength.

Then, I saw a faint light far in the distance.

It was the moon in the night sky.

Apparently, I had been buried outside the village. My dead body was still in the same bloodied clothes I had died in.

I found my fiancé's corpse buried beside me, so I tried to heal his corpse again. The only thought in my mind was to heal him. I silently continued holding the healing light against him.

How much time passed like that? Eventually, I realized he wasn't coming back to life.

After that, I headed for the village.

Why was I alive?

Why was I the only one alive?

Why did they kill him?

I went to find the answers to those questions.

Based on the situation, the one who was most likely to know was the baby's father. His house was on the edge of the village.

Night had already fallen over the village, and it was completely dark outside. No one was walking around. I made it to his house without passing anyone. I peeked inside the house from a gap at the front entrance.

It was a small, one-room house for a family of three. The father and mother sat at the dining table while the baby slept on a raised bed.

"We did a good job. Now I'll be able to open my own store. I can give you and this child a better life."

When the father said those words, the mother reacted with clear excitement. They must have dreamed of escaping their poor life in the village.

Before I knew it, my feet were moving. The run-down door opened with a creak. The couple noticed the sound and looked up at the entryway. When they saw me in my bloodied clothes—

"Eek!" The mother trembled in horror.

"H-How are you alive…?" The father was also speechless.

"Give him back…"

"Huh?"

"You said you'd be indebted to me for the rest of your life."

"…"

When I voiced my demand, the father made a hideous face. Was he feeling guilty about something? He averted his eyes from me.

"If you're indebted to me for the rest of your life, then give him back. Give him back to me. Bring him back to life."

"Eek…!" The mother jumped out of her seat and backed away from me in fear.

"D-Don't come any closer!" the father yelled. The sleeping baby was shocked into tears.

"What a cute child." I picked up the baby.

"Wh-What are you doing?! You'd lay your hands on a baby?!" The father glared at me as though I was the devil.

"Lay my hands? Why would you think I'd do such a thing? All I did was pick up a crying baby."

"That's because…!"

"Because what?" I approached the panicked-looking father.

"Y-You're being strange! There's something abnormal about you! You're clearly a danger to us right now!" The father yelled vague insults at me.

"You won't allow me to hold the baby because I look like a danger? Then would you rather I let go?" I almost laughed in spite of myself. Instead, I grabbed the baby by the scruff of the neck and lifted my arm up before the parents. If I let go, the baby would drop to the floor.

"Don't!"

"Please don't let go!"

The couple both screamed at once. The baby flinched and bawled harder.

"In that case, why don't we have a little talk? Tell me why he had to be killed. What exactly did we do to deserve this?"

"I-I don't know!"

"You're the one who brought them from the capital, no? You were just talking about how you did such a good job."

The father paled at my words. He must have believed I had overheard something unfavorable to him. All I heard was a brief mention of a job, but it was clear this father had done something for this to happen to us.

"I-It isn't my fault." Despite saying that, the father eventually gave in and started speaking.

It was nonsense.

Everything he said was complete nonsense.

The trigger was when our clothes resold for higher than expected. The buyer was the exceptionally well-dressed man in the village center earlier. He and his daughter—who hadn't come to the village—wanted to know who had made the clothes they bought.

In short, the father before me had let slip that we possessed more rare items like the clothes that were sold. That we had neat utensils that he had never seen before, precious metals, and a staff with the power of healing.

The noble and his daughter expressed a strong interest in our items. The man was especially curious about the healing staff I possessed.

On that day, the father went back to his relative's home without further discussion. But the next morning, a messenger from the noble summoned him back. When he arrived at the mansion—

"Good work. Thanks to you, my friend's stolen items have finally been located. Incidentally, would you be interested in cooperating to assure the retrieval process goes smoothly? You will be rewarded handsomely, of course."

He was given such an offer.

"So you were blinded by greed. You pinned a crime we never committed on us."

"Y-You're wrong!" the father argued back in a flurry when I glared coldly at him.

"I don't see how I'm wrong."

"I was threatened! I couldn't defy a noble; I would have been killed if I hadn't helped him. And the rest of the village is at fault as well! We were told they'd exempt us from paying tax for a while."

"So the entire village sold us."

At this time, I was surprisingly calm. Perhaps it was because the man's panicked excuses sounded so comical.

"W-We all tried to persuade your fiancé! The noble wanted to settle things peacefully if possible! If he had just handed over everything, he wouldn't have been killed! Yet he insisted on opposing the noble...!"

Was he trying to redirect the blame?

"Why did he oppose the noble?"

"It was a ring! He said it was for you, so he absolutely couldn't give it to them!"

A ring for me.

In other words...

"An...engagement ring...?"

Yes, it must have been an engagement ring.

He first proposed to me shortly before we wandered into this world, but at the time he hadn't given me a ring. He had wanted us to go shopping together to buy something I liked.

However, I told him I wanted to wear a ring he picked for me. So he'd bought it already...

We didn't have any money to buy a ring in this world.

The situation was clear. He had tried to protect it from being taken away by the noble. And then he was killed for it.

"Aha! Aha ha!" I laughed with tears running down my face. I wouldn't have been able to maintain my sanity otherwise.

But was there a reason to maintain my sanity?

"..." The couple before me watched me like I was being strange. Then, the baby started crying again. What a grating sound.

"Th-That's enough, isn't it?! Give me back my child! I told you the entire truth!"

"After killing my fiancé and taking away our hopes of having a child, you want your own child back?"

Could there be anything more selfish than this? Was it right to let a request like that go unpunished?

"I told you already, I wasn't the one who killed him! That noble was the one who killed him! The knights were the ones who killed him! And your man wouldn't have been killed if he hadn't defied them!"

In all likelihood, everything he was saying was true.

"I don't care about what you think the truth is. You were the one who blabbered away about our valuables and brought that evil noble here. That noble ordered his knights to kill my fiancé as a result. Are these not the facts?"

"That's...because I couldn't oppose the noble... And the noble could have been right about you stealing those items."

"Aha! You'd believe a noble you've never met before over the woman who saved your wife and baby's lives. You said you'd be indebted to me for the rest of your life, but you didn't believe in us in the slightest."

It was such a pathetic excuse to hear this late in the game.

"This is the truth to me: from the very beginning, there was nothing. This land where we were prepared to live out our days, this village where we thought we had gained a place to belong, the villagers whom we trusted enough to sell our belongings to save... All of it was a lie! We were betrayed by you all! You people killed him!"

Everyone was a liar.

We were fools for trusting them.

We never belonged in this village.

We didn't belong anywhere in this world.

Home was not where you made it...

What we lived in was hell.

I gradually grew more emotional and tainted with madness. The baby seemed to fear that, as the crying grew louder.

Then, at that moment—

"P-Please, I beg you... Give us back that child... Please... Please... We'll apologize for everything, but please." The mother begged me to return the baby; she probably feared the worst.

Meanwhile—

"Aaaah!" The father yelled like an animal and charged at me.

Whether he was unable to accept his own fault, or knew he was at fault but wanted to protect his child, I know not. Either way, he was a shameless man. That's why he was able to step on others for his own sake.

Enraged, he swung at me violently with the intent to kill, but—

"Rah!"

I materialized my staff in my left hand, which wasn't holding the baby, and easily knocked him down. I held back my strength.

"Ugh..." He fell back, knocking over some furniture. My restraint allowed him to remain conscious, and he heaved resentfully.

I couldn't forgive him.

Killing him wouldn't be enough.

How could I punish him with the same despair that I'd received?

I thought about it as I spoke to the fallen man.

"You said I was being strange. But the one who made me strange was you. I will not—I *cannot* forgive you people." I could no longer suppress my impulse with the little rationality I had left. I placed the baby in my hand down on the bed. When I lifted my staff overhead, the mother charged at me next. I brushed her aside just like I'd done to the father.

Then, I raised my staff once more.

"Stop…!"

I swung the staff down in front of the two of them.

"Aha! Aha ha ha!"

I laughed like a broken record.

No… I was the broken one.

From that moment, I was no longer human in body or soul.

The last one I killed was the father.

He yelled at me for killing his wife and child up until his last breath.

I accepted his words emotionlessly with the same rage in my heart.

The nobles had yet to leave the village, so I killed them and retrieved the engagement ring. I then made my way back to the village outskirts where my fiancé was buried, collected his body, and headed for the mountains.

I buried him in the place where we first arrived in this world. I figured that was the closest place to Earth.

Then, I killed myself to follow him.

If this were a story that ended with my death, there would still be salvation to be had.

But there was no salvation.

There truly was no salvation.

Apparently, I couldn't die.

Even when pierced through the heart.

Even with a slashed throat.

Even after bleeding out from cutting my axillary artery.

Whether I jumped from high ground or burned in a fire.

I was apparently incapable of dying.

I could heal from any kind of wound.

He was dead, but I had to continue living in this world.

I wanted to die.

I wanted to follow him.

But I couldn't.

It was mad.

This world was mad.

I hated it.

I hated this world.

What did I have to do to be able to die and join him again?

I traveled around, seeing the world with my own eyes...

But everywhere I went was the same.

No matter where they lived, humans were the same.

Humans were hideous creatures.

Even if they looked like harmless lower-class citizens, there was no telling what they were truly thinking. Everyone was selfish, forcing their own circumstances onto others. But if anyone posed an inconvenience to them, they'd antagonize them without batting an eye. At times, they'd group together to do just that. And when humans gathered together, they became dangerous beasts.

Yet they had no self-awareness. No one thought of themselves as wrong. It was only natural for others to be wrong. It was only natural for the people around them to accommodate their circumstances.

It was very difficult to believe in humans.

So why did people believe in other people so often?

Why did people think it was natural to believe in themselves?

No matter what words or actions were conveyed, there was no way of telling what someone else was thinking, what someone else was seeing...

And yet, people believed in others.

No, they believed in what they wanted to believe.

They averted their eyes from inconvenient truths. They sometimes hid them away.

They sometimes felt betrayed, enraged, and vengeful.

Were humans foolish creatures?

Were humans intelligent creatures?

Were humans ugly creatures?

Were humans beautiful creatures?

I didn't know if this world had a god, but if it did, only it would know the answer.

However, as a hero, I was apparently an agent of god.

If that was the case, was it my duty to present the answer only god would know?

I believe I was entrusted with Pandora's box by god. Was I unable to die because I had yet to fulfill that duty?

In that case, I had to open the box and carve it into the humans.

The fact that they were the most foolish creatures in this world.

This was my revenge, my crusade.

That's right. I will start a crusade.

I can tell there'll be no salvation at the end of this.

But I won't stop marching forward...

Because what I desire the most is despair.

I want to die.

⁕ Chapter 1 ⁕
After Return, Before Return

Immediately after returning from the Holy Democratic Republic of Erica, Rio made his way to his mansion with Liselotte and Aria. They proceeded to the dining room, where King Francois was coincidentally visiting at the same time.

As soon as they had all taken their seats, Francois looked at Rio. "I believed you could do it...and you truly did. Well done bringing Liselotte back. Thank you for your efforts, Haruto."

Rio gave a short nod and bowed his head. "It was nothing."

"Welcome back, Liselotte," Francois said, turning to her next. "I'm glad to see you safe."

"I've caused so much trouble for the country and everyone here... Please accept my deepest apologies."

"Don't let it bother you. Think of it as encountering an unlucky misfortune. The Saint's existence itself was a disaster..." Francois said, sighing at the memory of meeting Saint Erica. "I've asked someone to summon Cedric and Julianne, as well as Princess Christina and Princess Flora, who are close to you. They will arrive shortly, so show them that you're safe."

"Thank you for your consideration."

"Of course. The main discussion will start after they arrive, but I'm sure Haruto must be very confused right now. Did you hear about what happened to the mansion on your way here?" Francois asked, glancing at Gouki and Kayoko.

"No, I was told it would be better to wait for everyone to be present."

That was what Charlotte had said to him on the way here. She had spoken teasingly, but it was indeed the more efficient option.

"I see..." Francois hesitated, but made up his mind quickly after. "In short, invaders attacked the castle shortly after you left."

"Wha—?!" Rio and Liselotte both widened their eyes.

Francois paused, thinking about how to explain things in a way that wouldn't cause them excess concern. The assailants were deeply related to Rio's fated enemy, so he chose his words carefully.

"Rest assured. Although the scale of the attack was large, the matter was resolved with relatively little harm. It was all thanks to the efforts of this mansion's residents. I visited today in order to express my gratitude over the incident."

"Is that so...?"

Rio and Liselotte looked a little less anxious, but there was still too little information to dispel their confusion.

"Excuse me. Princess Christina, Princess Flora, as well as Duke Cretia and his wife have arrived." A female knight announced the arrival of the invited guests.

"Thank you for the invitation."

The first to enter after the knight were the foreign royals, Christina and Flora, but they promptly moved aside after giving their short greetings. They were probably being considerate of Liselotte's parents, Duke Cedric Cretia and Duchess Julianne Cretia.

"Your Majesty..."

As her parents, they wanted to call out to their daughter immediately, but as a duke's family, they couldn't do such a thing. With his position as a noble in mind, Cedric greeted King Francois first. That being said, his gaze and attention were completely focused on his kidnapped daughter who had safely returned.

"There's no need to greet me. I will not stand in the way of a father-daughter reunion," Francois said, dismissing the need for any noble etiquette.

"Thank you for your consideration. Oh, Liselotte!" After a quick bow, Cedric rushed straight over to his daughter. His wife Julianne was right behind him.

"Thank goodness you're safe…" she sighed, sweeping Liselotte, who had stood up to meet them, into a loving hug with Cedric.

"Mother, father…" Liselotte was unable to budge from their embrace. There were tears in her eyes and her voice was trembling. Everyone else in the room watched over the family quietly.

After some time, Cedric and Julianne turned to Rio and bowed their heads deeply.

"Sir Amakawa… No, Haruto. Thank you for bringing my daughter back."

"I acted of my own accord, so don't worry about it," Rio said, shaking his head.

"Oh my…"

Those words must have resonated in Julianne's heart, as she looked at her daughter with a sigh of admiration. Liselotte tried to feign composure, but her cheeks were tinted a shy pink.

"Thank you, truly…" Cedric smiled softly and shook Rio's hand, emphasizing his gratitude from the bottom of his heart.

"You're welcome. However, it might be a bit too early to celebrate. I have some bad news to report as well…" Rio said, looking at Francois.

"I expected as much. I also need to explain what happened over here to you. But let's start with your report first."

Thus, Rio and Francois explained to each other what they had experienced during Rio's absence.

Two days ago, on the outskirts of the Holy Democratic Republic of Erica…

The sun was just about to set behind the stone house set up in the woods.

"Mm…" Rio, who had been wounded in his battle with Saint Erica, opened his eyes.

Where…?

The familiar ceiling of the stone house greeted him. He tried to recall what had happened with his still-groggy mind.

"Sir Haruto…?"

A familiar voice called to him from beside his bed, so he turned to look that way. Liselotte was seated in a chair next to his bed, having nursed him while he was unconscious. Their gazes met.

"Liselotte…?"

"Umm, how are you feeling? If it hurts anywhere…"

Her hands hovered over his body, prepared to cast *Cura* to heal him.

"I'm fine. Nothing hurts."

Rio slowly sat up, moving his arms to check the condition of his body. He could feel his body was stiff from sleeping, but he wasn't in any pain.

"Thank goodness…!" Liselotte exhaled in relief, slumping over as all her strength left her. Her hovering hands settled on clinging to Rio's right arm on the bed, squeezing his hand tightly.

"…" The sudden contact to his hand almost made Rio flinch, but he stifled his body's reflexes with a gulp of air.

"Thank goodness… Truly…"

Liselotte was crying. Her head was hanging downwards, but both her slender body and lovely voice were trembling.

"Sorry, I must have made you worry," Rio apologized quietly.

"No, I should be the one to apologize! I've caused you so much trouble…"

Liselotte had lifted her face to argue back, but was looking down once again with the latter half of her words. Rio watched her like he was unsure of what to say.

"It was no trouble at all." He quickly gave her a gentle smile of assurance. Then, he moved his left hand and squeezed her hands softly between his.

"Sir Haruto?" Liselotte asked, looking up in confusion.

"I'm here of my own will. Being bedridden after charging in so triumphantly is pathetic of me, but I've never thought of it as a trouble caused by you." Rio spoke slowly, as though he were explaining things to a crying child.

"You're not pathetic at all." Liselotte's voice cracked as she spoke. She still looked like she was blaming herself.

"That's a relief to hear. I'm so glad you were unharmed. We both came out of this benefiting from something, so please don't look so upset," Rio said, the sharp outlines of his face easing in joy.

With that, Liselotte was unable to argue any further. Her body flinched a little in surprise.

"Okay…" she murmured with a small nod.

The two of them gazed at each other at close range, holding each other's hands.

The first one to react was Liselotte. Her emotions had spurred her to act far more daringly than she normally would have. Gazing into the eyes of the opposite sex while holding hands was a completely new experience for her. Once she realized this, she immediately turned redder and redder.

"O-Oh! I'm sorry!" Liselotte let go of Rio's hands in a fluster, backing away to create distance and ducking her head.

"No, I should be apologizing... I'm sorry," Rio said awkwardly. Although he had wanted to cheer Liselotte up, squeezing her hands back had been thoughtless of him.

"Oh, no, don't apologize. I was the one who held your hand first..."

"Then..." Rio looked up at the ceiling and thought for a moment, then rephrased his words with a grin. "Thank you very much."

"Wh-What are you thanking me for?"

"For nursing me back to health while I was unconscious. You stayed beside me the whole time, right?"

"Lady Aishia and Aria also took turns caring for you... All I really did was sit here, so you should thank the two of them instead."

"I see. Still, I appreciate how worried you were for me. Thank you so much, really."

"I-It was nothing... And I should be saying that to you. Thank you for coming to save me."

The embarrassment that had nearly faded came rushing back at Rio's honest admission of his true feelings. Liselotte looked downwards with a blush once again.

"It was no problem. So, where are Aishia and Aria?" Rio seemed to be feeling bashful himself, as he changed the subject awkwardly.

"I'm right here." Aishia entered the room through the open door. She had probably been listening to their conversation from the hallway, as she made her entrance as soon as Rio asked about her.

"Morning, Aishia," Rio said with a soft smile.

"Yup. Morning." As usual, there was no intonation to her voice, but even Aishia seemed to be in good spirits today. Her mouth was turned upwards in happiness.

"Thank you for coming back after the battle. You saved me." Rio recalled the battle with the Saint and thanked her before anything else. Just before he lost consciousness, Aishia had arrived to help carry him.

"It was nothing."

"How long was I out for?"

"Over a day."

"I slept for that long...?" Although his wounds had been healed, his physical body had taken a huge burden. The fact he could get by with just some bed rest was extremely fortunate.

"Liselotte watched over you the entire time. She hasn't had a wink of sleep."

Aishia and Aria also took turns caring for you was what she had said earlier, but Liselotte herself hadn't actually swapped out of looking after him.

Rio's eyes widened. "Wait, really? Please get some sleep," he said worriedly.

"U-Umm... I'm fine, this much is nothing," Liselotte mumbled. She hadn't wanted Rio to know that, so she shook her head with a tinge of shame.

"Sleep and rest are important for the body. I appreciate your concern for me, but please take care of yourself as well. Please."

She had acted that way out of concern for him—he couldn't scold her too harshly.

"She was beside herself with what to do if you didn't wake up because of her. Please go easy on her."

Aria entered through the still-open door while defending her master. She was carrying a water pitcher on a tray.

"Aria…"

Her attendant had spoken to support her, but the way her state of mind had been exposed left her even more embarrassed.

"As long as you rest after this, I have no objections," Rio said, watching her in concern.

"Yes. I was about to drag her to bed myself if she didn't sleep soon. Thank goodness you woke up before then, Sir Amakawa. Please, have some water." Aria filled a wooden mug with water and handed it to Rio.

Rio took a gulp of the water and sighed in relief. "Thank you… I feel better."

"I should be the one expressing my thanks. Because of your efforts, my master has been retrieved safely."

As soon as Aria placed the tray down on the bedside table, she knelt down to express her gratitude.

"There's no need for that. Like I said, I did it because I wanted to." Surprised by the sudden change in attitude, Rio tried to stop Aria in a fluster.

"That doesn't mean I cannot express my gratitude," Aria replied flatly, her head still bowed low.

"Yes. Thank you so much." Liselotte agreed with Aria and bowed her head alongside her attendant. Faced with the gratitude of both the master and her servant, Rio finally accepted their feelings.

"All right, all right… You're very welcome."

They continued to hold their heads low for a few more seconds, until Aria looked up to speak first. "Now, by your leave, I believe it is time for my master to sleep. Is that all right with you, Sir Amakawa?"

"H-Hey, I'm not a child that needs to be put to sleep..." Liselotte puffed up her cheeks cutely and glared at Aria. Aria had spoken up in a very serious tone, but her words had been chosen with humor in mind.

"Please do," Rio replied with an amused look.

"Right away. I will prepare a light meal for you after my master falls asleep. Please wait a short moment."

"Thank you. The earliest we'll leave for the Galarc capital will be after tomorrow, so please rest well, Liselotte."

"Fine..."

Thus, Liselotte allowed herself to be led out of the room, leaving behind Rio and Aishia.

"Where is this house located, by the way?" Rio asked Aishia, who was standing beside his bed.

"Several kilometers from the city where you fought the Saint. In the middle of the woods."

"I see. Did anything happen while I was asleep?"

"Not particularly."

"You said you were hindered by a skilled spirit art user as you were escaping with Liselotte, right? Is it safe to assume we haven't been followed?"

Rio recalled the matter of the spirit art user who had seen through Aishia's invisibility art. The stone house had a similar barrier that prevented it from being perceived, but a skilled spirit art user would be able to see through it.

In reality, the one who had interfered with Aishia's rescue mission to make Rio battle the Saint was Reiss, but there was no way for them to know that.

"Most likely, yes. It's possible the Saint was the one who got in our way," Aishia theorized.

"That is indeed a possibility..." Rio agreed.

The effects of the Divine Arms are extremely similar to those of spirit arts, he thought.

However, there was something else that bothered him. "But the spirit art user manipulated bullets of light to attack you, right?" Rio asked.

"Yeah."

"In that case..." Rio placed a hand on his chin and thought carefully.

Apart from the physical body enhancement and language interpretation, the abilities of Divine Arms seem to be limited to a single element. Satsuki's is wind, Sakata's is water, Rui's is lightning, Takahisa's is fire, the Rubia Kingdom's hero used ice in our fight, and the Saint's should be earth...

Magic and spirit arts that fired light orbs as bullets of energy didn't count under the six elements of fire, water, earth, lightning, ice, and wind. Thus, if the Saint had been the one to attack Aishia with light bullets, it would mean the Saint was capable of controlling something outside of the six elements.

Was it not the Saint who attacked Aishia? No, it's possible the Saint has learned how to use spirit arts instead of her Divine Arms...

After all, the heroes had all the groundwork for learning spirit arts laid down already. That was probably an effect of the Divine Arms—Satsuki had been the same. She could visualize magic essence from the moment she was summoned into this world.

239

They couldn't practice using spirit arts openly before Charlotte and the castle knights, so he hadn't taught her any more than the bare minimum, but she should be able to pick it up fairly quickly if she learned properly. That would create a hero that could use both Divine Arms and spirit arts.

There's also the possibility of her Divine Arms having more abilities. Satsuki said she didn't completely understand hers either.

At any rate, thinking about this any further wouldn't resolve anything.

"We can't discard the possibility of a third party interfering. Let's keep our guards up."

If it was the Saint that had obstructed Aishia, there was no need to be wary. Rio had killed her himself, after all. But if it was a third party, then they had to fear the possibility of an attack from someone else.

Of course, there was no need for Rio to say that out loud. Aishia already had it covered.

"Okay," she said, nodding obediently.

"Thanks. The other thing to worry about would be that beast… It seems most natural to assume the Saint was controlling it as well, but…"

He couldn't be sure.

"I could sense a spirit-like presence from that huge creature," Aishia stated simply, referring to the beast's identity.

"So it was a spirit after all?"

Rio had considered that possibility during the battle himself. But it had possessed so much power—more than a high class spirit would have had—and it wasn't a humanoid spirit. As far as he knew, all high class spirits and above were humanoid, so he wasn't sure if that beast could've been a spirit.

"I can't say for sure… The presence was really cloudy."

"The presence was cloudy?"

Humans couldn't detect spirit presences with their senses. When Rio looked like he was struggling to understand—

"People, spirits, animals, monsters, plants; any living thing has a presence. There are characteristics distinct to the presences of certain species, and there are variations in the presences of different individuals. Out of all living creatures, the easiest presence to detect is that of spirits and monsters," Aishia added.

"So the presence was most similar to that of a spirit?"

"But it was cloudy."

"Hmm…"

That was the expression it came down to. Rio hummed in confusion, not quite getting it.

"Monsters also have cloudy presences. So in that way, it might be similar to a monster? But it also felt really similar to a spirit."

Since it was a matter of intuition, Aishia struggled to describe it as well. However, although they didn't have an exact answer, it was definitely something similar to a spirit.

"I see. Could you sense anything else about the creature's presence?"

Aishia paused for a moment. "It was angry," she answered.

Spirits were sensitive to the emotions of others. They could sense them to a certain extent through the presences of others.

"Ah, I noticed that too," Rio agreed.

His impression may have been influenced by its overwhelming size—over a hundred meters in length—but its eyes were filled with a resentment greater than any word could describe. That was something Rio could observe even as a human.

"It was really, really angry. It was pitch-black." Aishia's description was short, but it resonated, painting a truly dreadful picture of the beast's wrath.

"Pitch-black… It was so angry, it lost all sense of itself?"

"Probably. It had lost all reason."

"What was it so mad for? I suppose it could have been mad at me, the enemy, but…"

When did he incur such enmity?

Sure, he had invaded the enemy's territory to retrieve Liselotte, which could have triggered the beast's wrath—but something didn't seem right about that.

"It didn't seem like the anger was directed at you. It wasn't angry at anyone there in particular."

"In that case, why…?"

What reason did it have to be so angry?

"Maybe it didn't know why it was mad itself. Perhaps it was blindfolded and left in a state of confusion, like it didn't know whom to direct its anger towards. All it knew was that anger was overflowing from within itself. That was the feeling I got from it."

"And that was what made it pitch-black?"

"Yeah." Aishia nodded quietly.

"I see… But for some reason, it seemed like it was rampaging in an oddly calm way. It was like I was fighting a cunning beast that had locked on to its prey."

The last attack that struck its own allies had caught Rio by surprise, but every other attack before then seemed to be controlled by the Saint to prevent destruction to the city. It had even feigned its death up until it made its last attack. There was something unpleasant about that.

"If it had lost itself to its rage, would it have been able to obey its master's orders so calmly?" Rio wondered out loud.

He could understand if the Saint had absolute control over the beast's movements. However, if that beast was something similar to a spirit, a contract wouldn't be enough to create such a connection.

In a contract relationship, both sides were equal. Spirits served their contract partners because they wanted to—they were still capable of moving about of their own will.

"That, I don't know."

That was a given. Aishia had never been in such a mental state.

"Of course..."

Rio sighed as though to expel accumulated mud. The lack of any confirmed information made him feel as if he were sinking deeper into a bog the more he thought about things. Waking up to such a heavy topic was tiring him out quickly.

However, that didn't mean he could stop to rest.

"If that beast was a spirit, then it's not dead, is it?" Rio asked. It was the most important thing he had to confirm right now.

"That depends on what kind of attack you used to defeat it. A spirit cannot die of wounds dealt to its incarnated body—any damage has to be done directly to the spiritual body. It's also possible to eradicate a spirit by making it expend essence until it can no longer maintain its spirit form."

That meant it was no good just damaging the physical body that was created when a spirit materialized. As long as it recovered its magic essence, it could reappear with its wounds healed.

"If I use spirit arts to directly attack a materialized spirit, I can do some damage to its spirit form, right?" Rio asked. He had once learned that in the spirit folk village.

"Yup. But it's difficult to deal enough damage to kill it. Against strong spirits, it's pretty much impossible."

"I see... Can you sense that beast's presence right now?"

"I cannot. Its presence completely disappeared shortly before I reached you."

"Honestly speaking, I highly doubt I managed to kill it. If killing the contract holder doesn't kill the spirit, then it's probably in its spirit form right now, too low on essence to materialize itself. I doubt there's anyone else out there with enough essence to supply something like that, but..."

If the spirit art user who interfered with Aishia wasn't the Saint, then that person could have been controlling the beast. But there couldn't be many people out there capable of materializing such a powerful spirit. It would be out of the question for a human. It would even be impossible for a high elf like Orphia, despite their abundance of essence.

But no matter who was controlling the beast, there was a high possibility it still existed in spirit form somewhere. And the next time it materialized, it might attack them again.

I'd rather not picture that...

Rio didn't have the confidence to say he'd win a rematch. He didn't believe he'd be able to prevent damage to the surroundings and protect others at the same time. He needed the strength to protect people if the worst should happen. Rio's face tensed at the thought.

"Let's look together. For a way to win the next battle. We can fight together next time."

She had probably read his fears. Aishia grabbed Rio by the hand as though to remind him he wasn't alone.

With that, Rio's expression softened a little.

"Thank you, Aishia… We'll have to find out more about that monster." Rio squeezed Aishia's hand back. He then smiled gently to clear the gloomy fog that had befallen him.

"Dryas and the others in the village might know something."

"Yeah. Let's ask Sara and the others when we get back."

There were many things he wanted to investigate.

It's highly likely that the Divine Arms are related to that beast. I'll need to ask Satsuki for her assistance, which might require permission from King Francois too.

He considered what he needed to prepare for a possible rematch with the beast. First, they had to return to Galarc as soon as possible. Rescuing Liselotte and bringing her back was the most important mission at hand.

"Now that you're awake, I'm going to check on things in that city," Aishia said, voicing the words in Rio's head first.

"I was just thinking of going as well…"

"You've still recovering. And your face might be recognized after that huge fight. I can check on things in spirit form."

"But you might end up in a fight with that spirit art user that hindered your escape."

"All the more reason for me to go, then."

There was no way he could argue with that reasoning. He shouldn't be pushing his recovering body.

"Fine… Then I'll leave it in your hands." Rio showed signs of uncertainty, but chose to rely on Aishia.

"You can count on me."

"There's just one thing I'd like you to check. I want to know how the people living in the city are reacting to the Saint's death. I need to report that to King Francois."

"Okay."

"If you can find the spirit art user, then please do so. But it isn't a top priority, so don't push yourself into a bad situation over it."

"Got it."

"Be careful out there. If you sense the slightest sign of trouble, you can run right away."

"Okay." Aishia nodded firmly. Even Rio would struggle to catch her if she devoted herself to fleeing. There shouldn't be a problem.

"..." And yet, Rio couldn't help looking at her worriedly. He looked like he was on the verge of insisting he went along anyway.

"You worry too much," Aishia pointed out, seeing right through him.

"Oh, well..." Rio mumbled evasively, unable to deny it.

"Believe in me a little," Aishia said to him.

"I do believe in you."

Rio tried to muster a forced smile.

"I'll be fine." Aishia's expression softened and she wrapped him up in a gentle hug.

"Umm..." Rio stiffened slightly out of embarrassment.

He and Aishia were normally close, often sticking together for everything, but being hugged out of the blue like this gave him a little shock. However, it was strangely comforting. Rio's body gradually relaxed, accepting Aishia's warmth. Some time passed like that in silence, creating a space where only the two of them existed.

The food's ready, but I can't enter the room... What should I do?

Meanwhile, Aria stood outside the bedroom awkwardly.

✦ Interlude ✦
Pandora's Box

The morning after Rio stabbed through Erica's heart, in the capital of the Holy Democratic Republic of Erica, Ericaburg…

A unanimous vote had just been passed.

"Our nation will now invade the Galarc Kingdom," Erica announced.

A declaration of war.

"Oooooh!"

The congress hall was immediately filled with enthusiasm.

"Saint Erica!"

"Saint Erica!"

"Saint Erica!"

"Saint Erica!"

"Saint Erica!"

Voices worshipping Saint Erica reverberated around the room. They were rejoicing, or they were angered by the vile Liselotte the Witch, who spouted convenient words pandering to the people while refusing to give up her own noble privileges.

By the underling of the Galarc Kingdom, Rio, who had marched into their capital city to take Liselotte back.

They were filled with more rage than they could endure.

They were seething to the point of their blood boiling.

It was an anger that wouldn't settle without retaliation.

That was why they rejoiced in the decision to invade the Galarc Kingdom. This would give them an opportunity to exact revenge.

It was the Galarc Kingdom that had started the fight with the Holy Democratic Republic of Erica. And the monarchy was an absolute evil that had to be eradicated from this world anyway.

That was their justification. There was no room for rebuttal. That's what they believed without a single doubt.

"Do not forgive Liselotte the Witch!"

"We must demonstrate our wrath to the despicable royal monarchy!"

"Execute the evil kingdom that oppresses the weak!"

"God will have vengeance! Saint Erica will give them divine punishment!"

The members of the congress yelled passionately.

"Please quiet down, everyone." Erica raised her right hand with a thin smile and called out to the noisy group. The congress members immediately fell silent.

"The congress vote has passed. We will now proceed down the path of confrontation with the Galarc Kingdom. Does anyone have any questions or comments?" Erica asked, looking around at the members.

"Saint Erica." Andrei, the prime minister and chairman of the meeting, sought permission to speak.

"Yes, Andrei?"

"Will we be announcing this decision to the people right away? The commotion yesterday has caused rumors to spread across the nation, and everyone is feeling anxious and enraged. Knowing that we're planning a counterattack may raise their morale."

Other members of the congress voiced their agreement one after another. They all wanted to spread the news to raise the fighting spirit of the nation. If they could appear reliable to the people, they would be able to gather support.

"It is exactly as you say, Andrei. As a concerned party of the nation, the people have the right to know. However, the problem lies with the Galarc Kingdom's Liselotte the Witch, who escaped." Erica acknowledged Andrei's opinion, then sighed dramatically.

"The problem..." Andrei's face twisted at the mention of Liselotte. He had been in charge of looking after her during her house arrest, so his feelings towards her were especially conflicted.

"As I previously explained, the young man who rescued Liselotte the Witch was severely wounded in the battle with the beast of the land I summoned. That was when he used the cowardly method of taking hostage Natalia and the others who came to my assistance."

That was the reason why Natalia and the others had died—or so Erica had explained when Andrei and the reinforcements came running after the battle ended. But they had no reason to doubt her. There was no way for them to know that their comrades had actually been killed by the beast of the land's attack.

"The young man fled after releasing an attack that enveloped all of us. He must believe that he killed me with that attack. However, he may possibly return to check on the situation after healing his wounds."

"And if he learns of our plan to invade Galarc, he'd be able to make the first move against us. Is that right?"

"Exactly." Erica smiled as though she were praising an excellent student.

When it came to war, information was key. Knowing the enemy movements was an advantage, while having the enemy know yours was the exact opposite.

"In that case, we must ensure that no one here makes any careless mention of the war," said Andrei. The conversation just now had made him more aware of the importance of protecting the nation's information.

"Indeed. Although we managed to catch on partway, he was skilled enough to retrieve Liselotte the Witch from a highly secure location. As we have no idea when he might send someone to spy on us, it would be best to enforce a gag order on all the congress members. The time and location of discussions must be strictly controlled, and code words should be used to prevent anyone from overhearing the plan to invade Galarc."

"I see…"

Erica stared into space to think for a moment, then suggested a name for the plan. "The name of the plan can be… Hmm. How about the Pandora Plan?"

"Pandora?" Andrei tilted his head at the unfamiliar word. The other members of congress showed similar reactions.

"It's from an ancient legend of a sacred treasure called Pandora's box. I took the name from there."

"Oh, a sacred treasure? That sounds wonderful."

Andrei and the other congress members were all born and raised in Strahl, where the people had a strong faith in the Six Wise Gods. Whether it was because it was a god's namesake or because it was Erica's suggestion, they were unconditionally in favor of the idea.

"It was a box of hope that a god bestowed upon mankind to bring them salvation. Pandora was the name of the woman entrusted with that box. Opening the box would bring salvation to the world."

The Pandora's box that Erica spoke of came from Greek mythology on Earth, but there appeared to be some errors in her retelling.

"That's exactly like you, Saint Erica!"

"Oh my, do you really think so?"

"Yes. Saint Erica is both a saint and a hero. A true representative of the Six Wise Gods. There is no one more fitting to be Pandora," Andrei stated proudly.

"Is that so?" Erica said with a saintlike smile.

"In that case, shall we go and retrieve the key to Pandora's box first?" she suggested.

"Where would that be...?" Andrei asked.

"The Galarc Kingdom, obviously. I also know of a potential site to begin hostilities."

"Oh my. When did you have the time to find that?"

Liselotte had only been rescued yesterday afternoon. Although they had officially voted to retaliate as a nation overnight, they had practically no plan at all. That was the case for everyone other than Erica, at least.

"I gathered all the information I needed of every country's political state, geography, and climate while I was traveling."

She had abducted Liselotte in the process of doing so, but that hadn't been her main objective while traveling. Of course, it was only normal for nations to scout this much out before weighing whether they should go to war or not.

"We can always count on you, Saint Erica," Andrei said.

"From this moment on, it's a race against time. I will retrieve the key to Pandora's box and present it to everyone."

"Are you going to Galarc alone...?"

"There are numerous minor countries from here to the Galarc Kingdom. If we march an army through their lands, we'll end up in combat with them instead. It would be unwise to go against a major power in a battle of resources. That's why I intend on taking only a small force with me by griffin. I will achieve victory with that alone."

Erica's combat strength had been proven already. That track record made her statement all the more persuasive.

"I see…"

"And so, I will be departing for the Galarc Kingdom today."

"T-Today?"

Andrei and the congress members stirred noisily at the sudden news. They were in high spirits from the decision to retaliate, but even they hadn't expected to suddenly put the plan into action.

"I said it was a race against time, didn't I? You shouldn't place too much trust in your ability to prevent information leaks. We may be able to fake my death in the meantime, but if the other side discovers my survival, they'll become warier. We must make the first move before then."

"I understand. In that case, should we go about hiding the fact you're alive right this moment? We've already spread the news that you won yesterday's battle across the capital…"

"There's nothing wrong with spreading news of our victory— that affects the morale of the people. What we must avoid is giving the other side conviction that I'm alive. The worst case would be for me to stay in the capital and get discovered by a spy. We must avoid letting them find my whereabouts."

If they didn't know that Erica was alive and moving about, they wouldn't prepare any countermeasures against her in advance.

"I see. And that's why you'll leave today."

"Exactly. That's why I'd like you to leave the beginning of hostilities to me. In order to reduce the risk of our plans being overheard by a spy, I wish to depart without openly explaining the invasion details. Is that agreeable to everyone?" Erica asked the congress members.

Her proposal was as good as asking for carte blanche, but—

"We have no objections!"

Only agreement came back from around the room.

"Thank you very much. I estimate I will return successfully in a month's time. Please look forward to it."

⁕Chapter 2 ⁕
Amakawa Haruto

It was early in the evening, just as the sun was about to set. One hour had passed since Rio first woke up.

Aishia was in the capital of the Holy Democratic Republic of Erica to conduct the investigation Rio had asked of her: that was, to check how the people of the city were reacting to the Saint's death, and to locate the unknown spirit art user.

In order to conduct the investigation, Aishia had decided to walk around the streets in her spirit form. Right now, there were many pedestrians on their way home from work.

There were currently quite a few manual laborers in the city, who were working on restoring the damage from the revolution. When Aishia peeked inside a lively bar, everyone at the tables was discussing the battle between Rio and the beast of the land. That was only natural, as it had only happened yesterday, and the beast of the land had been overwhelmingly huge. Aishia listened to the conversations for a while.

No one's talking about the Saint's death...

Everyone was discussing the battle, yet not a single conversation mentioned the Saint's death. There were people angry at Rio for attacking their city, but there was no sense of gloom. In fact, they were all speaking as though Erica had won. But why?

Was the Saint's death hidden from the people?

The most likely possibility was the higher-ups of the nation concealing her death. Announcing the death of the nation's leader would definitely shake the people, which was why it was the first thought that came to mind. But there was one other option—

Or is the Saint still alive…?

Aishia considered the possibility. She had personally witnessed Rio stab her through the heart from afar. She had also watched Erica take her last breath and die beside her.

At the end of the day, it was all rumors from a bar. Repeated hearsay could have twisted the truth, and some of the information may have been arbitrarily distorted to begin with. It was hard to imagine Erica was still alive.

But she should at least confirm the facts. And if she wanted to find out the truth, she had to search for Erica. Where was the Saint most likely to be?

I'll pay a visit to where the higher-ups are as well.

After leaving the bar, Aishia headed straight for the official residence of the head of state, where the security was particularly strict. When she looked down from the sky, she could count over thirty soldiers patrolling the grounds. There were lights on in the windows, where there were more soldiers patrolling inside.

The security is strictest here. This should be a good place to find any leads on the Saint. The spirit art user might also be here.

Aishia immediately decided to infiltrate the building. Sure enough, there were soldiers patrolling the inside of the building, but they weren't able to perceive her spirit form with their naked eyes. Aishia went from room to room without being seen by anyone.

I can't find the Saint.

But she couldn't find Erica anywhere in the building. The one people she saw were officials and patrolling soldiers.

Had Erica truly died? Or was she hiding somewhere else?

Should I look for someone talking about the Saint's death?

She considered eavesdropping on people, but the official residence wasn't a gathering of alcohol-loosened tongues like the bar. It could take forever for her to find someone talking about the Saint's death.

I can't sense any other spirits around, so...

That left the option of materializing and asking someone directly. It would be a more beneficial way of gaining information than eavesdropping.

What worried her the most was the unknown spirit art user that could be hiding in this city, potentially in this very building. If there was a spirit contracted to the user, it would be able to sense her presence. But not every spirit art user was contracted to a spirit.

Rio had asked her to search for the spirit art user if possible, so perhaps it would actually be better for her to materialize as bait. It was worth trying.

With that decided, Aishia had to find someone she could question. She went around the estate once more, and several minutes later—

There.

She spotted a man in the garden behind the building. He appeared to be a cook who worked at the official residence. He had just finished preparing dinner for the employees of the building and was taking a break outside the kitchen.

Fortunately, there were no soldiers patrolling nearby, so Aishia immediately set off to question him. She materialized behind him, activated a spirit art in her right hand, then touched the back of his head through his chef's hat.

"Wha...?"

Feeling the contact at the back of his head, the cook turned around. At that point, his mind was caught under Aishia's spirit art. His eyes went vacant as he looked at Aishia's face with an unfocused gaze.

There were many varieties of illusionary arts out there, but the majority could be split into two: those that sent fake information to the five senses, and those that affected the mind in the form of suggestions.

"Good evening."

The one Aishia was using placed her target in a daydreamlike state of hypnotism. It was a powerful illusion that could control the target's thoughts and actions to a certain degree when activated successfully.

The flaw of this technique was that the target had clear memories of everything up until the illusion was cast, meaning she had to cast it without being noticed.

"Oh, good evening. You're—ah, that's right. How can I help you?" The cook had no idea he was under a spell, convinced that Aishia was a friendly colleague of his.

"Is Erica alive?" Aishia asked bluntly.

"I don't approve of that form of address. It should be Saint Erica, no?" His belief in Erica was so strong, he showed faint indignation as he corrected Aishia.

"Is Saint Erica still alive?" Aishia repeated.

"What are you saying? Of course she is."

"Didn't she lose her life in the battle yesterday?"

"Of course not. She emerged victorious from yesterday's battle."

"Really?"

The Saint should have lost, yet everyone believed she won.

"That's right." The cook was adamant the Saint had won. He was in a hypnotized state, so his eyes were blank, but his tone was firm. He seemed extremely offended by Aishia's question.

"Did you see her return alive, then?" Aishia continued to ask.

"No, I didn't… She didn't return to the official residence yesterday as she had to deal with the aftermath of the battle."

"She didn't return yesterday… What about today?"

"She left on some urgent business this morning, so no."

"Left for where?"

"That's not something a cook would know."

"Who would know, then?"

"Hmm… Her close aide, Mr. Andrei, should know…"

"Andrei…"

The man with Liselotte yesterday?

Aishia recalled the young man who had been beside Liselotte when she was captured. He had been called Andrei—and she was pretty sure she had spotted him in the building earlier.

"Where is he now?"

"He should be in the congress hall, but it's almost time for dinner, so he should be returning soon."

"Will he return here?"

"Yes, Mr. Andrei lives in this building as well."

"I see…" Aishia mumbled. She stopped asking questions and thought about what to do.

Should I wait for Andrei here?

Going to the congress hall herself was an option, but searching for him would take time and she might miss his return. But just then—

"Mark, are you there? Mark?" a man called from the kitchen. It seemed like someone was searching for the cook.

"You're Mark?"

"Yes."

"I see."

Once she confirmed the cook's identity, Aishia changed her spell to suggest something new to him.

"I'm over here! What did you need?" Mark called out, loud enough to be heard from the kitchen. After a while, a middle-aged man appeared in the kitchen doorway.

Aishia immediately hid behind Mark. It was already dark outside, so she easily hid her small frame behind him.

"Ah, so you were outside. Mr. Andrei has returned. Please prepare his dinner."

The older man paid no notice of Aishia, speaking only to Mark. He immediately turned to head back inside.

"Oh, hold on a second. In that case, can you call Mr. Andrei over here?" Mark asked.

"Mr. Andrei? Why?"

"There's something I want to consult with him about. Preferably in private."

"Ah, I see. All right."

The middle-aged man looked curious, but returned to the kitchen to call Andrei out.

"Sorry. Please sleep for a bit." Once he had left, Aishia touched the back of Mark's head and stopped the illusion art, putting him to sleep through another spirit art instead.

"Mm…" Mark slumped over instantly. Aishia gently supported him, leaning him to sit against the outside wall. Once she confirmed he was fully asleep, she moved over to the kitchen door and hid herself in wait for Andrei. He came out less than a minute later.

"Are you here, Mark—mmh?!"

Andrei had stepped out of the kitchen door to look for Mark. But the very moment he did so, Aishia restrained him from behind.

"Good evening." Aishia undid the restraints after casting an illusion.

"Good evening. What are you doing here…?"

"I have something important to ask you."

"Oh right, that's why I was called out. What is it, comrade?"

Right now, in Andrei's head, he wasn't talking to Mark, but one of the kitchen-hand girls. However, since he didn't know Aishia's name, he referred to her as "comrade."

"Is the Saint alive?" Aishia asked right away.

"What's the matter? Why so out of the blue?"

"I want to know if the Saint is really alive."

"Why do you wish to know such a thing?"

Andrei was currently being directed to answer Aishia's question, yet he kept responding with his own questions instead of answering honestly. He probably had a strong reason to not answer her. At the same time, it was evident that Andrei was a strong-willed person.

"Because no one's seen the Saint alive."

"That's not true. I've seen her," Andrei clearly stated.

"Then what is she doing now?" Aishia asked pointedly.

Andrei hesitated before answering. "I'm afraid I don't know the answer to that."

"Why not?"

"She departed without telling any of us the details of her trip."

"She didn't tell anyone where she was going?"

"Yes. This is a national secret. So even if I knew, I wouldn't tell you."

"I see…" Aishia hummed in suspicion. Calling it a national secret made it sound like they were hiding the Saint's death.

"Are you sure she isn't actually dead, and you're just hiding that fact from the people? If everyone knew she was dead, they would be upset." Aishia voiced her suspicions, pushing closer to the core of the matter.

"Like I said, that isn't true. I understand you feel uneasy being unable to see Saint Erica, but she's on a very important mission. Please believe me," Andrei pleaded.

It doesn't seem like he's lying...

The information was obtained by loosening his tongue through an illusion. She had also hypnotized him to only tell the truth. This meant that Andrei truly believed the Saint was alive—that, or the Saint was actually alive.

Rio and Aishia were convinced the Saint was dead because they witnessed her take her last breath in person. That was why Aishia wanted definite proof the Saint was still alive, but...

"Ah..." Aishia suddenly stepped back from Andrei and returned to her spirit form. Doing so inevitably canceled the illusion cast on Andrei.

"Huh, what was I...?"

Andrei stumbled forward and snapped back to his senses. He looked around the area and spotted the cook, Mark, sitting asleep against the wall.

"Is something the matter, Mr. Andrei?" A man appeared at the kitchen door. It was the older man that Mark had asked to call Andrei over earlier.

"Umm..." Andrei cocked his head in confusion.

"Weren't you speaking to a girl out here?"

"No, I wasn't... I don't think..."

"I thought I heard the sound of you speaking with a girl, though... Why is Mark asleep over there?" the man asked, looking over at Mark curiously.

"I don't know either… What were you doing over here?"

Andrei was bewildered by his lack of memories. He figured the man might know more than him and questioned him in return.

"O-Oh, I was just…" The man immediately smiled awkwardly. He might have been eavesdropping out of curious amusement. Sensing that to be the answer, Andrei sighed lightly.

"At any rate, let's wake Mark up."

"Y-Yes, right away. Hey, Mark! Get up! What are you snoozing for after calling Mr. Andrei all the way out here!" The man started to scold Mark dramatically. Meanwhile—

Was this the work of a spy? It looks like I'll need to take better control of the flow of information…

Andrei became even warier.

After leaving the official residence, Aishia set out from the capital of Ericaburg. She was currently outside the city at the place where Rio fought the divine beast yesterday. She stood in the middle of the battlefield.

A spirit art user would notice the activation of this art.

She had just activated a particular spirit art. At a glance, nothing had happened, but what she had actually done was release a signal wave around the area that could only be sensed by spirit art users. Her goal was to lure out the spirit art user hiding in the Holy Democratic Republic of Erica—and to make contact if possible.

Rio had said there was no need to push herself to find them, but Aishia wanted to lure them out if she could. The ground was illuminated by moonlight, but it was hard to see. Anyone who came to check the signal would be spotted by Aishia first.

How long would it take them to come? Would they come at all? Would one hour be enough of a wait? Aishia stared in the direction of the capital as she waited.

She naturally found herself recalling the sight of the beast of the land standing where she was yesterday as it fired its powerful attack.

Back then, she could be mistaken, but when the beast of the land caught sight of Aishia, it felt like it had directed its negative feelings towards her. Rio hadn't noticed it, so it could just be her imagination, but...

"Was it just my mistake...?"

Was it because she had returned to the location where Rio fought the beast of the land? For some reason, it was only bothering her now. If she was right, and that beast had truly felt negative emotions towards Aishia—why?

Do I know that beast...? Or did the beast know me? That was the thought that suddenly came to Aishia's mind.

Aishia had no memories from before she woke up. Haruto accepted her for that, but it felt like she was forgetting something very, very important.

She existed for Haruto. That, she was certain of.

But there was something more important. Something that she had forgotten for a long, long time...

Was this some kind of forewarning?

She had an extremely uneasy feeling right now.

The next morning, Rio and Aishia were sparring lightly. Vigorous movement should be avoided immediately after healing a wound, but two days had already passed since the battle with the Saint.

Thus, the two of them had decided on some light sparring without weapons. Of course, to the average observer, it was more like a high-speed battle. And there was one such observer watching them from the entrance of the stone house—Liselotte.

Wow...

She had seen the two of them spar many times now, but she was still in awe every time. Plus, watching Rio move around like this really made it seem like he had recovered from his wounds.

Thank goodness, truly...

She had been beside herself with worry, wondering what she would do if something happened to Rio because of her. Seeing him moving about energetically today made her sigh in relief.

Rio and Aishia's back-and-forth exchange continued for another minute. Liselotte was still watching on in a daze as the two came to a sudden stop.

"Well?" Aishia asked.

It was hard to tell what she meant with just a single word, but Rio seemed to understand her through the lack of words and smiled.

"I'm feeling much better now. We can leave today," he replied.

"That's good."

"It's all thanks to you, Aishia. Thank you."

"You're welcome," Aishia replied happily, the faintest smile on her face. Her facial features were so perfect, she normally felt inhuman, but the expression on her face right now was very soft.

She's got such a beautiful face...

Liselotte found herself captivated by Aishia's beauty. She nearly forgot herself for the next few seconds, but now was the perfect time to approach them with their sparring finished. Liselotte snapped to her senses and took a step forward, but when she watched how intimate the two of them seemed, she couldn't move.

"..."

It was like she'd be intruding on a space for just the two of them.

After all, there was very little personal space between the two of them. They were speaking within arm's reach of each other. Aishia was the one who moved to shorten the distance between them, but Rio showed no sign of backing away in discomfort. He stood next to Aishia as though it was only natural to be right beside her.

What's the relationship between them, I wonder?

She had been informed about Aishia being a contract spirit to Rio while she was being rescued, but she wasn't wondering about any formal titles like that right now. She wanted to know the more substantial details.

It doesn't seem like they're lovers, though. From what I've heard from everyone else, Sir Haruto isn't dating anyone in particular.

There were many attractive women around Rio. A number of them clearly liked him as a member of the opposite sex. However, it seemed Rio had a rather negative outlook on romance and only interacted with them in a gentlemanly manner—or so Latifa had once told her. In fact, Latifa had offered the information without any prompting.

But it feels like Lady Aishia is special.

This was just Liselotte's own impression, but it didn't seem like Rio was as accepting of anyone being near him as he was with Aishia. Of course, he naturally let Latifa near him, but that was as his little sister rather than as someone of the opposite sex.

Just what made Aishia so special? It didn't seem to be something that could be explained as a strong bond or trust. Such things had been formed between him and the other girls too.

That's why Liselotte was unable to shake the feeling of Aishia being special to Rio. She was allowed to be closer to him than the other girls—but what did she have that the other girls didn't?

Perhaps he's actually in love with her, and just hasn't noticed it himself?

Rio wasn't the outgoing type with romance, and he didn't seem to have any intentions of forming a harem with multiple women. That much, Liselotte was certain about. He would only devote himself to one person.

What if there was something special about Aishia that could be linked to romantic feelings in Rio? Even if he had no romantic feelings right now, there was plenty of chance he could connect the dots in the future.

Would Rio fall in love with Aishia?

What is this...?

When Liselotte imagined that, for some reason, a hazy feeling suddenly overcame her. But she couldn't tell what the identity of that feeling was, which just left her confused.

"Are you not going outside?" a voice called from behind her.

"Aah!" Liselotte let out a cute yelp of surprise. She looked back to see her head attendant, Aria.

"D-Don't appear out of nowhere like that..." she complained.

"My apologies for scaring you. You were just staring outside so enviously, I couldn't help but give you a push."

"I-I'm not envious of anything, though."

"Sir Amakawa and Lady Aishia are outside, no?"

"Y-Yes..."

How did she know that?

"You looked like you were about to call out to them, but your sense of inferiority made you give up."

"Can you stop reading the mind of your master?!"

"It's an essential skill of an attendant."

"Guh…"

It was indeed a vital ability for an attendant.

I'd prefer it if you only activated that skill for work, though…

It was the duty of an attendant to serve their master in their daily life. It was clear Aria would merely reply that she was working right now, so Liselotte didn't argue out loud.

"Sir Amakawa is in great demand as is. He won't turn your way if you merely sit and stare," Aria said, giving her master advice.

"Why are you making it sound like I want his attention?!"

"Because no matter how you look at it, he has yours…"

Was it possible that she wasn't aware of it?

"Th-That's not true! I'm not some princess from a fairy tale, falling in love with the first person to rescue me from a pinch," Liselotte squeaked, averting her eyes.

She showed signs of falling for him some time ago, but does she actually have no awareness of her feelings, or is she just refusing to admit to it? Either way, her case is rather dire. At this rate, things will only get more complicated for my master.

Aria looked exasperated. Her master had received countless proposals, but she had lived only for her work until now. She had no experience falling in love with the opposite sex. This might even be her first love.

That thought put a smile on her face, but the future was rather concerning.

"What's that look for...?" Liselotte pouted, puffing up her cheeks cutely.

"Nothing. But if I were to offer one word of advice..."

"What?"

"If there's one thing I can say for sure, it's that you won't find a better gentleman than Sir Amakawa anytime soon. Don't regret your decisions." With that, Aria pushed open the front door.

"Stop saying weird things to make me feel self-conscious about it," Liselotte grumbled. Perhaps she already knew in her head, and her heart just hadn't caught up yet.

What am I thinking?! I'm practically admitting that I'm conscious of Sir Haruto...

She soon came to her senses and shook her head furiously.

This really is dire... Aria thought, watching her master's reaction with a sigh.

"What's up, you two?" Just then, Rio came over.

"G-Good morning, Sir Haruto," Liselotte replied first, feigning composure. But there was a clear blush tinting her cheeks.

"Nothing. I'm about to prepare breakfast, so please have a seat." Aria was her usual self. She bowed at Rio and Aishia before turning to head for the kitchen. But Rio called out to stop her.

"Let me make breakfast today. As an apology for all the worry I've caused."

"In that case, let me make it. I'm the one who should be expressing my gratitude," Liselotte immediately offered instead.

"No, it'll just be a simple Japanese meal..." In other words, there was no need to make a big deal of it.

269

"If I may be so bold as to speak, my master has been quite anxious as to how she can express her thanks. She's also well versed on the subject of Japanese meals. Would you kindly consider taking her up on her offer?"

Aria tactfully took the chance to assist her master. Like Rio, Aria was aware that Liselotte had memories of her past life—what she wasn't aware of was that Rio also had memories of *his* past life. In her mind, this was the perfect excuse for Liselotte to make breakfast for him.

Take this chance to win him over with your cooking.

Aria's intentions were clearly conveyed to Liselotte, who blushed shyly.

"How about we make it together?" Rio suggested. "There's all sorts of ingredients available, so we can both make a dish we want to make."

"That sounds wonderful," Aria agreed dramatically.

"Enough, Aria!"

"You two sure get along well." Rio chuckled.

"Umm... Please let me cook with you."

And so, Rio and Liselotte decided to make breakfast together.

"You really have everything..." Liselotte mumbled, looking around in awe. They were in the walk-in pantry connected to the kitchen.

"There's soy sauce, miso, and dashi, as well as every seasoning you need to make Japanese food. Anything raw or hard to preserve is stored in the Time-Space Cache, so just let me know if you need something you don't see here."

Rio opened the refrigerating magic artifact as he gave his explanation. The Time-Space Cache was far better at preserving foods than this fridge, so he only kept foods he planned on using soon in here.

"Wow, there's even seaweed and tofu."

"There's also natto, wild yam, and okra."

"Oh! I want to eat that…!"

The two stood before the fridge, checking the contents like that.

"Let's make something you want to eat. What would your dream Japanese breakfast be?" Rio suggested after he'd finished explaining all of the features of the kitchen.

"My dream breakfast… That would have to be rice and miso soup."

"I see. What ingredients do you like in your miso soup?"

"I can't decide! I like tofu, but how about radish and abura-age? Since there's soy sauce, I'd like to eat the tofu with that."

The prospect of eating Japanese food again seemed to have stimulated Liselotte's soul as a Japanese person, as her voice was brimming with excitement.

"We can also chop the radish leaves and make a stir-fry."

"That sounds great! It'd go well with rice too."

"Is there anything else you'd like?"

"Hmm… Maybe a grilled fish…"

"We can season it with salt and serve it with grated radish. That would be nice."

"That sounds delicious!"

They settled on a breakfast menu in no time at all, then returned to the kitchen to finally begin cooking.

"Who normally does the cooking in your mansion, Sir Haruto?"

"Miharu and Orphia take the initiative to make our meals. Everyone else helps out here and there. Do you normally cook for yourself, Liselotte?" Rio asked back. Although she was the daughter of a duke, she clearly seemed familiar with cooking.

"I leave all the cooking to the chefs when I'm at home, but when I'm developing new recipes for work, I cook myself. The fastest way to recreate the dishes I ate while I was in Japan is to make them myself."

"So that's why you're so good at cooking."

"Thank you for the compliment. Back when I was Minamoto Rikka, my parents managed a family restaurant, so I learned a lot by helping them. That experience helped a lot."

"My experience as Amakawa Haruto has helped me a lot too."

"You also cooked when you were Amakawa Haruto?" Liselotte asked a little hesitantly. They both knew that the other had memories of their past life, but they hadn't had many opportunities to discuss it quite like this.

Of course, she had always wanted to talk to Rio about his past life, but Rio wasn't the type to talk about himself. Would it be rude to ask prying questions to someone like that? Such considerate worries had kept Liselotte from broaching the subject until now.

"Yes. I lived alone from my high school years to university. I also worked part-time jobs at restaurants and learned a bit there."

Rio explained how he was forced into learning by necessity, showing no reluctance in discussing the topic. This eased the self-restraint Liselotte had maintained until now.

"Amakawa-senpai. Ah..."

Liselotte unconsciously called Rio "Amakawa-senpai," then immediately panicked. It was a blunder she would normally never commit; it had slipped out when she brought the Minamoto Rikka side of herself to the forefront.

Rio blinked in surprise. "Senpai…you say?"

"Oh, no. Umm… I may have mentioned it before, but I knew you in my past life… And you were my upperclassman, so I would have called you 'senpai.' S-Sorry for bringing it up out of the blue." Liselotte bowed her head, blushing furiously.

"Is that so…?" Rio replied curiously. He wasn't completely unaware of a girl named Minamoto Rikka, but he only knew that she was a high school girl who rode the same bus as him. He didn't think she'd seen him any differently to how he saw her, but perhaps that wasn't the case…

Liselotte read Rio's question off his face and hurriedly added to explain, "I didn't have the chance to say this before, but I knew you when you were in high school as well."

"Umm… Did we meet somewhere then?"

"I suppose you could say that. I don't expect you to remember, though—we only met once during the cultural festival of your high school. You happened across me and helped me out when I needed a hand. But…"

"But?"

"But there's another reason I knew about you… My cousin actually attended the same high school as you."

"Oh, I see now." Rio finally nodded in understanding.

"My cousin's name was Fujiwara Mafuyu. Do you remember her?" Liselotte asked nervously.

"Fujiwara… Yes, I remember." He looked through Amakawa Haruto's memories and a certain girl came to mind.

"You remember her?" Liselotte sighed in relief, smiling happily.

"Yes. She used to hang out with someone named Chizuru a lot."

Chizuru was one of the loud and lively girls in his school.

"Oh, you even remember Chi-san."

"You called her Chi-san?" Rio smiled in amusement, surprised by the unexpected acquaintance they had in common. Mafuyu was one of the more introverted girls, but Chizuru often invited him to hang out after school. That was why he could still recall them.

"I also called my cousin 'Fu-chan.' I was still in middle school back then, but the two of them were my best friends. I often played together with them."

"So that's why you were at the school festival."

"Yes. Thank you for helping me back then."

"You're welcome, though I doubt I did anything special."

"No, no, you were really cool."

"Aha ha. Thanks," Rio chuckled shyly.

"I'm sure Fu-chan would be shocked to hear that I'm cooking alongside Amakawa Haruto in a world where I was reborn after I'd died." Liselotte looked into the distance longingly.

"Maybe."

"Besides..." Liselotte started to say, fixing her gaze on Rio's face.

"Besides?" Rio made eye contact with her.

There was still one thing she had yet to tell Rio: that Fujiwara Mafuyu had been in love with Amakawa Haruto. That was something she had learned from Chizuru, rather than Mafuyu herself.

It was why Rikka had always known about Amakawa Haruto: she had always supported Fujiwara Mafuyu's crush. The young man her cousin loved had been reborn into this world and was standing before her.

"It's nothing. Sorry, I got a little sentimental there."

After some hesitation, Liselotte decided not to tell Rio. No, she couldn't tell him—though she didn't know the reason why herself.

"Right." Rio was a little puzzled by the averted topic, but he readily moved on.

"Amakawa-senpai," Liselotte said slowly, immersing herself in the sound of the words.

"It's a little embarrassing to be called that," Rio mumbled, scratching his cheek.

"May I call you by that name again, sometime in the future?" Liselotte asked seriously. She didn't appear to be making fun of him, so Rio granted her wish pleasantly.

"Sure... If you want."

It felt like he had gained another connection with someone, which made him feel happy. No, it probably wasn't his imagination. Acting cowardly out of the fear of others... Acting brave to be liked by others... That was how people accumulated connections.

"Hehe," Liselotte giggled, feeling how their relationship had deepened. The same feeling applied to Rio.

"We've stopped moving. Let's get back to cooking."

"Yes sir!"

At Rio's suggestion, they resumed cooking.

Meanwhile, Aishia and Aria had been watching over the two of them from the living room behind them. They had quiet personalities, so their conversation hadn't been very lively, but the silence between them wasn't uncomfortable either. Aishia wasn't the type to feel awkward over any silence in the first place, and Aria understood that after their recent experience of living together.

I was worried about what would happen between them for a while there, but...

"Let me thank you once again, Lady Aishia." Aria looked away from her master in the kitchen to address Aishia, who was seated beside her.

"Sure." Aishia nodded in return, her expression soft as she watched Rio. Her side profile was beautifully alluring even to Aria, who found herself swallowing her breath.

"..."

If Aishia had any romantic feelings for Rio, she would be an extremely formidable rival to her master. Aria almost pitied Liselotte—but it seemed Liselotte was yet to accept her own feelings, so it wasn't a concern for now.

And it wasn't only Aishia. Once they returned to Galarc, Rio would be surrounded by charming girls who were attracted to him. Aria was certain that her close friend Celia was included among them.

Who should I support between my master and my close friend...?

Aria grimaced at the difficult position she was left in.

But at least I can cheer for my master without any reservations while we're here.

With that thought, she resumed watching over Liselotte, who was happily standing in the kitchen.

❖ Chapter 3 ❖
Report

In the dining hall of Rio's mansion, located on the Galarc Castle grounds...

It was just the day before that Rio and Liselotte made breakfast together, listened to Aishia's investigation report after eating, and departed for the Galarc Kingdom that very morning. Rio had carried Liselotte and Aishia had carried Aria as they flew through the sky, arriving in the capital of Galtuuk in the span of one day.

Rio and Liselotte were currently reporting everything that had happened to them to François and the others. Liselotte started with what had happened during her abduction, explaining the state of things in the Holy Democratic Republic of Erica.

This was followed by Rio's explanation of how he rescued her—that is, his fight with the giant creature called the beast of the land. He described how it had attacked him, wiping out Erica's own allies in the process, and how the battle ended with him piercing Saint Erica through the heart. Yet despite this, the people of the Holy Democratic Republic of Erica believed she was still alive.

"And that is everything that happened up until my return," Rio said, concluding his report.

"Hmm... I see it was the right choice to send you after all." Francois, who had carefully listened to the entire report without interrupting, hummed in deep thought and commended Rio.

"But I have returned without resolving the issue. I apologize for my failures."

"Saint Erica's survival, and the monster called the beast of the land…"

"Yes."

"Your apology is unneeded. Take pride in your results. The duty you were entrusted with was to retrieve Liselotte and set an example for the foolish nation that stepped out of line. You succeeded on both accounts. I knew from the start that these goals had the potential to provoke a counterattack—the scale of the counterattack being greater than expected is not a failure on your part."

"Thank you for the kind words…" Rio bowed his head, his expression still concerned.

"If the Saint is truly alive, then the issue is rather headache-inducing. I'm sure the beast of the land is also a tremendous monster to be reckoned with."

"If that monster were to attack, there would be nothing left of the capital. As long as the Saint's survival is unclear, it would be best to watch out for any incoming attacks."

"Suppose the capital were to become the battlefield… Would you be able to drive off the monster, having won against it before?"

"I cannot guarantee I would win a second time… Even if I could, the capital is highly unlikely to get by unharmed."

"I see. If someone like you is saying that, then this cannot be dismissed lightly. But do you truly believe the Saint is alive?"

"It shouldn't be possible…I think…" However, he couldn't say he was absolutely sure. That was what his choice of words was implying.

"You're certain you pierced your sword through her heart, no? You also confirmed her pulse had stopped. When you infiltrated the capital the next day, you were unable to spot the Saint alive anywhere."

"Yes."

"It seems most reasonable to assume the leaders of that country are hiding the Saint's death, as you previously pointed out in your report."

"Indeed, it is exactly as you say."

"Hmm. Then let me confirm this: can you think of any means for a stopped heart to start beating again?"

"I cannot…"

It was possible to heal a heart the moment it was stabbed, but the damage he dealt to the Saint had been enough to kill her instantly. It would have been difficult to survive even if she had had her physical body enhanced when he stabbed her. Controlling one's magic essence when fatally wounded was extremely difficult. She wouldn't have been able to heal herself in such a state, and even if she activated the spell, she wouldn't have been able to maintain it long enough to heal herself.

There was a possibility she was healed by someone else nearby, but even then, there was little to no chance of survival.

"I see. I agree it would be more reassuring to have some kind of confirmation that the Saint is truly dead, but you are aware of the difficulties of proving a death with no corpse, yes? You weren't able to locate the corpse even after looking for it."

"I can go and search for it again," Rio suggested. He wouldn't have the duty of escorting Liselotte back this time, so he could take his time investigating.

"You've just returned after fulfilling your duty. You may appear fully healed, but you were terribly wounded in battle, were you not? Remember that you need your rest as well," Francois warned Rio with a somewhat exasperated sigh.

Indeed, leaving for the Holy Democratic Republic of Erica immediately upon bringing Liselotte back to Galarc was bordering on overwork. All the girls sitting present nodded along in approval to Francois's words.

"But…" Rio hesitated under all of their gazes.

"If the need arises, I will make an official request for your assistance—but until then, restore yourself in this mansion. I have other options available to me, such as sending spies to hide in their capital or an official envoy to probe their attitude."

"I understand…" With that, Rio finally backed down.

"I would also prefer for you to remain in this capital as a form of defense. As I mentioned earlier, there was a bit of an incident here that was unrelated to the Saint. I'd like you to focus on protecting the castle in the meantime," Francois said, finally moving on to the incident that occurred while Rio was absent.

"What happened?"

"The castle was attacked three days ago."

"By whom…?"

"The remnants of the Heavenly Lions."

"What…?!" The moment the Heavenly Lions were mentioned, Rio froze. It went without saying that he believed it was his fault.

"I've heard that the group has some deep animosity for you, but there's no clear evidence that the attack was for the purpose of revenge on you. That is how I see it, at least," Francois immediately said. "We captured some prisoners, but they all died without warning. It was just like what happened to the attackers that appeared on the night of the banquet. You understand what I'm saying, right? This removal of witnesses is the exact way of the Proxia Empire." Francois let out another sigh, this time out of irritation.

"But they targeted this mansion, didn't they?"

He had seen traces of what had been combat scattered across the castle grounds on his way here, but the area surrounding the mansion was particularly damaged. In fact, a whole section of the building had been clearly destroyed.

In other words, they had attacked with the knowledge that Rio lived here—or so Rio assumed.

"Indeed, this mansion was targeted. They also made some statements that implied they were after revenge against you."

Everyone in the castle knew that much, so Francois didn't bother to hide the fact the mansion had been at the center of the fighting.

"Then surely…"

Surely that meant their goal was to have revenge on him, did it not? A dark shadow fell across Rio's face.

"Even if their goal was to have revenge on you—so what? This is the royal castle of the capital. As the king, it is my duty and my pride to protect it. No matter what connection you may have with the assailants, it became the kingdom's problem the moment they attacked the castle. My failure in preventing invasion is not your blame to take," Francois stated clearly.

"Besides," he continued. "There were many important figures gathered in this building at the time of the attack. Lady Satsuki, Princess Christina, Princess Flora, and Charlotte. Three princesses and one hero—if they were after someone to take hostage, it would only make sense for them to come here."

All four of the girls named were present in the room. Francois looked around at each of them as he mentioned their names.

"Flora and I have been targeted by them before," Christina added in support. "The Proxia Empire is connected to the Arbor family and the Beltrum Kingdom. There's nothing strange about their coming after the leaders of the Restoration."

Flora shot out of her seat to add her theory, defending Rio intently. "That's right! It'd even mean that Sir Haruto's mansion was targeted because we were here, making it our fault…!"

"Well, that's one possibility. It could also be my fault the mansion was targeted," Satsuki said, agreeing with them.

"The mercenaries of the Heavenly Lions targeted Sir Haruto's mansion, where multiple figures of importance were present at the time. That is the objective truth. With more than one candidate for the attack, there is no need to point fingers at anyone. Everyone is innocent until proven guilty—if anyone is to blame, then it's the attackers. That is why Sir Haruto's apology is unnecessary."

With a smile that wouldn't take any objections, Charlotte shot Rio down before he could apologize further.

"Fortunately, there wasn't much damage done, thanks to the efforts of Lord Gouki's people and the girls here. If anything, I should be thanking you all." Francois chuckled, looking around the room.

"Thank you very much, everyone…" Rio bowed his head, expressing his deep gratitude for everyone. No one immediately stepped forward to say something on behalf of the others, as they all accepted his words happily.

"Speaking of which, I don't see everyone here." Rio noted that Latifa, Alma, and the rest of the Yagumo group were not present.

"Let me just say this first—Alma was injured in this incident," Sara replied first.

"Wh…?" Rio's expression instantly stiffened.

"You're not allowed to apologize to Alma either," Orphia interrupted. "Because it's not your fault. Her wound has fully healed already; she's resting in another room with Suzune just to be safe."

"I understand… Then I shall thank Alma and Suzune later."

"It isn't something you need to thank them for either. We're all friends here, and we just did what was natural," Sara mumbled somewhat shyly.

"Hmm? Did you say something, Sara?" Orphia asked with a grin. She was sitting right beside her, so she had heard her words clearly.

"It's nothing!" Sara feigned ignorance in embarrassment.

"Heh heh." Miharu and Celia giggled at the sight of the two of them.

"Komomo and the others are waiting outside the city. Everyone should be doing well, so there's no need for concern," Gouki said.

"I can see why you and Kayoko are here now. Thank you so much for coming…"

"We ended up intruding upon the castle in an unexpected manner, but I'm glad we were able to help."

"Indeed."

Gouki and Kayoko both bowed their heads respectfully. Unaware of the relationship between them, Francois and Charlotte watched on curiously. The couple was old enough to be Rio's parents, yet they showed this kind of attitude towards him.

"They were amazing, you know? Gouki and Kayoko defeated all the mercenaries as soon as they arrived. It was a great battle!" Satsuki gave them raving praise.

"There were monsters that appeared along with the attack, but the Saga couple assisted in subjugating those as well," Francois added.

"Monsters appeared?"

"Yes. Black orbs fell from the sky, releasing swarms of monsters. According to Lady Celia, the same monsters appeared during the attack on Amande."

The monsters they were referring to were revenants.

"They were humanoid monsters that moved nimbly. The strong ones that appeared at Liselotte's mansion," Celia explained to Rio.

"Those things…"

"I don't want to believe it, but it seems the Proxia Empire—or perhaps the Heavenly Lions—have a means of controlling monsters. That's the only possibility I can see based on the situation."

"So it seems…"

"However, there's an even more troublesome monster out there. It wasn't as formidable as the beast of the land you fought, but a giant skeleton knight appeared," Francois said, referring to the Hero Killer Draugul.

That prompted a reaction from Aishia.

"A giant skeleton knight?"

Everyone's gazes focused on her.

"Do you know something about it?" Rio asked.

"It might be Reiss… I ran into him while you were in the Paladia Kingdom."

"Ah, back then…"

Rio remembered what she was referring to. It was around the time he had achieved his revenge against Lucius and returned to the Galarc Kingdom. Reiss had appeared before Celia and Aishia, whom he had left in Rodania. He fled when Aishia chased after him, turning into a monster when cornered—and was then defeated.

According to Rio's memory, Celia had reported her encounter with Reiss to the Restoration, and it would have reached Christina and Francois's ears. However, she hadn't mentioned Aishia chasing after him. Doing so would require explaining how Aishia was guarding her in spirit form.

"Reiss is the man acting as the ambassador for the Proxia Empire, no? He was the one dispatched to the Beltrum Kingdom… Did that truly happen?" Francois asked Rio.

"Yes, it happened. But I'm not sure where to start explaining…"

If he were to explain things truthfully, he'd have to start with how Aishia was a spirit and everything else he had kept hidden until now. Rio struggled to answer.

"It was when Princess Christina and Princess Flora were kidnapped by Lucius. Do you remember when I reported that I saw Reiss?" Celia explained on behalf of Rio.

"I remember."

"Indeed."

Christina and Francois exchanged a look before nodding in turn.

"That was back when Haruto was absent, and Aishia was secretly guarding me," Celia revealed honestly. Hearing that, Rio held his breath. But he didn't think someone as intelligent as Celia would slip up like this, so he kept an impassive look on his face.

"Umm, they know that Aishia is a spirit," Celia clarified, giving a short summary of the situation to clear Rio's woes.

"Ifritah, Hel, and Ariel fought alongside us when the invaders attacked," Orphia added. "That was how Lady Aishia came up."

"So that's what happened. No wonder…"

No wonder they had come to meet him at the gate earlier, Rio thought. The spirits had detected Aishia's presence, and there was no need to hide that any longer.

"Well, that's how it is," Francois said heartily, making fun of Rio's surprise.

"I'm sorry, I didn't think it was good to speak about spirits freely…"

"No worries. Records of spirits exist in literature, but I've never heard of anyone seeing them in person. It's clearly not a topic to speak about openly. It would be one thing if it were just uncommon, but the value in that rarity could bring even more trouble."

In this world, in this era, rare talents and fortunes had to be hidden to stay out of trouble. That was one of the secrets to success.

"Indeed, it is as you say..." Unsure of how far the knowledge of spirits had spread, anxiety filled Rio's face.

"There were many people who witnessed the spirits during the fight, but only a select number of trusted figures know that they were spirits. Don't worry about it."

Rio sighed in relief. "Thank you for your consideration."

"No problem. We can't have any more needless trouble happening around you. That aside, she really looks no different from a regular human... Besides her appearance, which is so unhuman she almost looks divine... I mean. Let's get back on topic."

Francois was nearly captivated by Aishia when he turned to look at her, but the steel reasoning power of a king prevented him from trailing off-topic. He returned his gaze to Rio and asked, "What were you saying about Reiss?"

"We believe that the skeleton knight may have been Reiss's true identity. That was the form he took on when he fought Aishia. We've also seen him summon monsters."

"So Reiss's true form is a monster?"

"The transformed skeleton knight didn't leave an enchanted gem, so he may not be a monster... If he has the ability to summon monsters, he may be a being of a higher existence than just a regular monster."

"Hmm. If there are spirits that look no different to humans, there may be monsters that look no different to humans as well."

Controlling monsters is taboo for anyone who believes in the Six Wise Gods. It's heresy. His existence would even be considered on par with the King of Fiends from the Divine War, as recorded in the sacred scriptures.

Francois thought in his head, refraining from deviating the conversation.

"Right," Rio nodded with a contemplative look.

"Now that I think of it, I may not have finished him off. That might be why there was no enchanted gem," Aishia added beside him. Rio listened to her words, then turned to Gouki who actually fought the knight.

"Did he leave an enchanted gem when you defeated him?"

"No, I didn't see anything of the sort. Did anyone else?" Gouki asked, looking around at Celia, Sara, Orphia, and Kayoko who had fought with him.

"Nothing…"

"I don't recall anything like that."

"Nope."

"Me neither…"

It seemed that no one had seen it.

"Did you fight as well, Celia?"

"Yes, I did," Celia said, blushing proudly.

"Wasn't it a strong monster, though?"

"I can fight as well, you know? Although I do need to be protected while casting my magic…"

"I knew you were an amazing sorcerer, but…"

"Oh, it was a tremendous spell," Gouki praised, having seen Celia use her magic in person. "She blew up the shield we were struggling against in a single blow, taking out half the body with it. If Lady Celia wasn't there, it would have been a much harder battle."

"It was stronger than anything we can cast, wasn't it?"

"Yes. It truly was a sight to see."

Orphia and Sara both sang praises of Celia as well.

287

"Th-That doesn't matter right now. We're in His Majesty's presence, so please continue with what you were saying. Something about Reiss's identity, right?"

Celia urged Rio to continue speaking, hiding her embarrassment.

"Yes, err... As you may have heard from Sara and the others already, spirits are extremely sensitive to the presences of others."

Despite his confusion, Rio resumed his explanation.

"Presences, you say?"

"You can think of them as invisible waves, unrelated to magic essence. Perhaps as spiritual existences, they can feel the souls of other creatures? That's how I see it, anyway."

"I see. And?"

"Presences tend to have similarities within their species. Spirits feel like other spirits, humans like other humans, and monsters like monsters. However, Reiss sometimes feels like a spirit, and sometimes feels like a monster..."

"Hmm. So when she saw him transform into the giant skeleton knight, she felt a presence that wasn't that of a monster?"

"Yes, though there's no way to be certain... Aishia actually defeated that skeleton knight back then. We wondered if Reiss died in that battle, but..."

"Considering there was no enchanted gem left behind back then—and the reappearance of the same knight now—he may still be alive?"

"Yes."

"I see... But to think that a giant like that could be defeated alone... It seems I'll never cease to be surprised."

Francois had only watched things take place from the ground, but the menacing sight of the Hero Killer Draugul had been burned into his eyes. He had seen how it flew around unaffected by the intermediate and high grade spells, so he was amazed that Aishia had defeated it alone.

"Spirit girl—Aishia. I wish to ask you a question," he said to Aishia.

"What...would you like to ask?"

Aishia replied plainly at first, then added more polite words to show respect for the king.

"In your eyes, how strong was that skeleton knight?"

"He had tough defenses. But once I got past that, he wasn't too hard to defeat."

"The people gathered here are strong enough to represent their respective nations. How would they compare to him?"

"In a one-on-one battle, no one here would fall behind in terms of overall strength. They might not be able to defeat him without breaking through his defenses, but that doesn't mean they'd lose."

"I see. In that case, it would be best for someone to act as a decoy while another prepares a powerful magic spell to break through. What do you think of this strategy?"

"That would be the best option if you were taking him on in a group. However, if your attacks were ineffective, it might be difficult to stop him from rampaging about. He's highly mobile, so it'd be a challenge to hit him from afar. You'd have to be careful there."

"It sounds difficult, but now I can adjust our training regime in preparation for future monsters like him. Thank you for the valuable opinion."

"Sure thing... I mean, you're welcome."

"Incidentally—I know you defeated it by yourself, but how would Haruto have fared?"

Francois knew that Rio was strong, but he didn't have an exact image in his head. He figured this was a good chance to ask about it.

"..."

Aishia looked at Rio to check if she was allowed to answer. Rio nodded to convey that he didn't mind.

"It wouldn't be a problem for Haruto. He could even take on multiple at once."

"Multiple at once... Ha ha ha! No, I apologize. I should have guessed, but he truly is a remarkable man. It seems I underestimated you yet again," Francois said to Rio cheerfully. First the King's Sword Alfred, the strongest man of the Beltrum Kingdom, then Lucius, the veteran commander of the Heavenly Lions. The boy named Amakawa Haruto had overcome such influential figures to prove himself. And now he had defeated a beast of even greater size.

He had known that Rio was stronger than those renowned across the world, but it was clear that there was still no limit to his strength.

"I have one more question, spirit girl. If that skeleton knight were to fight the beast of the land, who would win?"

"The beast of the land."

"An immediate reply, hmm?"

"Not even an army of skeleton knights could take on the beast of the land. The most they could do is buy time."

"I see. The beast of the land must be quite the monster. I can see why Haruto is wary of the Saint's survival," Francois said, sighing tiredly. He then turned to Rio. "According to your report, it seemed like the Saint was in control of the beast. And it's possible the beast is a spirit, you said?"

"Yes."

"I've learned a lot over the course of defending the castle from this incident. Things about spirits, and things about spirit arts. Lady Sara explained how the power hidden in the Divine Arms closely resembles the phenomenon of spirit arts."

"Indeed," Sara confirmed.

"If the beast of the land is a divine beast summoned and controlled through the Saint's hero powers, would it be correct to assume Lady Satsuki could do the same?"

"I considered that possibility as well..."

Rio looked at Sara and Orphia's faces, nodding together. The two had the same thought after hearing Rio's report earlier. Their gazes all gathered on Satsuki.

"Wait, what? I don't know how to summon such a scary-sounding beast!" Satsuki protested in confusion.

"What about Sir Hiroaki, Princess Christina?" Francois asked Christina, the representative of another organization with a hero.

"Such a thing has never been mentioned to me..."

"In that case, we cannot say for sure whether it is a hero ability. Even if the beast of the land is a spirit, the Saint may have formed a contract unrelated to her powers as hero, no?" Francois asked, turning back to Rio.

"I doubt it's truly a spirit, but the possibility exists."

"Why do you doubt it?"

"As I said earlier, spirits can sense the presences of other spirits. Aishia said the beast of the land felt similar, but fundamentally different from a spirit's presence."

"Right…"

"Besides, a spirit with that much power should be humanoid in shape."

Isn't that right? Rio looked at Sara and Orphia to confirm. As spirit folk, they knew more about spirits than he did.

"Yes, that should be the case… But there are people more knowledgeable than us about spirits, so Orphia and I will find the time to go ask them about it," Sara offered. She was probably referring to the elders of her village.

"I see… Then I shall leave the investigation of that matter to you," Francois agreed.

"There's one thing I'd like to check too…" Rio stated, raising his hand.

"What is it?"

"Has there been any record of a beast like that appearing in the literature about heroes?"

"There's no such mention in any of the sacred scriptures or apocrypha. I also had all the pseudepigrapha searched through after Lady Satsuki was summoned, but the possibility still exists. I'll have them investigated once more."

Firstly, sacred scriptures were scriptures that were personally inscribed by the Six Wise Gods and transmitted widely until the present. They contained accounts of the Six Wise Gods and the heroes, as well as an extremely simplified history of the Divine War.

Rio had seen them in person at the Royal Academy, but their contents were abstract, and the texts themselves were very short.

Additionally, apocrypha were the supplementary texts that kingdoms produced to explain the abstract contents of the sacred scriptures. The religious belief in the Six Wise Gods was controlled by the royal families of each kingdom, so they usually recorded the origin of the royal family and other matters convenient to the ruling class. They also included additional descriptions where necessary.

Furthermore, because the apocrypha were different for every kingdom, wars had previously occurred over their contents. Thus, there was now a diplomatic and unspoken understanding that no kingdom would interfere with the apocrypha of another.

Finally, pseudepigrapha were the supplementary texts written by civilians without the approval of the kingdom. They weren't treated as heresy just for being written without approval, but the authors would be punished if they wrote anything inconvenient for the kingdom. Thus, most pseudepigrapha were written anonymously and released in single volumes, with very few in circulation. They were referred to as pseudepigrapha for their lack of credibility.

In short, apocrypha were the texts produced by the kingdom, while pseudepigrapha were the texts created by civilians. If Hiroaki were here right now, he'd probably call both a type of historical fantasy novel.

"There aren't that many in our possession, but I'll ask the Restoration to search through the pseudepigrapha in Rodania as well," Christina chimed in, offering her assistance.

"That would be helpful," Francois said, nodding. "Now, I would like some time to organize my thoughts. If there's nothing else to discuss, let's call it a day."

He tried to wrap up the discussions for the day, when—

"Umm, this might not be the place to ask, but I do have a matter that should probably be approved by the king as well."

Satsuki raised her hand.

"What is it, Lady Satsuki?" Francois asked.

"I'd like to ask Haruto for a favor," she said, turning to look at Rio.

"Yes...?" Rio looked puzzled, having no idea what Satsuki could want from him.

"You mentioned how the Divine Arms' abilities are extremely similar to spirit arts. I'd like you to give me proper instruction on how to use my powers."

"Are you saying that because you want to become stronger?"

"Yes. I... I want to be stronger."

"May I ask why?"

With the beast of the land in mind, Rio had been thinking of explaining the existence of spirits to Francois and asking for his permission to seek Satsuki's assistance anyway. Thus, this development was most welcome to him—but that was only if he considered himself. He still wanted to know how serious Satsuki was and what she was thinking.

Besides, there was also the issue of what the Galarc King thought about Satsuki's pursuit of greater power.

"I was frustrated. When this mansion was being raided by the attackers, everyone else was fighting while I hid somewhere safe... I joined the fight eventually, but I was only able to watch on when the skeleton monster appeared. That's why I want to become stronger. I want to be able to fight with everyone when something happens."

Satsuki laid bare the feelings in her heart. All that was left was to confirm Francois's intentions.

"Practically speaking, will your instruction in spirit arts actually draw out the abilities of Lady Satsuki's Divine Arms?" Francois asked Rio.

"Yes... I've given her some simple advice before, and that was enough for her to show visible improvement. If I were to teach her properly, she would probably improve far more dramatically."

"I see... In that case, I would like to make the same request. Would you be able to provide proper instruction to Lady Satsuki?"

"After fighting the beast of the land, I was hoping to ask Satsuki for her help in finding out more about Divine Arms anyway. It would be my pleasure to accept." Rio placed his right hand over his chest respectfully.

"Then it's decided. You may use the rear garden of the castle if you so wish, but if you would prefer to train somewhere out of sight, then you may leave the castle as well."

"I can leave the castle?"

Satsuki's eyes widened. Although it was for the sake of training, the others also showed signs of surprise to hear that she was allowed to leave so easily.

"You've never been prohibited from leaving in the first place, no? I would express my disapproval if the situation were unfavorable, but that doesn't apply to cases where you have a proper reason for going out and understand the risks."

"Well, that's true..."

"I thought I had made my trust in you clear. I would prefer it if you informed me of your plans before leaving, but I won't oppose your outings if Haruto is accompanying you. You may arrange the details with Charlotte later."

"Yes, please do." Charlotte nodded happily. It was clear from her expression that she was hoping to take advantage of the opportunity and leave as well.

"Then let us end talks for real this time. I'm sure the Cretia family has much to discuss. Please lend them a room in the mansion to catch up with each other," Francois said to Rio and Charlotte, showing consideration for the family that probably wanted to have a proper reunion in private.

"Then allow me to show you to a spare drawing room. Princess Christina, Princess Flora, please remain here. Will that be acceptable, Sir Haruto?" Rio owned the house, so Charlotte sought his permission.

"Of course."

And so, the group dispersed.

"I will return to the castle first. Charlotte, come see me in my office after you're done showing them to the room."

"Understood."

"And Haruto, may I ask you to escort me there?" Francois asked, getting up from his seat. He had his own personal guards, so he usually didn't ask Rio for an escort.

"Sure... Gladly."

The unusual request caught Rio off guard, but he agreed quickly with a smile.

After Francois left the mansion, he ordered his usual guards to follow from a distance. Thus, he and Rio began making their way to the castle.

"I didn't say this earlier, but there's something else I'd like to share with you," he said abruptly to Rio, who was walking diagonally behind him.

"What is it?"

"Before I do, I'd like you to keep what I'm about to tell you a secret from Lady Satsuki. I do not wish to give her needless worry over an uncertainty. Understood?"

"I understand." Rio had figured there was something else Francois wanted to discuss privately from the moment he asked for an escort, but it seemed to be a heavy topic.

"A thought came to mind when you mentioned the Saint might still be alive. Could it be that heroes cannot die? Or at least not to a sword through the heart."

"Why do you think that...?"

"When Lady Satsuki was summoned, I had all the pseudepigrapha in the kingdom gathered. One of them stated that the heroes were tenacious with bodies that seemed immortal. I recalled that when you mentioned it."

"Immortal, you say? In the unaging, undying way?" Rio was taken aback by the fantastical terminology.

"Indeed. However, at the end of the day, the source is a pseudepigraphon written by an unknown author. I dismissed it for the lack of credibility, but your fears reminded me of the text."

"In other words, you believe the Saint might still be alive, Your Majesty?"

"Who knows? It is hard for me to believe that someone can survive a sword through the heart. And if the heroes were truly immortal, the ones that fought in the Divine War should still be alive now."

If immortality meant eternal life, then they wouldn't be able to die of old age.

"No one knows what happened to the heroes of that time, right?" Rio asked.

Such as where they died, or where they went.

"There are folk tales of the heroes establishing the kingdoms, but there are no specific details of what happened to the heroes after the Divine War in any of the ancient texts."

If they vanished after the war, is it possible they returned to their original world?

Rio thought in his head.

"It's strange how there's no record of what happened to the key figures of the Divine War... Is it possible for me to view these ancient texts as well?" he asked, seeking permission to read the apocrypha and pseudepigrapha. He was unlikely to find an answer to the aftermath of the heroes, but it was possible he could discover something new. Pseudepigrapha in particular were texts that kingdoms didn't want to be seen, so they weren't available for everyone to view.

"Very well." Rio received permission without any resistance from the king.

"Thank you very much."

"Of course. It has to do with the reason why I summoned you here like this."

"By which you mean...?"

"It has to do with the heroes' powers. There were many anecdotes of the heroes in the pseudepigrapha, but it is difficult to determine what is true or not due to the abstract nature of the ancient scriptures. Immortality is one such example—I shouldn't utter this even as a joke, but I don't suppose you'd be willing to stab Lady Satsuki to confirm?"

"No..." Rio shook his head, gulping.

"Your instruction may awaken the power sleeping within Lady Satsuki. I fear the control of a monster like the beast of the land and the possession of an immortal body might be too much for a young girl to bear. It is enough to destroy a human's heart."

"..."

"Lady Satsuki is smart, honest, and possesses a strange charm that draws others to her. However, she is only a normal girl. At least, that is how I see her. What are your thoughts on this?"

"I feel the same way."

"In that case, I make this request of you as a man. I'd like you to guide her as necessary so that she isn't swallowed if her power grows to be too much. Can you do that for me?" Francois stopped walking and turned around to face Rio.

"Is it...? Is it something I can do?" It was an important role. Rio couldn't agree to it without due consideration.

"I believe you can. You too have far more power than a single person can bear, yet you haven't been swallowed by it. You didn't accept my request immediately, and I wish to entrust this to you precisely because of that."

"I understand..."

"I'm counting on you."

Seeing Rio nod politely, Francois bowed his head deeply in return. While they were talking, they had arrived right before the front entrance of the castle.

"We've arrived at the castle. Accompany me for a while longer."

It seemed Francois wasn't done speaking; he walked into the castle without waiting for Rio's response. As the king, Francois stood out even at the best of times, and Haruto Amakawa was the hottest topic nowadays. They attracted much attention as they walked through the castle together, eventually reaching Francois's office.

"Go on, have a seat."

"Thank you." Rio sat down on the lower seat that Francois, who had sat down first, offered.

"Hmm…" Francois nodded in silence for a moment. Rather than being undecided on a topic, it seemed he was hesitating over how to approach the topic he had in mind.

Time passed like that until Charlotte arrived at the office. "Excuse me."

Francois gave her permission to enter the room.

"That was rather fast," he said in slight surprise. Only a minute had passed since they sat down.

"I had a feeling there was something very interesting to be discussed, so I entrusted Princess Christina and Princess Flora to Lady Celia."

"I see. Well, have a seat."

"Thank you."

With an eager and cheery reply, Charlotte sat right beside Rio on the three-seater sofa. She was practically clinging to him.

"…"

They weren't even betrothed. No, even if they were betrothed, doing such a thing in front of her father, King Francois, was somewhat troubling. Very troubling. Rio casually shifted to the side to gain some distance from Charlotte, but she merely shifted over to fill that gap.

If he moved aside any farther, his actions would be seen as unnatural to Francois, who was seated across from them. Rio gave up on distancing himself further.

"Heh heh." Charlotte smiled impishly.

"Hm…" Francois watched the two of them curiously, but eventually began to speak. "I have some questions about the existence of spirits and spirit arts. Lady Sara and her friends gave me a brief explanation of the topic while you were absent. I searched through ancient texts afterwards and found mentions of casters of such techniques existing in the Strahl region in the past."

Rio pulled himself together and answered through feigned composure. "Yes, though the techniques have been lost from Strahl for a long time. I've barely encountered any spirit art users throughout my travels of the Strahl region."

"Barely, meaning there has been at least one?"

"That would be Reiss."

"I see... I think I can understand the reason why spirit arts became obsolete in Strahl: because sorcery and magic are the miracles given to mankind by the Six Wise Gods. Worship of the gods would have prioritized sorcery and magic over spirit arts. And if magic is easier to learn than spirit arts, it would be more convenient to use for military purposes as well."

"It is exactly as you say."

"However, there is a group of people who have passed down the use of spirit arts to the modern era."

Francois paused, staring closely at Rio seated opposite him. "You are one of them," he said, stressing his words.

"Yes..."

"It seemed that the Yagumo nations we were once connected with had no knowledge of the Six Wise Gods and used no sorcery or magic. Instead, they had techniques that were similar to spirit arts. The ancient texts also said that elves, dwarves, and werebeast species excelled at such techniques."

"..."

At first, Rio couldn't see the point of the conversation, or why Charlotte had been summoned to sit in on it, but now he had an idea of what Francois was getting at.

"That was when I wondered—could Lady Sara and Gouki's groups all hail from outside the Strahl region?"

He had just discovered that users of the lost art of the Strahl region had gathered around Rio in droves. Someone as wise as Francois would naturally consider that possibility. Charlotte seemed to be similarly intrigued about it, as she looked up at Rio's face.

"You need not answer if you do not wish to do so."

Just as Rio was about to answer, Francois spoke over him.

"No, it is as you have guessed. Everyone originally lived outside of the Strahl region."

He had deduced this much already. Rio didn't attempt to cover up the truth. He had trust in Francois and Charlotte.

"As I expected... In that case, will you tell me about your relationship to the Saga couple?"

This was the true question that Francois wanted to ask Rio. A couple old enough to be his parents was treating him with deep loyalty. It was impossible for it not to pique interest.

"The circumstances are a little complicated. I'm afraid I must ask that you keep this an absolute secret."

"Hmm. Just to confirm, is it something that Charlotte may listen to? My daughter's at that age where she's brimming with curiosity. I invited her to sit in on this conversation as she would only probe around if I tried to hide it from her."

"It was my intention to explain things to Your Majesty and Princess Charlotte anyway. I also wish to inform Satsuki, so I'll talk to her again later."

"Very well. Make sure you keep this confidential, Charlotte."

"Of course," Charlotte agreed in a truly pleased voice.

"Firstly, my parents are immigrants from the Yagumo region..."

And so, Rio disclosed his relationship with Gouki and Kayoko, and the circumstances of his parents. The explanation took several minutes. He had already explained it once to Miharu and Celia, so he was used to talking about it.

"I wondered if there were special circumstances surrounding your identity, but I hadn't expected royal blood…" It was certainly a shocking revelation. Francois sighed heavily to suppress his surprise.

Rio raised his hand, seeking permission to speak. "Your Majesty. May I ask one more thing?"

"What is it?"

"There are more than ten others that traveled to the Strahl region with Gouki. I'd like to invite them into my mansion. Would that be an issue?"

"That mansion belongs to you. You are free to invite whoever you wish."

"Thank you very much."

Rio bowed at the approval that was readily granted.

"Why not just make them your vassals?" Francois suggested. "That complies with their own desires, does it not?"

"That's…"

"I understand you do not want that. However, I plan on rewarding them for their meritorious deed in defeating the giant skeleton. If you have any intention of employing them as vassals, I can bestow them with the rank of an honorary retainer. That will make their lives far more comfortable if they are to live in the castle— something which you should know well yourself, no? Well, you can discuss this with them."

Rio paused, then nodded stiffly. "I understand…"

"And that just leaves… Right. There's something I wished to ask you. Charlotte, you may excuse yourself first." Francois suddenly changed the topic.

"All right…" Despite her confusion, Charlotte stood up and exited the room. The door clicked closed behind her. Just what were they about to discuss?

"Do you have any interest in marriage with Lady Satsuki or Charlotte, or perhaps both?"

Rio fell speechless, freezing for a long moment. He eventually snapped back to his senses and squeezed out the words, "Surely you jest."

"I see. Well, just keep it in mind." Francois smiled suggestively.

"…" Rio couldn't reply.

"You may return to the mansion now. Please instruct Lady Satsuki well."

With those final words, Francois showed Rio to the door.

"Please excuse me." Rio left Francois's office.

"I was waiting for you, Sir Haruto. That was quick."

Charlotte was waiting outside, beaming from ear to ear.

"Yes… It was just a brief question." He refused to inform her that he had been offered her hand in marriage.

"What did you talk about?"

"You'll have to ask His Majesty…"

Charlotte held her curiosity to the forefront, stepping forward forcefully. Rio faltered for a reaction.

"Ahem." A light cough resounded. There was a middle-aged noble standing a short distance away from Charlotte. This man was the head of the second major duke family in the Galarc Kingdom, on par with the Cretia family—Clement Gregory.

"Oh my, I almost forgot you were there, Duke Gregory. If it's my father you're after, he's still in his office. Why don't you go inside?" Charlotte asked.

"I'd like to have a word with that man too," Gregory said, glaring at Rio. Even to a bystander, it was clear he felt animosity towards Rio.

"How can I help you?" Rio had greeted Duke Gregory briefly during the banquet. He hadn't felt any particular hostility back then.

"Sir Haruto has just returned from a long journey," Charlotte interrupted in an annoyed tone. "He's very tired, so could you please keep it brief?"

"Then, Sir Amakawa. Where were you during such an important time? The Heavenly Lions attacked the castle in your absence. It seemed their attack was focused around your mansion, but what is your relation to them?"

Duke Gregory rapidly began interrogating Rio, though it would be of no surprise coming from the head of a duke family. Despite being in the Second Princess Charlotte's presence, he wasn't about to read the room and back down easily. His position allowed for that.

"I…"

"Excuse me, Duke Gregory." Charlotte cut in before Rio could reply. Her expression was cheerful, but the gaze she turned to Gregory was cold.

"This topic has already been discussed with my father. Sir Haruto was out on a mission to rescue Liselotte. He's just returned from fulfilling that mission. Someone as quick-eared as you should be aware that Liselotte has returned, no?" she stated.

"So it was you…" Duke Gregory looked discontent that Rio had gained another achievement to his name.

"…"

Without saying another word, Charlotte knocked on the door to the office. She forcibly ordered the knight guarding the door to open it. "Open up."

"Yes, Your Highness."

"Father, Duke Gregory has come to pay you a visit." She waved Duke Gregory into Francois's office.

⚜ Chapter 4 ⚜
Training and Investigation Begins

The next morning was clear and comfortable.

"Mm, nothing like the taste of sweet, sweet freedom!"

Satsuki looked up at the sky and stretched in delight.

"Sweet freedom…" Rio chuckled, standing across from her.

"I mean, I'm finally able to leave the castle openly. It's a mood thing, okay?"

As Satsuki had said, they were currently in uninhabited plains outside the capital. Francois had given his permission to leave, so they decided to start training outside right away.

Incidentally, they had traveled to this empty plain by horse carriage. It would have been faster to fly on Ariel, but they had only explained the existence of spirits to a select few people in the castle. The plan was to tell the public that they were mounts that could be summoned through magic artifacts, and they couldn't be used very often.

"But I don't think there was a need for Char and the others to come along, was there?" Satsuki said, looking at Charlotte, Louise, and the few guards that had accompanied them. The female knights were the ones that had fought at the attack on the mansion, so they had witnessed the spirits and spirit arts already. They were the few people who knew of the circumstances besides Charlotte, Francois, and the Cretia couple.

"It's because this is the first session. I need to report to Father on how it goes."

"You say that, but you're probably planning on making an excuse to come along each time…"

"Perhaps I will. It's lonely for me to stay back by myself."

Like Charlotte said, the others present there were Miharu, Celia, Aishia, Latifa, Sara, Orphia, Alma, Gouki, and Kayoko. Some of them had other things to do, but staying in the castle meant being unable to practice spirit arts freely, so they had used this chance to come along.

"If you're going to observe, please stay in this."

Rio used spirit arts to manipulate the ground. In the blink of an eye, the earth rose and created a small pavilion with low windbreak walls. At the same time, Alma used the same spirit art to set up a simple stable a short distance away.

"Spirit arts are truly amazing…"

Charlotte's eyes widened at the feat, which couldn't be accomplished through magic.

"*Dissolvo.*"

As the finishing touches of the pavilion, Rio used the Time-Space Cache to take out a table and chairs. The atmosphere was perfect once he'd prepared some cold drinks.

"You're basically a Doraemon…" Satsuki had been watching him set up the pavilion with interest, but the moment he took out cold drinks, her expression turned half-exasperated.

"What's that…?" Charlotte asked.

"It's a creature that can make anything appear out of thin air."

"I'm only taking out what I originally stored," Rio corrected with a wry smile.

"But I'm sure you have many more tremendous things stored away. He was hiding a magic artifact like that, after all."

Charlotte was informed about the Time-Space Cache after the outside training sessions were decided on. Francois was also made aware.

"There aren't many things more amazing than this artifact. It's all food and furniture inside anyway."

The only artifact on par with the Time-Space Cache would be the teleport crystals.

"Is that so…? So there are *some* things."

"W-Well, I'll introduce you to the others if the necessity to use them arises. We'll run out of time if we don't start training," Rio said, forcefully brushing off the topic.

"In that case, Sir Haruto, I will go with Lady Orphia to pick up Komomo and the others."

Gouki spoke up, giving Rio a timely escape from his dilemma.

"Yes, please do."

Rio took the chance to nod firmly. Gouki and Orphia were to move separately from here. They had to pick up the rest of the Yagumo group waiting in the stone house.

"Come out… Heh heh. Well done."

Orphia summoned her contract spirit, Ariel. Ariel rubbed its face against Orphia happily, and Orphia patted its head gently.

"Please get on, Gouki."

"Many thanks." Gouki leaped up and onto Ariel's back. Orphia used spirit arts to fly up softly.

"We'll be back soon. See you later."

With those words, they departed from the skies. The group sent her off, waving.

"Let's do our own training over there," Sara said, leading Miharu, Celia, and Latifa away.

This left Rio and Satsuki in front of the pavilion, as well as Charlotte and Louise's knights, who wanted to observe, and Kayoko, who wanted to remain as a guard. Aishia and Alma were also there to survey the power of the Divine Arms.

"Shall we begin as well?"

"Sure! Please, give me your guidance!"

Rio and Satsuki distanced themselves from the pavilion.

"Kayoko," Charlotte called out.

"How can I help you, Princess Charlotte?"

"Would you be willing to give these girls a little training as well?"

"What about your guard?"

"This place is made for sparring. Everyone else is nearby, and Lady Aishia and Lady Alma are right here. It should be safe to spar nearby, no?"

Kayoko thought for a moment, then looked at the knights standing close. "I understand... Is that all right with you all?"

"Yes, please!"

Louise, their commander, nodded energetically. Thus, Kayoko began training Charlotte's knights off to the side.

Rio and Satsuki moved a hundred meters away from the pavilion.

"What do you want to be able to do by controlling the wind?"

"I want to fly!"

"That was a quick response." Rio chuckled at the sight of Satsuki's eyes shining eagerly.

311

"Because...it's like a dream! Who wouldn't want to fly?" Ashamed of how childish she was acting, Satsuki blushed faintly.

"Then let's make today's goal to be able to fly slowly."

"Wow, is it something that can be learned in a day?"

"It's a fairly difficult technique, but if the Divine Arms works how I think, then it should be possible."

"Really? That makes me even more fired up."

It was clear from her expression that she was raring to go.

"But first, before I teach you how to fly..."

"Yes?"

"Spar with me."

"We're always sparring..."

"You can release all of your Divine Arms' abilities today."

"So not just the physical body enhancement, but the wind control as well?"

"Yes. We can fight to our hearts' content out here. Whether it's close combat or ranged, you can use your Divine Arms to level whatever attack you wish against me."

Rio moved to a position with no one behind him. It seemed he truly wanted them to fight to their hearts' content, as he'd said. They normally sparred with the rule of Satsuki using a spear and limiting her attacks to close combat, but now that limit was gone.

"Hmm..." The corners of Satsuki's mouth turned up in amusement. Although she didn't have much pent-up stress from constantly suppressing her abilities, she had never been able to fight while maximizing all of her hero abilities before. And with Rio as her opponent, she could trust that he would be fine facing her.

"So, come at me when you're ready," Rio said, drawing his favorite sword from the sheath at his waist.

"You're not going to say, 'Ready, go'?"

"Nope."

When she saw Rio nod, Satsuki materialized her Divine Arms as a short spear and held it ready. She then started running without a word. Her initial velocity surpassed what could be achieved with a physical body enhancement alone as she approached Rio.

She's got the basics of using wind to accelerate.

Rio watched her movements closely as he evaded to the side with ease.

"Wh…!"

Satsuki's momentum carried her past the spot where Rio stood. But she used her leg strength to force a change in direction, approaching Rio once more. She swung the spear in her hand over her head.

"…" Rio didn't lift his sword. He nimbly ducked under the swinging spear instead.

"Kuh!" Satsuki continued swinging her spear at point-blank range, but…

"No way… Why do I keep missing?"

Her attacks couldn't hit him. Rio had his sword in his hand, but he hadn't braced it once since their match began. He was evading Satsuki's attacks by movement alone.

"I'll be evading every attack I can," he said, provoking Satsuki. At present, all they were doing was their regular sparring, but at a faster speed.

So he wants me to use more of my abilities, right?

Satsuki immediately guessed the intention of Rio's provocation. It was most likely—or rather, almost certain—that he was holding back on her greatly during their daily sparring matches. That was vexing for her.

313

But if she was allowed to use her Divine Arms, she might be able to win one over him. Or at least, she hoped so.

"How about this, then?!"

Satsuki sent magic essence to the tip of her spear, then swung it from outside of contact range. A fierce wind blew from the tip, rushing at Rio to send him flying.

However, instead of being blown away, Rio gently rode the wave of wind up into the air. He proceeded to land a short distance away in one smooth movement. Satsuki was almost captivated by the sight.

"I-I'm not done yet!"

She snapped back to her senses and charged once again. From that point on, each swing of Satsuki's spear created a powerful burst of wind. If her opponent had been the average knight, they would have been blown away along with the rest of their squad.

"Your attacks are monotonous."

For some reason, Rio wasn't sent flying. In fact, he no longer even floated—he stood on both feet and moved freely. The only times he floated up was when he leaped of his own accord.

"H-Hey, the wind I'm controlling is hitting you, right?!" Satsuki shouted, implicitly questioning why he was able to move so calmly under such fierce winds.

"I'm interfering with the flow of wind you created. Firing a blast of wind straight at a wind spirit arts user isn't going to amount to an attack."

"Spirit arts users are outrageous…"

"Here's a hint. If you want to use a wind attack against a wind spirit arts user, try something like this. I'm going to show you an example, so try and deal with it yourself."

"Okay, sure." Satsuki braced her spear once again, facing Rio warily.

"Now then…"

A whirlwind formed around Rio, kicking up dust and obstructing Satsuki's vision.

"Wha…?!"

The whirlwind started moving towards her. It was an attack that also served as a smoke screen. Satsuki moved to the side, out of the range of the whirlwind, but…

"I'm over here." Rio's voice came from behind her.

"Huh?!" Satsuki spun around in a panic. There, Rio stood out of range, sword braced at the ready. He had a spell ready and waiting, whirling around his blade like a violent storm.

If this were a real battle, her opponent wouldn't bother calling out to her. Satsuki would have been helplessly blown away by the wind attack behind her.

"Your back was completely unguarded."

Satsuki hung her head in frustration. "I see… I'm so simpleminded."

"You're just lacking combat experience. Once you've gained some experience, it shouldn't be a problem for you. Now, let's try that attack once again."

"I'll stop you perfectly this time."

"Okay, then…" Rio leaped high in the air, distancing himself once again. Once he landed, he created the same whirlwind, releasing it towards Satsuki one more time.

"…"

Satsuki carefully focused her attention on what was behind her, but…

"This time you were too focused on your back."

Rio was standing boldly before her. The instant Satsuki's attention had gone to her rear, he had moved into her blind spot.

"Argh!" Satsuki groaned in frustration.

"I directed your attention to what was behind you, so you thought I would come from behind, didn't you? Psychological warfare like this is vital to a battle between spirit art users. If you can catch your opponent off guard, you can gain an advantage in a single blast of wind. And if you can lead them into a psychological battle, you'll have the potential to overpower someone with more technique than you."

"So it would be the height of foolishness to challenge someone stronger in a straight battle of power or technique. Got it."

That was exactly what Satsuki was doing just now.

"You've practiced how to read your opponent's movements in your regular sparring. The rules we've changed to today have increased your attack options, so just think of it as a more complicated version of reading your opponent."

"Yeah… Okay. You're right." Satsuki hummed in thought.

"Also…"

"Also?"

"You're a very gentle person. I can tell you're holding back," Rio said, smiling.

Satsuki blushed in embarrassment. "That's not true…"

"Today's goal isn't to instruct you on how to fight, so I'll leave the commentary at that. What can you do with that weapon of yours, Satsuki? Show me without holding back."

"Fine. I'll show you. Let's do this again from the top."

Satsuki refocused her mind on the battle with a look of determination.

"All right. I'll also add an attack every now and then, so watch out," Rio said, before moving an acceptable distance away from her.

"Here I come!" Satsuki dragged the tip of her spear through the ground, then flicked it up at Rio with a blast of wind. A cloud of dust filled the air.

Rio moved to the side, out of the range of the approaching dust cloud. Satsuki sent another cloud of dust towards his new location. They repeated this until the entire field was obstructed by dust, when Satsuki charged forward.

Is this meant to be a smoke screen?

She wouldn't have made her vision worse for no reason. If it was just a dust cloud, Rio could make one by controlling the wind as well.

I can hear the sound of the ground cracking. She must be setting something up.

Satsuki was doing something on the other side of the dust cloud. In order to see how she would use her ingenuity to fight, Rio decided to wait.

Shortly after, a corner of the dust cloud blew away. One portion of the air cleared before countless stones started flying his way, carried by a windstorm.

She's using the stone she crushed as projectiles.

Rio swayed smoothly, evading the flying stones. Just as he confirmed that Satsuki wasn't standing in the spot where the air had cleared, another section of the dust cloud blew away, and stones started flying out from there. But they couldn't hit him either. He swayed from right to left, evading the stones. Before long, his vision of the field was almost clear.

That must be the last spot.

Rio looked at the last remaining section of the dust cloud. Wind blew aside the cloud, and stones came flying once more. At the same time, the air above the field completely cleared—but there was no sign of Satsuki anywhere.

I see...

Rio predicted her next move and took a sudden step back. Immediately following that, Satsuki swooped down on the spot where he had just stood. She had been trying to swing her spear down on him, but his movement had caused her to miss.

"It's not over yet!"

But Satsuki didn't falter at that. She kicked the ground and accelerated using her wind, closing in on Rio and swinging her spear down at him.

Rio evaded her while retreating, then used wind spirit arts to fly back. Satsuki also used her wind to leap high into the air, pursuing Rio. Once she reached a height of twenty meters or so above the ground, she wrapped her wind around herself and swung her spear up.

She's focused on the fight. Good.

Rio lightly evaded to the side in midair.

"Ngh." Without falling to the ground, Satsuki came to a stop in the air. She was naturally floating as she pursued Rio. Her physical body enhancement had also improved, as her movements were gradually getting faster.

Just as I expected.

Right now, Satsuki was drawing out the power of her Divine Arms unconsciously. Hiroaki had done the same the last time Rio fought him. The more absorbed they were in the battle, the more of the power they could draw without realizing it.

According to Rio's theory, Satsuki and the other heroes understood how to use their Divine Arms instinctively, just like how living creatures knew how to walk and breathe. That was why she was able to use her power better when she was moving instinctively than when she was thinking about it.

However, the problem was whether she could continue using that ability once her concentration was worn out. She had to be able to do so consciously.

For now, she's succeeded in drawing out her power. All that's left is…

Rio decided to try a light counterattack. He braced his sword ready for the first time this match, making a dramatic swing that Satsuki could block with her spear easily.

"Wha—?!"

Satsuki braced her spear at the last moment, blocking the sword. Unlike when she was on the ground, there was no surface for her feet to stand against in the air. With his sword pressed against her spear, Rio shrewdly adjusted the angle of their positions until his back was towards the ground and his sword was towards the sky.

"H-Huh?!"

Satsuki's body was lifted by a wind, boosting her up into the air. The distance between them instantly expanded to ten meters, and Satsuki yelped in shock.

Rio prepared several bullets of magic essence wrapped in wind, then fired them successively towards Satsuki. He could control their trajectory, so they were all sure to strike her like this. He planned on redirecting them at the last moment if he needed to, but he believed she would be able to handle them without a problem, and they didn't contain enough force to cause a severe injury anyway.

"E-Enough!"

Satsuki gathered essence to the tip of her spear and slashed down the approaching bullets. Once she saw that there were no bullets left, she sighed in relief. But then she saw how far the ground was below her and came to her senses.

"W-Wait, help! How do I get back down?!" she shrieked, panicking.

She's forgotten how she flew by herself, huh? How ridiculous...

She was failing to control her ability consciously because she had obtained the ability without learning any of the necessary basics. There were times where she had no control at all and just activated her abilities at maximum power. This was something she had in common with Hiroaki. Rio continued to watch her for a while, until...

"H-Haruto!"

It seemed that flying consciously was just too hard for her. Rio sheathed his sword and began to fly towards her. He slowed down just before crashing into her, gently catching her in both his arms.

"..."

Satsuki opened her eyes fearfully.

"Good work today," Rio's smiling face said to her.

"R-Right... Thanks."

Satsuki blushed, stammering her gratitude.

"Let's go back to the ground. I'll give you my review then."

Thus, the two of them descended.

A short distance away from the pavilion where Charlotte was observing from...

"Aww, man... I couldn't land a single hit." Satsuki hung her head in disappointment.

"There were holes in your plan, but it was a good plan overall. I liked how you broke up the terrain to use as projectiles. You started flying by yourself to attack me, but I guess you didn't notice that part."

"Y-Yeah... I was so immersed in fighting..."

So she had been flying unconsciously after all.

"Activating your abilities consciously will be your next goal."

"Flying by myself is so much scarier than being carried while flying. I'm shocked."

"A major hurdle to the spirit art of flying is overcoming the fear of heights. Your emotions have a large influence on your abilities."

Spirit arts brought about phenomena by conveying the imagination of the spirit art user into the mana in the atmosphere. If the caster feared falling, then the activation of the art would also become unstable.

"At the end of the battle, all I could think about was how scared I was of falling."

"That's normal, and you need to know the feeling of fear. Otherwise you may hurt yourself flying while your control is still lacking."

What was most important was to remain calm and unaffected by those emotions.

"I see…"

"You know that you have the foundations for flying. Work hard from here."

"Yup! Oh, that's right. There's one other ability I want to be able to use."

"What is it?"

"You know how there are times when you move as though you teleported?"

"…Like this?"

Rio demonstrated the move that came to mind. He distanced himself from Satsuki and immediately moved back beside her.

"Y-Yes! That! How do you do that?" Satsuki asked excitedly. To her, it truly appeared as though he teleported.

"You know how you used wind to accelerate yourself midbattle?"

"Yeah. I'm able to do that by imitating you. I wanted to move fast like you…"

"If you can do that, then you've got the foundation for it as well. It's a technique that's necessary in flying spirit arts as well."

"Hmm…"

"However, it's harder and more dangerous to do than flying. You'll need another ability besides the spirit arts…"

And so it was difficult to learn overnight, Rio explained.

"What kind of ability?"

"Hmm… You know how I told you about extraneous movements in combat?"

"Ah, right. Something about how when the opponent braces their weapon, you can read their next move by using that."

"Right. This is related to that, but have you heard of a telegraphed punch?"

"A punch…that you communicate?" Satsuki asked in confusion. It seemed she had no idea.

"If someone suddenly swung their fist before you, you'd think they're about to hit you, right?" Rio held his fist up in a swinging pose.

"Yeah, I'd be shocked. So that's an extraneous movement."

"Yes. This pose tells your opponent you're about to punch them, which is why it's called a telegraphed punch."

There were no telegraph systems in this world, which is why this was a method of explanation he could only use with Satsuki.

"I see."

"Aside from that, things like kicking, swinging your weapon, or running are actions that people unconsciously recognize as tells."

Rio assumed each one of the poses he mentioned.

"Yeah. I can easily tell which pose is what. Removing these kinds of movements is the purpose of martial arts forms, right?"

"Yes. You might have realized this already, but I remove all of those kinds of movements when I accelerate. That's why it gives the illusion of teleportation."

By moving from a complete stop, relying on only the spirit art to move, and refraining from making any other action, he could move as though a section of a video had been skipped entirely.

"I think I get the logic. You're basically running without making a running pose, right? And at an extremely rapid speed."

"It's more like flying than running, but yes. This technique is especially effective against opponents facing you—if you look from the side, it's clear I'm moving without running," Rio said, then flew to a spot a short distance away. This time, instead of moving forwards to Satsuki, he passed by her.

"Umm, you're so fast I can't follow you with my eyes... How many kilometers per hour are you even going?" Satsuki complained with a grimace. She couldn't even tell whether he was flying or running.

"Let's see. I change speeds depending on my distance to my opponent, so it isn't consistent, but... Even at my fastest speed, I cannot surpass the speed of sound."

"Th-The speed of sound?! Oh, but less than that... Still, that's amazing."

The speed of sound was 340 meters per second. Converted to kilometers per hour, it was a little under 1,200.

"I've surpassed it once before, but doing so creates a phenomenon known as a sonic boom. It's a great burden on the body, and there's a limit to how much relief the arts can provide."

That's why he normally set his own limit to a subsonic speed. For the record, he normally flew at a slower speed when traveling—an average speed of 100 kilometers per hour.

"S-So you can surpass it if you want to... Well, no wonder it looks like you're teleporting."

Even at a subsonic speed, he could cross a hundred meters in a single instant. He could approach his opponent in the blink of an eye.

"That's why it's dangerous. The movement takes a single instant, so you have to control everything from activating the art to stopping it in that instant. If you're inexperienced at casting, you'll risk colliding with your opponent and other obstacles. It's also difficult to change your trajectory while accelerating. If you don't choose your timing properly, you might self-destruct."

"And I have to think about how to attack after moving..."

"Yes. The ideal situation is to attack the moment you finish moving."

"That isn't a human technique, is it?" Satsuki eyed Rio in suspicion.

"It is a very difficult technique. That's why you should first focus on using spirit arts to fly."

"Okay! Oh, by the way..."

"Yes?"

"Do you have a name for it?"

"A name...for what?"

"For your high-speed movement."

"No, not particularly..."

None of the spirit arts Rio used had any particular move name. There were some casters that found it easier to imagine their techniques by giving them a name, but Rio had never felt the necessity.

"Instant movement, or instamove for short. Or maybe accelamove, short for accelerated movement. Or maybe even *Shukuchi*, like the ancient martial arts?"

"Shukuchi isn't a martial art, but a fable from ancient mythology..."

"Spirit arts are plenty similar to ancient mythology."

"I suppose…"

He personally disagreed, but he wasn't able to explain why, so he didn't say so out loud.

"They're the same in the sense that they're both fantasy techniques. So, regarding your high-speed movement: how about Shukuchi? I believe the origin of the word comes from the ground shrinking underneath your feet. Yup, it fits you perfectly."

"Well, I don't mind either way… You seem to care a lot about the move name, though."

"Because it's pitiful for such an amazing move to not have a name!"

"I'm honored you think that way." Rio smiled happily.

"Right…" At Rio's joyous face, Satsuki looked to the side shyly.

"Then let's go back for now. I'd like to give a lecture on spirit arts and check out your Divine Arms a little more."

Thus, Rio and Satsuki headed back to the pavilion.

And so, they moved on to investigating Satsuki's Divine Arms. What they wanted to know was whether something like the beast of the land was sleeping within her weapon as well.

Seated in a circle under the pavilion were Rio, Satsuki, Aishia, Alma, and Charlotte.

In the past, Rio and Alma had done a simple investigation of Satsuki's Divine Arms in private. However, they only knew that the spear was special, and nothing else. It was a completely out-of-place artifact, and they had no way of studying what sorcery was in it, or how it was made.

They didn't know about the beast of the land back then, so they hadn't considered the possibility of something similar to a spirit sleeping within the weapon. Besides, multiple heroes had materialized their Divine Arms in front of Aishia before, but she had never sensed the presence of a spirit from them.

But they were yet to conduct an investigation under the assumption that something was sleeping within. And so…

"Okay, can you lend your Divine Arms to Aishia?"

"Sure. Here you go, Aishia."

They decided to have Aishia, the spirit, take it in her hands and investigate it herself. This was the same action that Dryas had done on Rio the first time he had visited the spiritfolk village with Aishia sleeping within him.

At any rate, if there was something like the beast of the land sleeping within the spear, it would be dangerous to trigger it carelessly. The chances of something terrible happening were low, but investigating in an unpopulated place like this was for the best.

"…" Aishia stared at the spear she accepted from Satsuki in silence.

"How's it look, Aishia?"

"I can't feel any spirit presence when it's materialized as a weapon. But there's definitely a connection between the spear and Satsuki. I could tell as soon as I touched it."

"Huh, so that's how it is…" Satsuki looked between the weapon and her hands. Naturally, she couldn't see anything with the naked eye.

"Is it like the path between a contract spirit and us?" Alma asked Aishia.

"Yeah, it's similar to that."

"Is it impossible for there to be a spirit in the weapon, Alma?" Rio asked Alma. As a dwarf, she had more profound knowledge when it came to spirits and weapons.

"There are some spirits who choose an object to represent them instead of a contract. Like a spirit that resides in a tree, for example."

The spirit who resided in a tree was probably Dryas. Since Charlotte was present, she purposefully avoided saying her name.

"However, spirits prefer to reside along leylines—places where the land is abundant with magic essence. I've never heard of one choosing to dwell in a weapon. If it were something like a spirit stone, then I could understand, but…"

Satsuki's Divine Arms had no spirit stones embedded as decorations.

"I don't know what a spirit stone is, but the item that summoned the heroes is an ancient artifact called a sacred stone. Is it possible for a spirit to reside in that instead?" Charlotte asked.

"That is another possibility. But the sacred stone disappeared when Satsuki was summoned, right?"

"Yes. Father believes the stone became the Divine Arms."

"If the sacred stones are spirit stones, is it possible for a spirit to reside within them and transform into a weapon?" Rio asked, seeking Alma's opinion once again.

"As far as I know, such a technique doesn't exist… But it doesn't look like time-space sorcery is being used when the weapons are materialized. It looks similar to the phenomena of spirits materializing…"

"I had the same thought. In this case, instead of there being a spirit inside the sacred stone or Divine Arms, it's more like the Divine Arms itself is a spirit?"

"If that's true, then the Divine Arms would have two forms: a weapon form and a beast form… Three if you include the sacred stone form."

"Can spirits have multiple forms?"

Alma shook her head slowly. "Not to my knowledge…"

"Whether the Divine Arms is holding a spirit or is a spirit itself, I can't feel any presence in its current form," Aishia chimed in.

"I see. In that case, the beast of the land might not be part of the Saint's Divine Arms…"

Alma groaned in thought. The more they investigated, the more possibilities emerged. There was no way of reaching a conclusion.

"The connection between Satsuki and the Divine Arms… I'll try following that link to see if I can probe further."

Aishia suddenly stood up with Satsuki's spear in hand. She proceeded to walk out of the pavilion, followed by Rio and the others.

"Are you examining the Divine Arms right now?"

Sara, Miharu, Celia, and Latifa, who were training separately, came up to them. Kayoko and Louise's knights also came over to watch.

"It might be dangerous, so everyone should stand back," Aishia said, distancing herself.

"Everyone stand behind me just in case." Rio stood in front of the group to be ready to protect them.

"It's a little scary…" Satsuki was trembling faintly. An unknown beast could be residing within her Divine Arms, so it was only natural.

"We're just examining it, so I don't think anything will happen. This is just in case," Rio said reassuringly.

Meanwhile, Aishia began her examination. With the spear in both hands, she closed her eyes, following the connection between the weapon and Satsuki to dive within. Thus, she reached the visualization of the world within the Divine Arms—

I can't see anything...

It was pure white. It was as though there was a thick fog covering everything, preventing her from seeing more than a few centimeters to the front.

If she hadn't followed the path between Satsuki and the weapon, she wouldn't have been able to dive within here. She had barely been able to do so by relying on that connection.

There's a wall.

When she followed it farther, she bumped into a barrier. It wasn't visible to the eye, as her vision was filled with nothing but white. Just what was on the other side of the barrier? Aishia tried to push her way through.

Just then, the wall was stained with something black. The darkness crossed the wall and attempted to cover Aishia as well.

"Huh?!" Aishia immediately withdrew from the Divine Arms, snapping her eyes open. She stared down at the spear in her hands, bewildered.

What...?

The darkness that crossed the wall had been trying to tell her something before she broke away.

I...

Was there something she was meant to be doing? Was there something she had forgotten? She didn't know why, but that was the feeling flooding into her right now.

"What's wrong, Aishia?!" Rio noticed the abnormality and came running over immediately.

"I'm fine..." she replied, swaying on her feet. However, her face was extremely pale. She was even whiter than she usually was.

"Ai-chan!"

Worried about Aishia's state, Miharu came running over soon after to support her body.

"Did you see something?" Rio asked nervously.

"I couldn't see anything," Aishia muttered. "It was pure white, then pitch-black, but…"

She looked at Rio's face, followed by Miharu's. She felt like there was something she had to tell them, but the words wouldn't come out. She looked unusually anxious.

"All right… Let's stop here for today."

Seeing her in such a state, Rio decided to stop the investigation on the Divine Arms.

⁕ Chapter 5 ⁕
A New Match

The problem occurred two days after they began training. Precisely speaking, it happened just as they were about to board the carriage outside the mansion.

"Halt! Sir Amakawa! Is Sir Amakawa present?" a voice called across the garden of the mansion. It was Clement Gregory. He was accompanied by dozens of nobles—members of his faction, most likely.

Out of the people present, the one who knew Duke Gregory the best was Princess Charlotte, followed by Rio and Satsuki who knew his face. Everyone else made confused faces, unaware of who he was.

Having been designated by name, Rio had no choice but to reply. But before he could do so, Charlotte stepped forward in his place.

"What do you want, Duke Gregory? Visiting without an appointment like this. I believe my father has forbidden anyone from entering Sir Haruto's property without permission."

Which I know you are well aware of, Charlotte's fed-up tone clearly implied.

"That is why I'm waiting outside the mansion like this."

It was a ridiculous technicality, but Duke Gregory seemed to feel no guilt about it.

So he knew we planned on leaving and decided to ambush us like this.

It was hard to believe someone on the inside had leaked their schedule. They had probably seen them leave the mansion at this time yesterday and assumed they would do the same today. Charlotte instantly deduced that in her head.

It's an annoyance, but this may be a good chance.

Despite her annoyed sigh, she started devising a delightful plan in her head. It was about time this duke was taught a lesson.

"Even then, this is too insolent of you. Marching here in such great numbers without a prior appointment," Charlotte protested unhappily.

"My apologies. However, this is a matter that involves the kingdom and the great hero, which I just could not leave unresolved," Clement replied in a dramatic tone.

"Is that really all you're after, coming here in droves?"

"Yes."

Rio and the others watched their exchange in silence. At this point, the first impression of those without any knowledge of Duke Gregory wasn't looking too great.

Just then—

"What is the meaning of this commotion?"

Francois arrived.

"Your Majesty." Duke Gregory and his men bowed their heads respectfully, but Charlotte didn't miss the smile on his face.

He's prepared for Father's arrival. It seems like all the pieces are in place.

A large group had been waiting outside a mansion they were forbidden from entering. Naturally, Francois had been alerted of the situation immediately—even before Rio and the others noticed. In other words, this development was exactly what Duke Gregory wanted.

Like Charlotte, Francois could see through Gregory's intentions easily. He addressed him undauntedly. "Answer my question."

"I wish to make a direct appeal to Your Majesty with regards to a matter regarding the kingdom and the great hero. It involves Sir Amakawa and Duke Cretia as well."

"What?"

"I've heard that Sir Amakawa is currently serving as the hero's instructor."

Duke Gregory faced Francois without fear.

"What about it?"

"The truth is, there are many people who are unhappy about it. Can Sir Amakawa really serve as the hero's instructor properly?" Duke Gregory looked at Rio with suspicion. It wasn't very commendable, but using inflammatory speech to rile the opponent up was the oldest negotiation trick in the book. However, it was a method that only worked when the opponent was of equal or lower status. In a situation with Francois and Satsuki, who were clearly above him in status, Duke Gregory's success depended on his skill and Rio's reaction.

"..."

Rio accepted the words with a straight face. Meanwhile, the people around him felt antipathy at the words just now. It showed considerably on the faces of some of them.

"You witnessed Haruto's abilities yourself at the night of the banquet, did you not? Why do you feel he is unworthy?"

"I won't deny he has the ability. But isn't he too young to be an instructor? I hear he is even younger than the hero."

"Hmm. That's true. Come to think of it, you're only sixteen, aren't you Haruto? I forget myself sometimes."

Francois's eyes widened faintly before he let out a hearty laugh. Rio frowned at his reaction.

"It isn't a laughing matter. For the sake of the kingdom, a proper and worthy instructor should be appointed to guide the great hero. Someone like this is…" Duke Gregory made his claim in an indignant, emotional tone.

"Is what?" Francois asked calmly.

"Frankly speaking, I don't think he is to be trusted."

"Wha—?" Satsuki was unable to suppress her anger any longer. She spoke out angrily, glaring at Duke Gregory with her brows furrowed.

"You don't even know where he's from! Just because he's done a few good deeds—"

"Well, if you ask me, I find you much less trustworthy," Satsuki snapped without any hesitation, interrupting Duke Gregory's words.

"What…? H-How rude! I am a duke! You may be a hero, but that is uncalled for!"

After being taken aback, Duke Gregory expressed indignation.

"Aren't you the one being rude to Haruto, the honorary knight? Just coming here in such a large group is rude enough to begin with."

"That is because our dissatisfaction has reached the limit. I understand he has made meritorious achievements, but you've bestowed on him a royal mansion within the castle and given him free rein to do as he pleases. He's invited an unknown group of armed people onto the castle grounds, and keeps taking the hero outside the castle without proper guards."

The unknown group of armed people Gregory referred to was probably Gouki's group. Perhaps Sara's group was included as well. In reality, Duke Gregory glanced at them as he voiced his concerns.

"The attack that occurred the other day was only repelled thanks to the efforts of those present here," Francois pointed out in defense of the group.

"But that attack was aimed at Sir Amakawa in the first place, was it not? Those men were clearly targeting this mansion."

It seemed they weren't making a fuss here for no reason. They had prepared plenty of material against Rio. Duke Gregory didn't back down easily and continued to blame Rio.

"That hasn't been confirmed as fact. And I believe you're deviating off topic, no?"

Duke Gregory's original point in question was whether Rio was worthy of being Satsuki's instructor.

"It's very much related. The point is that someone of unknown background cannot be entrusted with instructing the great hero. Is there a need to leave the castle just to train? Unless you can explain exactly what you are doing without hiding a thing, we cannot accept it. What if the hero is placed in danger because of him?"

"In short, you cannot trust Haruto. That is what you want to say?"

"Well, he does have multiple achievements to his name. I'm not saying he cannot be trusted, only that you should reconsider who should be instructing the great hero in an impartial and fair way that everyone can accept. We must control things to ensure the hero isn't negatively influenced."

"Control…?"

Satsuki had been watching on unhappily, but that word was particularly irritating to her.

"Excuse me!"

Before she knew it, she was raising her voice.

"Yes, Lady Satsuki?" Francois sighed with a pained expression.

"Why are you trying to decide who should instruct me without my consent? I *want* Haruto to teach me. Shouldn't that leave no room for argument?" Satsuki said with a subtly angry and twitching expression, all the while keeping an otherwise-cool smile on her face to remain calm.

"I'm saying this for your sake, great hero. It isn't discussed openly, but there are rumors spreading of how you and Sir Amakawa are in an intimate relationship, which is why you favor him so much."

He wasn't selected for his ability, but out of lust. Is that what you want people to believe? Duke Gregory was implying.

How shameless. It's only your faction that's spreading such rumors, Charlotte thought with a cold expression.

"What did you say?" Satsuki said furiously.

"Calm down, Satsuki," Rio called out to her, grabbing her shoulder. Then, he whispered so that only she could hear, "He's trying to rile you up and hinder your calm judgment."

"Haruto…" Although she was still infuriated, Satsuki managed to regain her composure.

"Sir Amakawa. I am asking for your answer," Duke Gregory said, glaring at Rio without hiding his disgust.

"I am against the idea of disregarding Lady Satsuki's opinion. I am also opposed to the word 'control.'"

It was a statement made precisely because he saw Satsuki as a human, not a hero. Satsuki seemed to understand that, as she smiled happily.

He's using the hero as a shield… This scum doesn't even have enough independence to express his own thoughts. He's a disgrace to all nobles—no, to all men.

However, Duke Gregory thought otherwise. He believed the hero was a political asset that had to be controlled and used effectively. As a hero, he thought it was only natural for her to accept that.

"Hmph." Duke Gregory clicked his tongue in annoyance. "You are only able to say such things because you have no responsibility. Your attitude is inappropriate for nobility—it's the mindset of a commoner. Corrupting the hero with such folly..."

"Let me apologize in advance, Haruto. Sorry," Satsuki suddenly said.

Rio could tell she had quietly snapped. "For what?" he asked.

"I'm about to drag you into this."

"I don't mind that."

"Thanks. Make sure you beat him thoroughly," she whispered so that only he could hear, then turned to Duke Gregory with a fearless smile. "Fine. If you're so insistent, I'll give you an equal chance."

"Oh?" That was exactly what Duke Gregory wanted. His mouth turned upwards in a twisted smirk. "Then how should we go about deciding?"

He hurried the discussions along before Satsuki could change her mind.

"You're unhappy with Haruto's abilities, right? Then why don't you prepare instructors you're happy with and have them face Haruto in a match? You wouldn't possibly dream of recommending someone weaker than Haruto, correct?" This time it was Satsuki's turn to taunt Duke Gregory.

"Of course... However, as this is the great hero that is to be instructed, I wish to prepare an instructor for each field." Duke Gregory didn't falter.

"What I'm seeking from Haruto is instruction in the use of the Divine Arms and battle techniques. There's no need to compete in any other areas. Please restrict the field to the topic of combat."

"Well, I suppose that is fine."

"That, and I want you to apologize to Haruto. And you must agree to never interfere in my business again," Satsuki added.

"Wait…" Duke Gregory expressed reluctance.

"Clement. Lady Satsuki has agreed to your demands. It is only right to accept hers in return," Francois immediately interrupted, blocking off any possible objections.

Your impatience in demonstrating your power has made you negligent in measuring your opponent, Clement.

Francois had wanted to see how things would develop, so he had watched over the scene quietly until now. He was prepared to intervene and adjust things as necessary, but he was mostly unneeded this time.

"I understand…" Duke Gregory nodded stiffly.

"Then it's decided. Is that okay, King Francois?" Satsuki asked.

"As long as you are fine with that, I have no objections."

"Thank you very much. Can I leave the rules and appointment of an umpire to you as well?"

"Of course. When will the match take place?"

"I am available whenever. I could even go today," Rio answered first.

"I also have a candidate selected already. However, I will need the time to summon them here, so could I please be given a three-day allowance?"

"Very well. Then the match will be held in three days' time, when the afternoon bell rings three."

Thus, the match between Rio and Duke Gregory's instruction candidate was decided.

"Heh heh… Just try and beat Haruto if you can."

It seemed Satsuki had a lot of pent-up rage, as the smile on her face was more like an evil grin.

"Satsuki must be really angry. Well, she has reason to be," Latifa said as she witnessed Satsuki in such a state.

"Yeah, she does."

Latifa, Celia, and the others offended by Duke Gregory were dumbfounded. They were all aware of Rio's abilities, so none of them doubted his victory. Satsuki had arranged things well, so all that was left to do was watch on.

"This concludes the discussions. Gather in the training grounds in three days' time," Francois said, turning to return to the castle first. He glanced at Charlotte before his departure, and she quietly followed behind him. Duke Gregory and his men also took their leave, and Rio and the remaining people returned to the mansion.

Half an hour or so later…

"I have returned."

"Pardon the intrusion."

Charlotte returned to the mansion. She was accompanied by Liselotte, whom she must have run into while at the castle. The door of the dining room connected to the entrance hall was left open, so Rio and the others were able to welcome them back while they prepared lunch.

"Welcome back, Char. And welcome, Liselotte. We're just about to have lunch. Everyone's waiting, so let's talk while we eat."

Thus, the group had their meal together. The rest of the Yagumo group had also moved into the mansion, so it was a large gathering. The number of people made it difficult to seat everyone at the same table, so they set up multiple tables in the dining room for people to change seats every day.

Since they wanted to hear about the incident with Duke Gregory today, Rio and Satsuki sat with Charlotte and Liselotte.

"How should I put this...? It's nice. Eating here in this house, I mean. It's warming," Liselotte said, looking around the room with a smile.

The majority of the residents had been raised in an environment far from hierarchical society. To them, it was only natural to have meals together.

"I've also become used to these kinds of meals. On the occasions where I take my meal alone in the castle, I feel so bored by myself. The meals here are healthier and better tasting too." Charlotte placed a hand against her cheek and sighed elegantly.

"I get it. Especially since the castle likes to serve oily foods first thing in the morning... And the meals I had alone when I was first summoned here were tough too," Satsuki agreed keenly.

"Your heart was closed off back then," Charlotte added.

"Yeah..." Satsuki had a faraway look in her eyes, recalling how she believed she was alone in this world back then. "Oops, got a little emotional there. Sorry," she said in slight embarrassment.

"Speaking of apologies, we must apologize for something as well. I am terribly sorry for the discourtesy you were treated with earlier, Sir Haruto, Lady Satsuki." It was at this point that Charlotte brought up the topic of what happened with Duke Gregory earlier.

"I would like to apologize as well." For some reason, Liselotte apologized after Charlotte did.

Satsuki exchanged a look with Rio, who was seated beside her, then tilted her head in confusion. "Uh, it's not something you two need to be sorry for... And why are you apologizing when you weren't even there, Liselotte?"

"It's related to the factions of the royal court, so it's a little complicated..." Charlotte began. According to her, Duke Gregory had been impatient until quite recently.

The two leading noble families of the Galarc Kingdom were Duke Cretia's and Duke Gregory's respective houses. However, ever since Liselotte had established the Ricca Guild, Duke Cretia's power had grown dramatically.

On top of that, Duke Cretia's house had strong ties to the honorary knight that had recently made numerous achievements.

Meanwhile, Duke Gregory's house didn't have any notable achievements to its name. At this rate, a huge gap in power would be created between the two houses during Clement's generation. He probably couldn't forgive himself for that.

Thus, Duke Gregory was constantly on vigilant watch for opportunities to show his presence—or to sabotage Duke Cretia.

"Because I was abducted by the Saint, Duke Gregory's house has regained momentum. The consequences of that were shifted onto the two of you. I'm very sorry." Liselotte bowed her head at Rio and Satsuki once again.

"That still doesn't mean it's your fault."

"Right. If you're going to say that, then the Heavenly Lions' attack on the mansion was what originally caused Duke Gregory to move."

Satsuki pouted sullenly. "In the first place, I don't like his ulterior motive of rising by stepping on others. He claims he's acting for the sake of the kingdom, the sake of the king, and the sake of the hero, but in the end, he only wants what benefits himself."

"Indeed, it is exactly as Lady Satsuki says. That is why we've been dealing with them before they could reach you until now, but we failed to stop Duke Gregory this time."

With the protection of Charlotte and Francois, who wasn't here at the present, Duke Gregory's faction was completely kept in check. On top of that, Rio kept gaining more achievements. The frequent rewards he received from the royal family made Duke Gregory direct his discontent towards Rio.

Then, when he realized there weren't many opportunities to make contact with Rio, he chose to make a bold move.

"Because of his position, Father has to remain impartial to both sides until the matches are over, but he's stated that he doesn't mind if you beat him up without holding back. So, Sir Haruto, please teach him a lesson he'll never forget."

Despite her radical words, Charlotte grinned cheerfully, creating cute dimples.

"That's right! Beat him to a pulp, Haruto!" Satsuki clenched her fists in a fighting pose as she cheered Rio on.

"I'll do my best…" Rio nodded with a wry smile.

Three days later, as the afternoon bell rang three times…

With his beloved sword at his waist, Rio stood in the training grounds of the castle. Facing him were two men who seemed to be the instructors Duke Gregory had prepared for Satsuki, with Duke Gregory beside them.

"Haruto. Clement has a proposal." Before the match began, Francois came to the center of the training ground and personally spoke to them.

"What is it?"

"Out of consideration for Lady Satsuki's education, I wish to split the matches into the fields of spears, martial arts, and enchanted swords."

"I don't mind."

Francois had asked him to instruct Satsuki in the field of spirit arts out of the hope that it would improve her handling of the Divine Arms. That's why they should have been competing in the field of spirit arts, but Duke Gregory was unaware of the existence of spirits. Thus, he had probably been told that the instruction was regarding enchanted swords.

"Hmm. There are two instructors prepared by Clement, but only one of you, Haruto. You'll be at a disadvantage like this. If you have any protests, I will allow you to fight on another day. You may also nominate a substitute."

"Thank you for the consideration. But in order to secure an instructor for Lady Satsuki, I'd like to settle things today. I can fight three times by myself without any issue."

"Is that so?" Francois chuckled heartily. Meanwhile, the man facing Rio with a spear in his hand looked a little discontent.

"Then, spears, martial arts, enchanted swords: which would you like to start with?"

"With all due respect, please allow me to fight first."

The man with the spear stepped forward. He seemed to be aged in his early twenties, and had a masculine face. He was dressed in a knight uniform and carried himself with dignity.

"This is William Lopes, the deputy commander of the First Order of the Galarc Knights. He normally serves to protect the kingdom's borders. The weapon in his hand is an enchanted sword— an enchanted spear, if you will."

"As introduced, I am William Lopes. I volunteered myself when I heard there would be an opportunity to spar with the renowned Black Knight. Pleased to make your acquaintance." William introduced himself and offered his hand for a handshake.

"I'm Haruto Amakawa. I'm honored to be granted this opportunity to face you. Let us have a good match." Rio extended his hand and shook William's.

I expected him to be moving on the orders of the duke, but...

While he didn't seem to be in the best mood, his first impression was honest and favorable. However, whether William himself was a good person or not, if his family was affiliated with Duke Gregory's faction, then he had to follow their orders. It was too dangerous to judge him based on his first impression alone.

"If you possess an enchanted spear, then you must be the instructor for the spear and enchanted sword training."

William glanced at the other man beside him, then nodded. "That is correct."

At that, Duke Gregory looked like he wanted to say something.

"In that case, would you like me to fight with an enchanted sword or a spear first?"

"I would like to request a fight against your enchanted sword," William replied immediately.

"Oi, Sir Lopes." Unable to control himself any longer, Duke Gregory interrupted.

"What is it, Duke?"

"Don't go changing the order we agreed on."

"Is something the matter?" Rio asked William and Duke Gregory, tilting his head.

"I merely wish to fight with my opponent at his strongest. Fighting against someone tired from successive battles wouldn't be considered a victory," William replied on Duke Gregory's behalf.

"I see…"

That was probably why he had looked discontent when he heard Rio agree to three consecutive matches in a row.

"Sir Lopes. You must win, understand?"

"Of course." William nodded without taking his eyes off Rio.

"If you're done introducing yourselves to each other, let's begin. You may use the abilities of your enchanted sword, but you are forbidden from injuring your opponent with it. Either stop your attack before making contact or limit yourself to blows that can only deal minor injuries."

"Understood."

Rio and William both nodded respectfully. Once Francois finished explaining the rules, he left the umpiring to one of his subordinate knights and returned to the spectator zone where Satsuki and Charlotte were. Duke Gregory and the remaining candidate followed behind him.

Furthermore, as the match was open to the public, a considerable number of people had gathered to watch.

"Now, both sides take your places. Ready your weapons," the umpire said.

Rio and William both held their weapons ready.

"Begin!"

Thus, the first round commenced.

The two of them stepped forward without hesitation. The first to attack was William. He launched a sharp thrust aimed at Rio. Although the spear he used was a short spear, it still had a longer range than a sword, so that was the most natural move to make.

However, Rio was more than aware that the other side would make the first move, considering the differences in their reach. He aimed the point of his sword at the spear and diverted the thrust.

Once the spearhead was sent veering to the side, he took the chance to step right up to William.

"Hah!" What a spear user disliked the most was for an enemy with an adaptable weapon to come up close to them. Thus, William's reaction was swift—he withdrew his spear as Rio moved forward, retreating immediately.

Rio moved forward to close their gap as William counterattacked to prevent the sword from coming within reach. The battle seesawed between offense and defense. With physically enhanced bodies, they ran around swiftly, probing each other for openings like threading a needle.

He's fairly strong.

Rio felt William's strength firsthand. He was certainly worthy of his position as the deputy commander of the First Order of the Galarc Knights. He probably hadn't reached Gouki and Alfred's level, but he had considerable abilities. If he fought Sara with the condition of only using physical body enhancements, he would probably best her.

In a corner of the spectating space, Gouki hummed to himself in interest. "Ho ho, the opponent uses his spear very well. Although a spear has the advantage over a sword, it's no easy feat to block Sir Haruto's sword. I would love to spar with him myself."

Charlotte expressed her surprise. "I expected Sir Haruto to end the match in an instant, before his opponent could even react…"

"Spears are a rather difficult weapon to approach from the front. On top of that, there's no knowing what ability is contained in that spear. Considering that, he's probably chosen to take his time with the battle," Gouki explained. "However…"

"Ngh…"

The balance between Rio and William toppled. By catching William within reach of his sword, Rio had gained the advantage.

"As you can see, Sir Haruto is winning in weapon technique. If his opponent continues to hold back his spear's power, at this rate…" The match would be settled in seconds. But before Gouki could say those words…

"Haaah!"

Sensing he would lose in a few more blows, William activated his enchanted spear's ability. He stabbed the stone spearhead into the ground. Then, an ice spear shot up before him.

"Wh…?" Rio retreated at the last moment, escaping the reach of the ice spear.

"You truly live up to the rumors, Black Knight… No, you surpass them. Marvelous." With sweat running down his brow, William praised Rio with a refreshed look.

"I'm honored." They were still in the middle of a match, so Rio's reply was awkward.

"Sorry. You wouldn't have known the abilities of this spear, and the ability is rather lethal, so I didn't want to use it. But it seems it'd be ruder to hold back against you."

"Not at all…"

"This spear is a family treasure that has been passed down by generations. I will now use its abilities without reserve."

"Then I shall do the same." He had been wary of activating his weapon's abilities before his opponent as Duke Gregory could potentially find fault with it, but that was no longer necessary. Rio decided on using his wind from that moment.

"Indeed. Here's to a fair fight!"

Rio and William separated from each other by ten meters, bracing their weapons. One moment later, they both started running.

A wind wrapped around Rio's body as he moved forward. The sand around him was blown up into the air, creating a dust cloud that hid him from view.

"Wait, that's—!" Satsuki cried, recognizing the move as the one Rio used against her yesterday.

"Humph!" William didn't seem to want his vision obstructed, so he created countless ice arrowheads at the tip of his spear and released them. The thin arrowheads pierced holes in the dust cloud, making the spectators stir.

"Hah!" Unsure of the attack he sent into the dust cloud, William stabbed his spear at the ground. At that, several ice spears appeared in a circle around him. He was probably covering all his blind spots, wary of an attack after Rio obstructed his field of view.

Wow, he could tell he would be approached from behind in an instant. Amazing.

Having received an explanation on the move from Rio yesterday, Satsuki was impressed William had seen through it in one go. Their exchange of blows was very enlightening. Rio had indeed gone around behind William, and had been blocked by the ice spears.

"There you are!"

William swung his spear as he turned around, aiming the countless ice arrowheads at Rio.

"What?!"

However, instead of being struck by the arrowheads, Rio disappeared from William's view.

Was that Shukuchi? Satsuki thought, but even watching from afar, she could see his movement speed was rather slow. He was still faster than any human could run, but it was easily ten to twenty times slower than the Shukuchi speed she knew. His trajectory was also curved instead of a straight line.

The reason why it looked like Rio had disappeared in spite of that was because he hadn't used a single muscle of his body, entrusting the wind to move him. And with the curved movement, Rio had come right up to William in the blink of an eye.

Like a floating cherry blossom petal, the way he closed the gap was truly elegant. Gouki was so captivated by the sight of Rio's movement, he muttered to himself in admiration. "He truly moves wonderfully…"

In a single instant, he moved to this position with no extraneous movements at all…!

By the time William spotted Rio with his eyes, it was already too late. Rio had his sword pointed just before William's solar plexus.

"This is my loss. I surrender." Unable to react in time, William admitted his defeat.

At the conclusion of the first match, the training ground burst into cheers. It was a splendid match that even had the spectators heated up, and it had ended in Rio's undeniable victory. The only area that wasn't cheering was the corner where Duke Gregory's faction members had gathered.

"Damn it, Lopes!"

Among them, Duke Gregory was unable to contain himself and ran towards William the moment the match was over.

"The numerous rumors of the Black Knight were no exaggeration. I can assure you of his abilities. Even without holding the rest of the matches, I would have no qualms entrusting him with the great hero's instruction like this."

William praised Rio openly, showing no frustrations over his defeat.

"You... How dare you...?!" Duke Gregory immediately reddened.

"I know how you feel about Sir Amakawa, Duke, but I believe he is far more trustworthy than that mysterious man over there," William said, glancing at the man standing behind Duke Gregory. The man was the second candidate Duke Gregory had prepared as Satsuki's instructor.

He appeared to be in his mid-thirties and was wearing combat clothes, though not those of a knight. Compared to a genuine knight like William, he seemed rather frivolous in appearance. There was something dark and creepy about him.

"Guh... If that's how you'll be, then—Gilbert! It's your turn! This man is useless!"

Duke Gregory gave up on William and turned to entrust the match to the remaining man.

"As I told you in advance, my field of expertise is hand-to-hand combat utilizing enchanted swords in the form of knives. The plan has veered slightly astray, but...well, I'll do my best."

The man named Gilbert shrugged, then started walking towards the center of the training grounds where Rio waited.

Damn it, if only Lopes hadn't ignored the plan and challenged him in enchanted swords first... On top of that, he just had to lose in such an unsightly manner.

The original plan had been to fight with spears and martial arts for the first two matches, then challenge him in enchanted swords in the third match after he was fatigued. By watching him in the first and second matches, they could adjust their approach in the third match.

But William had chosen enchanted swords for the very first match, ruining their plan. At least, that was how Duke Gregory saw it.

I paid Gilbert an exorbitant amount up front to hire him. If he loses like this, all my money will be wasted! This better work out...

Fearing that Gilbert wouldn't be worth the money he had paid, Duke Gregory glared at his back hatefully.

"Those clothes... Is that man not a knight from this kingdom?" Celia, who was spectating the matches, asked.

"He's probably one of Duke Gregory's private soldiers, but I've never seen his face before. I've never heard any rumors of excellent soldiers under his command, though..."

It seemed like Charlotte didn't know anything about Gilbert either.

"It's a pleasure to meet you. My name is Gilbert." With a fake smile on his face, Gilbert bowed.

He has no family name...? Is he not a noble? Rio thought.

"I'm Haruto Amakawa. It's nice to meet you." He quickly returned the bow.

"As you may have guessed already, I am not a noble. I have been serving under Duke Gregory for a long time, valued for my skills. When he approached me with this offer, I agreed, as I wanted to see the great hero with my own eyes."

"Is that so?"

"Despite my appearances, I am a faithful believer of the Six Wise Gods. I don't have much experience in jobs like this, but even if I am unsuited for the role of the instructor, I would love to have an audience with the hero."

Gilbert revealed a little more about his background and glanced over at Satsuki in the spectator zone.

"I see."

"The great hero, disciple of the Six Wise Gods. I wondered what kind of person they would be, but she seems no different to a normal girl. Although that might be rude of me to say out loud."

"She's just another human like us," Rio said.

"I see..."

Gilbert looked a little disappointed. Unsure of the reason for that disappointment, Rio tilted his head in confusion.

"The second match will now commence. Sir Amakawa, this is your second consecutive match, but is it really fine?" the umpire knight asked Rio one last time.

"It is."

"Then the martial arts match is a contest of pure martial arts. The use of any weapons or magic is forbidden. Is that understood?"

"Yes."

"Understood."

The two responses overlapped each other. For the record, Rio had left his sword with the umpire at the end of the first match.

"Both sides, take your places."

Rio and Gilbert stood five meters from each other and assumed their fighting stances. That being said, neither made a show of clenching their fists. They both took deep breaths, lightly assuming fighting stances while remaining calm and composed.

Several seconds later...

"Begin!"

At the umpire's signal, the match began.

"..." They both held their stances while slowly approaching each other.

Hand-to-hand combat that relied on pure physical abilities was always more boring to watch than battles with enchanted swords. The gallery probably believed that as well.

"Grah!" Once the exchange of blows began, their movements were truly transcendent. That didn't mean they were moving about extravagantly—as far as their leg movements went, one would step back if the other stepped forward. That was all.

What was moving at a speed too fast for the eyes to follow was their hands. However, they weren't throwing flashy punches around either. They were quietly moving their hands, aiming to land the winning blow while fending off the opponent's advances.

It was a silent exchange, but it was also speedy. Because of that, the spectators held their breaths in silence as well. Rio and Gilbert knocked each other's hands out of the way, creating the sound of fabric brushing against each other.

Eventually, Rio's fist found the first opening in his opponent's defenses.

"Ugh…!" With a dull impact, Gilbert's body was blown backwards. But that was because he had guarded himself with both arms, jumping back to release the force of the blow. He hadn't sustained any damage.

"Goodness me… Sir Amakawa, was it? Your techniques are far beyond others of your age," Gilbert grinned.

"You are quite a formidable opponent yourself."

In contrast, Rio's gaze was somewhat wary. During the short exchange of blows, he had felt there was something strange about him.

"Hmm…" Gouki, who felt something odd from where he was spectating, furrowed his brow. "Kayoko, dear, that man…"

"Yes. He reeks of blood. I doubt he's done much decent work up until now."

"Indeed. Well, it shouldn't be a problem for Sir Haruto either way…"

The Saga couple decided to watch over their master. Meanwhile—

"Personally, I'd like to end this soon, but… Perhaps you could give me a bit more of your time," Gilbert said.

He quietly stepped forward. Rio also stepped forward to meet him. Like that, their exchange of blows resumed.

They relaxed their muscles to reduce extraneous movement, weaving their attacks through the openings between their concentration and breaths. Detecting the attacks of their opponent and diverting their trajectories. Their fighting styles were similar, but different.

Rio's style of martial arts involved using a kick or punch at just the right moment to throw his opponent's body off-balance.

I knew it... This person's martial arts are clearly based around the use of a knifelike weapon. Is his fighting style based off assassination techniques? Or the hand-to-hand combat of some country's militia?

Gilbert's martial arts seemed to be refined for the use of a weapon to efficiently kill an opponent. Every time they passed, a fist extended directly towards Rio's body, aiming for his vitals as though there were a knife in his hand.

Another example was how he continued using attacks that involved moving his hands, but never attempted to grab Rio. He persistently kept trying to send his hand forward, aiming for the vital spots of the body. It would be one thing if he were aiming to land a blunt strike, but he merely seemed to be aiming for a certain spot as quickly as possible—there was no force behind his strikes. On top of that, he kept using his arm to deflect Rio's blunt strikes, as though he were holding a knife in his hand.

Are these truly assassination techniques? Does that mean this person is an assassin?

Did Duke Gregory intend on teaching Satsuki assassination techniques by employing this man as an instructor? Had he chosen anyone who seemed capable of victory, regardless of their occupation? Either way, it didn't make sense.

Gilbert distanced himself from Rio, then grinned eerily as he spoke suggestively. "My apologies. I can't quite break the habit in my hands."

"You're…" Rio stopped moving and faced Gilbert.

"Now that you've learned my secret, I am no longer able to win against you. I do not wish to reveal any more of my techniques either. That being said, I have my employer's order to consider…" Gilbert glanced at where Duke Gregory stood in the spectating space. "If possible, I would appreciate it if you could defeat me as painlessly as possible. I dislike being hurt, you see."

It was as good as a declaration of surrender.

"I have no intention of attacking someone with no will to fight. If you do not wish to fight, please surrender clearly." Rio shot down his request swiftly.

"Good grief. In that case…"

Gilbert sighed tiredly and charged towards Rio. He thrust his fist straight forward, as though to plunge a knife into Rio's heart.

But before he could reach him, Rio grabbed his arm and performed a one-armed shoulder throw. Gilbert was cleanly slammed against the ground.

"Ah, you are a kind person," Gilbert muttered the moment he was thrown. Once he was lying faceup on the ground, he added, "May the Six Wise Gods grace you."

"Halt! The winner is Sir Amakawa." At the umpire's declaration, the second match ended in Rio's victory.

Afterwards, Rio and William fought one more round using spears, which also ended in Rio's victory. Thus, Duke Gregory's plot to drag Rio down from the role of Satsuki's instructor was completely thwarted.

But if today had just ended like this, Duke Gregory would still have been spared from the worst day of his life.

"That was wonderful, Haruto." At the end of the third round, Francois entered the grounds to praise Rio.

"Thank you."

"I cannot imagine anyone better suited for the role of Lady Satsuki's instructor. That was proven today. Isn't that right, Clement?"

"...Yes," Clement rasped, barely managing to nod. The truth of three consecutive losses had been thrust in his face. He wanted to retort, but he had no means of doing so. The man named Clement Gregory wasn't opposed to acting shamelessly for the sake of his goals, but he was also aware that fussing further would just be a disgrace.

"And so, Lady Satsuki's instructor will continue to be Haruto. The method of instruction will also be left to his discretion," Francois declared in a loud voice so that the spectators could hear.

Just then, a knight came running over in a panic. "Your Majesty!"

"What is it? We're in the middle of something here."

"I-I am terribly sorry for interrupting, but this is an emergency," the knight panted.

"Speak."

At Francois's word, the knight shot a pitiful glance at Duke Gregory's face. "We have received notice that the capital of Duke Gregory's territory has fallen. His son, the governor, has been taken hostage."

"Wh...WHAT?!"

Duke Gregory's scream echoed across the training grounds.

⁕ Chapter 6 ⁕
Quiet Invasion

Duke Gregory's territory was located at the northernmost end of Galarc. The Cretia family of the south, and the Gregory family of the north; since the dawn of history, these two duke families supported the kingdom from one end to the other.

However, the events that were to happen to the Gregory territory today were never before seen in history.

Early afternoon that day, before the three matches were held…

A group being led by Saint Erica was staying in Greille, the capital of Duke Gregory's territory. Erica gathered the group in a room of a peasant inn to address them all.

"Everyone, what did you think of this city after walking around yesterday?" she asked cheerfully, looking around at the faces of her companions.

"By which you mean…?"

The companions exchanged confused glances with each other.

"We are about to seize this city and commence our invasion of the Galarc Kingdom. You will all be seizing this city with me. Not because I want it, but because *you* wish to do so of your own accord. That is why I want to hear about what you saw, where you stood, where you went, and what you felt. I had you look around the city by yourselves for this purpose," Erica explained, looking around at everyone's faces once again.

"It's a very big city," one young man eventually said. "Far bigger than the capital of our nation. If a suburban city is this big, then the capital must be even greater…"

A similarly aged woman seated nearby spoke up after him. "Will we really be able to seize a city this big by ourselves…?" she asked worriedly. The total number of their party, including Erica, was ten. A mere ten people.

Erica aside, even if they enhanced their physical abilities, the other nine each only had the strength of a knight at most. How could they storm such a large city and seize control of it? They were probably worried about that.

"What are you getting fainthearted about? We have Saint Erica's beast of the land on our side!"

"That's right. If the divine beast rampages a bit, this city will fall in an instant!"

There were others who were confident about seizing the city. They believed in Erica's beast of the land. However…

"You mustn't misunderstand, everyone. We are indeed invading this kingdom. However, our enemies are the royalty and nobility ruling this country, not the innocent people of this land. Summoning the beast of the land within the city would be a catastrophe. I cannot sacrifice the people of this land for no good reason," Erica said, expressing her reluctance to call the beast of the land to capture the city.

"So we must take over this city without the use of the divine beast…?"

"Yes."

"How in the world are we supposed to do that?"

Could they occupy a city with a mere ten people?

"With Saint Erica on our side, we have nothing to fear from their army."

"Indeed. Even without the divine beast, we can still take over the city easily."

"But there's only ten of us. Saint Erica cannot use her full power while keeping the residents unharmed, and if there's someone as strong as the man who attacked our capital here…"

"Hmm…"

The optimistic people who believed in Erica's strength fell quiet. They were probably recalling Rio, who had fought with the beast of the land on equal footing. If a warrior like that appeared, even Erica would struggle against multiple opponents at once.

"Indeed, it would be a little bothersome if someone like him appeared. But I have no intention of losing," Erica answered. "This isn't a battlefield where we hurl all of our forces at each other. We are infiltrating the enemy's territory, making the first move in a local war. There are plenty of ways to succeed."

"Ooh…!"

The group looked at Erica hopefully.

"What do we have to do?"

"Shall we increase the number of our allies first?"

"Increase our allies? Do you mean we should call for reinforcements from home?"

"No, there are plenty of allies in this city already."

"Was another squad dispatched along with us…?"

The group looked surprised. They hadn't heard of such a thing.

"No. I am talking about the people living in this city."

"The people…living in this city…?"

Nine of them made faces that said they'd never thought of that.

"Like I said before, our enemies are the royalty and nobility ruling this kingdom. There is no need to antagonize the innocent residents of this land. They are the victims that have been oppressed by the rulers, so they will join forces with us." Erica gave them a saintlike smile.

"Of course…"

"Yes, that's exactly right!"

"They'll become our allies!"

One after another, the group raised their voices in agreement. They believed that the people of this city would agree with Erica's teachings, just as they had when she first appeared before them.

"There are a few reasons why I selected this city as the starting point of our invasion. First, as it is located right along the border, it is constructed in a manner that is very easy to defend. On top of that, it is governed by one of the top nobles of the kingdom, making it a considerably large size. The more people living here, the more potential allies are available to us. If everything goes well, we'll be able to obtain a powerful base and many allies in one go."

The problem was whether things would go well or not. But for better or worse, the people here all had the utmost faith in Erica.

"…" They all saw their imminent victory. Even those who were unsure earlier looked confident now.

"The royalty and nobility of our nation were also overthrown by the power of the majority. If every single person living in this city became our ally, the Galarc Kingdom would be helpless. They couldn't possibly kill them all. Don't you agree?"

"Yes!"

Everyone's voices overlapped with each other.

"Then, in order to save our comrades from the tyranny of the nobles, let's first bring them over to our side."

Erica and her party left the inn in high spirits and made their way to the square connected to the main street of the city. However…

"There really are so many people here…"

Perhaps it was because they were all countryside dwellers that had never left their tiny nation before. When faced with the bustling street, far livelier than the capital of their own country, they felt daunted.

"There's nothing to fear."

Erica was the only one who marched through the square without the slightest hesitation. Behind her, the rest of the party nodded at each other before following her footsteps with resolution. Erica stopped before the fountain in the square. As for what she was doing in a square where so many people were gathered—

"Your attention, everyone!"

It was an appeal. Erica raised her voice loud enough to be heard over the noisy square, calling out to the people passing by.

"…"

The people paused, turning to her in silence. They looked at her with questioning gazes. Before she lost their attention, Erica continued.

"Don't you all think it's strange? We pay the noble class so much in taxes, yet they do nothing for us. If anything, they look down on us like we deserve to pay them tax. They think of us as dirty commoners."

She looked around at the faces of those closest to her, presenting her radical opinion to them. An unknown woman had suddenly started a speech in a corner of the city. Her loud voice attracted quite a few gazes, some of which were unimpressed. However…

"Thanks to the taxes we pay, the noble class live in fancy mansions and estates, wear fancy clothes, eat good meals, have warm clothing, and sleep in soft beds. Yet we are forced to live humble lives in our cramped homes."

Erica paid no mind to their dubious gazes, pressing forth with the presentation of her theory. Her speech was entirely extremist in a class society ruled by royalty and nobility.

But as the contents of her speech related to the lifestyle of the people, there were many who were listening in spite of their suspicion. Perhaps they were unhappy about having to pay such high taxes as well, and were only holding their tongues out of fear of the noble class.

"We are forced into absolute submission by the noble class. We must obey their every order, no matter how outrageous. We must constantly live in fear, praying that we won't be targeted by the wrong noble. Even though we are all the same humans... What is it that makes them so different to us?"

By the time Erica asked that, there were quite a few people who had come closer, be it out of interest or empathy. She had put into words the things they couldn't say themselves.

"Young lady," an old man chimed in.

"Yes, sir?"

"You know we can't defy the nobles. I understand exactly what you're saying, but you should leave it at that for your own good. The soldiers will be coming soon."

The old man expressed concern for Erica's well-being. In a class society, there was no freedom for commoners to criticize the positions of power. Inciting the antipathy of the noble class was like begging for punishment.

Erica met the old man's eyes and smiled gently. "You're a very kind person."

Just then, having heard the commotion, soldiers came running over—as the old man expected.

"What's going on here?!"

"What are you doing?!"

They were members of Duke Gregory's private army, hired to serve the role of police. It was the lord's duty to maintain public order within his territory.

"Eek!"

The reaction of the gathered people was swift. The moment they noticed the soldiers, they scattered away from Erica.

"Aah!" someone screamed. It was a little girl who had been pushed by the wave of fleeing people and fallen to the ground.

"Ow…" She must have grazed herself in the fall. There was blood flowing from her knee.

"Oh, dear me." Erica immediately approached the girl. She then materialized her Divine Arms and brought the end towards the knee. The end glowed with a healing light, closing the wound.

"Ooh…" The people scattered about stirred noisily at the appearance of a fine staff and a healing method they would never normally witness. They had distanced themselves from Erica out of fear of the soldiers, but they were now giving her even more attention than before.

"Off you go now."

"O-Okay. Thank you, miss!" The girl bowed nervously before running off.

"Hey, woman. What is that staff?" The soldier who came running was taken aback by what happened and questioned Erica about her staff. But the other soldier beside him interrupted with a gasp.

"Excuse me, ma'am. Would you happen to be a noble?" he asked politely. The reason for his question was her staff—only nobles and top-class adventurers possessed magic artifacts containing sorcery. The clothes she wore weren't particularly extravagant, but they were clean and of good quality. It would be bad for them if she was a noble. That was what he was probably thinking.

For the record, nobles that possessed territories—such as Duke Gregory—tended to have many vassals without a court rank. The soldiers working in the area generally came from such vassal families. They were treated as quasi nobles and guaranteed better lifestyles than the average commoner.

"No, I am not a noble."

"A renowned adventurer, then?"

Top-class adventurers tended to have connections to high-ranking nobles, so regular soldiers had to be careful with how they treated them. However, Erica openly disclosed that she was neither of those things. "No. I am a regular citizen no different to everyone else here."

"What...?" The soldiers exchanged confused looks, having assumed they were dealing with someone of important social status.

"Where were you hiding that staff? No—why do you have such an item? I've never heard of a magic artifact containing the sorcery to heal."

With a clear change of attitude, the soldier that had spoken politely to Erica gruffly questioned her about the staff.

"This belongs to me. Is there a problem?" Erica tilted her head curiously.

"Where did you get that staff from?"

"Why do you want to know that?"

"Because that staff is clearly a valuable item. There's no way a normal commoner would have such a thing."

"Are you saying you don't believe this belongs to me, by any chance?"

"That's right."

"This item is mine."

"Then prove it."

"How?"

The soldier sneered as though to taunt her stupidity. "If you can't prove it, then it clearly doesn't belong to you."

It was evident from his attitude that he had determined the staff wasn't hers.

"I suppose I have no choice, then. How about this—I can make it appear and disappear at will. Does that serve as proof?" Erica asked. She then made her Divine Arms vanish and reappear.

"…" The soldiers were speechless; it should have been pretty convincing proof. However…

"…No," they denied.

"Why not?"

"The governor needs to make the final judgment."

"Judgment of what?"

"Someone else might be able to make that staff appear and disappear too. He will be the judge of that," the soldier replied, voice cracking.

"Would you like to try for yourself, then?" Erica offered her staff out to the soldiers.

"…" One of the soldiers hesitantly accepted it. He stared at it closely, as though captivated by the sight, and gulped. He could tell that it was a far better item than any of the steel batons supplied by the army.

"How do you make it disappear?" the soldier asked, eyes glued to the staff.

"It's nothing special. I tell it to disappear in my head and it disappears. The same for when I want it to reappear."

"What...?" The soldier holding the staff grunted. He was probably thinking the word "disappear" in his head, but the staff showed no sign of vanishing.

Eventually, the soldier holding the staff reddened in anger. "I can't do it!" he shouted.

"That's because you're not the owner of that staff," Erica snickered.

"Guh... The governor will still be the judge of that. We will hold on to this."

"You're coming along too." The soldiers gave Erica their verdict.

"No. I do not want to go with you." Erica refused them flatly. The way she clearly stated her own opinion against people of power must have been satisfying to watch, as there were many curious onlookers around them.

"What did you say?"

Humans were creatures that responded to betrayed expectations with anger. Erica's defiance immediately soured the soldiers' moods.

"Give me back my staff," she said. The staff in the soldier's hand vanished.

"Hey! Return that!" the soldier yelled in a fluster.

"That's funny. Why should I return something that belongs to me?"

"There's still no proof it belongs to you!" the soldier snapped irrationally.

"Everyone! Who do you think is in the wrong here: me, or these soldiers? They're trying to steal an item from a commoner just because it seems valuable. No doubt they intend on claiming it for themselves, coming up with whatever excuse they can to confiscate it. Does this appear fair to all of you?"

Erica addressed the onlookers that had watched the entire scene from the start, seeking their opinion.

"N-No one said that much!" the soldiers refuted, flustered at how she had pointed out their ulterior motive.

"Is that so? Well, I'm sure whatever you say must be the truth."

Erica stared at the soldiers coldly. "You insolent... Enough! Return the staff!"

"I refuse. Actually..." Since the beginning of the conversation, Erica's tone had been extremely calm. "Do you have any proof I made the staff disappear in the first place?" she asked.

"You said it yourself! The staff disappears when the owner wants it to!"

"Oh, are you acknowledging the fact that I'm the owner, then?"

"No! I-It was just a figure of speech!" the soldier yelled with a panicked look.

"So it disappears when I want it to disappear, even though I'm not the owner? Do you have proof? Please present evidence that the staff disappears even when someone who isn't the owner wants it to disappear."

Her words must have been retaliation for the way the soldiers demanded proof from her earlier. The onlookers who had seen the whole thing play out from the beginning caught on immediately.

"Ha ha!"

Someone among the onlookers laughed loudly in delight.

"That's...!"

They had been humiliated before the public. The soldiers turned red as their emotions got the better of them, and they opened their mouths to argue. But no words came out. They were probably at a loss for what to say. Eventually, they realized they wouldn't win a verbal argument.

"Enough! You're under arrest for the obstruction of public order!"

The soldiers took out their batons and prepared to suppress Erica for her insubordination.

"Heh heh." Erica chuckled, and the fight with the soldiers commenced.

Over ten minutes passed in no time. Erica was still locked in battle with the soldiers. But the soldiers she was currently fighting weren't the same ones that initially confronted her—those two were lying around somewhere in this square. The whole square was covered in over fifty soldiers, all of them defeated by Erica's hand. Excited onlookers were gathered in one corner of the square, along with the party that had followed Erica from their homeland.

"Heh heh heh."

No matter how many soldiers she defeated, more reinforcements came running intermittently. But Erica faced them all with a cool head.

"Damn it!"

"Are the direct troops of the governor still not here?!"

Meanwhile, the soldiers surrounding her all looked rather pale. Their allies had been knocked out one after another, so it was only natural. They probably wanted to run away.

This is as much as I expected. As I thought, there's no one as strong as that boy.

Erica thought as she glanced at the cowering soldiers. She had been wary of the appearance of someone as strong as Rio, but none of her opponents had been particularly threatening so far.

"This way!"

Just then, a new group ran into the square. There were roughly thirty people on horseback. Noticing the reinforcements, Erica directed her gaze over at them.

Oh? These soldiers look a little stronger.

The troops were clearly dressed in better equipment than the other soldiers. Their uniforms resembled the knight uniform of the kingdom's military. They were all part of Duke Gregory's private army—an elite unit of the finest soldiers.

The onlookers clamored at the appearance of the governor, who ruled the city on Duke Gregory's behalf.

"Hey, it's the lord's personal army!"

"The governor is here too!"

"Will that lady be okay?"

The elite forces dismounted from their horses at a distance from Erica, stepping down onto the ground. But one man remained sitting on his horse. He was Duke Gregory's second son, Maxim Gregory. The eldest son of the family was employed in the capital.

"Hey, woman! You must be the one causing this commotion," Maxim shouted, glaring down at Erica on horseback.

"That would be incorrect," Erica replied, answering him boldly before the thirty troop members. "This commotion was started by two of your subordinates, not me. I believe they're lying around somewhere in this square."

"What a mess you've made here… You should hope you don't regret your actions."

Maxim glanced at the disastrous state of the square with disgust. She had openly fought with soldiers that served nobility. It was pretty much the same as bringing disgrace to the noble himself. No matter the circumstances, this situation was unacceptable.

"I permit the use of excessive force. Enchant your physical abilities and apprehend her."

"*Augendae Corporis!*"

At Maxim's order, the elite troops all chanted the spell in unison. Once they'd finished preparing for battle…

"Seize her!"

They were given the order to arrest Erica. Three soldiers immediately approached Erica, surrounding her from different sides. All three were armed with police batons.

The elite troops had been mobilized. There was nothing else that could be done here. The majority of the onlookers in the square were thinking that. However…

"Wha…?!"

Their expectations were defied. In a single swing from left to right, Erica defeated all three of them.

"Guh…"

They weren't dead, but their wounds were anything but superficial. The men who had been mowed down writhed, groaning in pain.

Maxim gasped in shock at the sight. "What did she…?"

But he immediately snapped back to his senses.

"All units!" he yelled.

Before he could command them to charge forward, Erica was running towards the elite troops. She slipped right into the midst of them.

From that point on, it was a one-sided scene of brutality. Against the soldiers that hesitated to raise their hands in fear of friendly fire, Erica swung her staff without a care. Some of the troops attempted to block the attack with their batons, but they were no match for Erica's strength with only their physical abilities enhanced.

"Wh-Whoa…"

The nine subordinates that accompanied Erica joined the residents of the city in watching with bated breath as the lord's army was helplessly suppressed. The nobles they feared didn't seem so scary right now.

"D-Defeat her! Defeat her! Defeat her...!" Maxim ordered, getting his horse to back away so he could distance himself from Erica. But even as he did that, the number of his unharmed subordinates decreased moment by moment.

What people sought in fiction wasn't a boring and ordinary life.

They wanted stories of the unreal and extraordinary.

For example, a hero appearing to punish the evil nobles... A story of poetic justice. Something simple and easy to empathize with.

That was how to seize the hearts of the people.

Eventually, all the knights and soldiers besides Duke Gregory's son had fallen.

"Whooooooooo!" The onlookers roared in joy, praising Erica as they looked down on the nobles.

Maxim's decision was rapid. He quickly yanked the reins, ordering the horse to change directions and flee.

"You're not getting away."

Erica slammed the end of her staff into the ground. A wall of dirt several meters tall rose before Maxim.

The horse neighed and tumbled over in shock.

"Ngh...!"

Having fallen from the horse, Maxim rolled on the ground and groaned. Erica walked towards him.

"Gah...!" Maxim tried to scramble back.

"There's no need to be frightened. I merely wish to confirm something. If you answer me honestly, I will spare you from any pain."

"I-I'll answer!"

"All right. If I'm not mistaken, you are the governor of this city?"

"Th-That's right."

"The lord is absent right now, so that makes you the head of this city, correct?"

"Y-Yes. As the second son, I am in charge of the city when my father is away."

"I see. Then there's something I need you to do." Erica smiled sweetly, her mouth twisting into a grin.

"Wh-What…?"

"In the name of Saint Erica, I am making a declaration. As of this moment, this city will become a territory of the Holy Democratic Republic of Erica. This is a declaration of war to the Galarc Kingdom. Tell that to the Galarc King for me."

At this very point in time, a state of the Holy Democratic Republic of Erica was created. It was just a short while before Rio won his matches against William and Gilbert.

⁕ Chapter 7 ⁕
Their Respective Intentions

"How dare they…?!"

Duke Gregory's anger echoed in a council room within the castle.

"Calm yourself, Clement."

Seated in the throne room of the Galarc Castle, Francois sighed. Furthermore, they weren't the only ones in the room. Duke Cretia and the other leading nobles of the kingdom were in attendance, seated within the room.

In addition, Rio, Liselotte, and Satsuki were also present. The three of them stood behind Francois.

"How do you expect me to be calm?!" Duke Gregory replied, baring his emotions at King Francois. "My land—my territory was taken! Because of those two!"

He pointed at Rio and Liselotte and glared.

"Why do you blame Haruto and Liselotte?"

"The Cretia daughter is the one who started the conflict with that ridiculous Saint!"

"And?"

"Wh…?"

Francois encouraged him to continue with indifference. That reaction was unexpected to Duke Gregory, whose face twitched.

"And it was Sir Amakawa who invaded that Saint's country and worsened the situation! Oh, but he did such a wonderful job

375

rescuing Cretia's daughter, was it? No, he did a half-cocked job—and now my territory has been invaded! It's all because of this imbecile!" This time, he criticized Rio harshly.

"Firstly, you claim that Liselotte caused the conflict with the Saint, but that is incorrect. The Saint intended on disputing with our kingdom from the very beginning. Any city ruled by a person of great importance would have been fine with her. She just so happened to target Amande."

Francois calmly dismissed Duke Gregory's claims.

"Guh... Well, what about Amakawa, then? You said so yourself, Your Majesty—that the Saint had most likely died by Amakawa's hand. What do you have to say to that now? She's very clearly alive, isn't she?!"

"I did preface with the fact that her corpse wasn't found."

"Even then, it should have been easy to imagine that the Saint would be enraged by Liselotte's rescue and escalate things. That's why he should have settled everything properly! He made a real mess of things with his inadequacy!"

"You seem insistent on blaming Liselotte and Haruto for this, but the Saint invaded a land completely unrelated to them. According to your claims, shouldn't she have targeted Amande or Haruto's mansion for revenge? In the first place, you seem to be blaming Liselotte for being attacked in the first place. Does this mean you should be similarly criticized for the attack on your land?"

"Grr... You're just arguing in circles."

"Haruto said he stabbed the Saint through the heart. He confirmed her pulse had stopped. Do you consider that an inadequate job?"

Out of desperation, Duke Gregory expressed his distrust for Rio with extreme resentment. "Did he truly pierce the Saint's heart? How do you know he isn't lying?"

"He is not a man who would tell such lies," Francois answered without any hesitation. It was proof of his utmost trust in Rio.

"You…" Duke Gregory's eyes widened so far, his bloodshot veins were in danger of bursting. He swallowed his words, unable to argue back against the king, but everyone could see his discontent rising higher and higher by the moment.

"The greater matter of importance right now is what to do about Greille. Declaring a vital city of our kingdom an exclave of the Holy Democratic Republic of Erica is not something that can be overlooked. That is why I will first send a team to scout the state of the city. Once they confirm that the Saint is alive, we will attempt subjugation," Francois said.

"This is no time to be acting so complacent!" Duke Gregory snapped once again. "Forget the reconnaissance team and send the enchanted airship fleet immediately to snatch the city back!"

"No, we mustn't underestimate the Saint's power. From what Haruto has described, her power is a true threat. If she is still alive, then it would be unwise to send soldiers charging in recklessly."

"The beast of the land, was it? Hmph, I find it questionable whether such a monster even exists. Everything that boy says rouses suspicion."

It seemed Duke Gregory had nothing but distrust for Rio. It also seemed like he disliked Rio. To be precise, it seemed he didn't want to believe him *because* he disliked him.

"I know that you dislike Haruto and are panicking right now. But while this issue involves your territory, at the same time it is a national emergency. As king, I cannot allow you to let your personal feelings affect your judgment in this matter."

He would prefer to dismiss Duke Gregory from his position, but things were never that easy. Though he was the king, there was an arrangement with the nobles that even he had to obey. If he wanted to dispossess a lord of his territory, it had to be for a clear and objective reason such as a serious crime on the lord's part.

Breaking that arrangement and dismissing a lord one-sidedly would create animosity from every noble in the kingdom. At worst, the kingdom could fall into pieces. In this incident, it was impossible to use Duke Gregory's dislike for Rio as an objective reason for dismissal. That being said...

"I do not particularly dislike him," Duke Gregory said, having detached his emotions to regain some of his composure. "But if Your Majesty insists, then I will cease my objections. However, would you please consider my opinion on two counts?"

Although he nodded in agreement, it was unlikely he had discarded his resentment for Rio.

"What are they?"

"The first is regarding the reconnaissance team. You must require someone familiar with the geography of the city. Please use one of my subordinates for that role."

"That is a reasonable request. However, my personnel will also be in that team, so do keep that in mind."

Duke Gregory glared at Rio in annoyance, figuring he would be one of those selected. But he didn't voice his disapproval out loud.

"Understood," he continued, moving on with the conversation. "And once the Saint has been subjugated, please deploy the military to recapture the city as swiftly as possible."

As the lord of a territory, this was another reasonable request. Francois hadn't wanted to send in the military when the beast of the land could appear, but not sending a single soldier was out of the question. Refusing here would potentially create dissent from every other territory lord as well.

"Very well. Then I will have a thousand soldiers on standby."

Francois gave a number that could be mobilized easily in an emergency.

"A thousand, you say…?"

The word "merely" was omitted, but it was certainly implied.

"I cannot imagine the Saint would have brought that many forces with her into the city. A thousand should suffice in regaining control of the city. Increasing the numbers would result in longer preparation time as well. I wish to prepare all the necessary personnel and supplies today, so they can depart to resolve the situation tomorrow."

A swifter resolution was better for Duke Gregory as well. Besides, his territory was only a few hours away from the capital by airship. If they needed more reinforcements, they could request more without too much effort. Thus, Duke Gregory chose to obediently back down.

"I understand. Thank you for your consideration."

Meanwhile, in Greille—the capital of Duke Gregory's territory—Erica had completed her takeover of the consulate, which was constructed as a fortress.

She had taken Duke Gregory's second son Maxim as a hostage. It took no effort to disarm all the soldiers and use the transmission artifact to send notice of Greille's takeover to the Galarc Castle.

However, there were some people who opposed her in spite of the second son being taken hostage: Duke Gregory's third son and his followers. Immediately after Erica made Maxim use the magic artifact to declare war on the capital, they attacked with no regard for the hostage's life.

"Your little brother doesn't seem to be a fan of yours," Erica chuckled. She was seated in a lounge chair in the office, across from the similarly seated Maxim.

"…" Maxim was staring downwards with a conflicted expression. Lying in front of him was his little brother, his magic sealed with a collar. The third son had believed that if he could eliminate Erica after his older brother's huge blunder, he'd obtain a once-in-a-lifetime opportunity to move up into the governor position. Of course, his attempt to do so had resulted in his own capture.

"In order to recapture the city, I would have done the same… It was the right action as a noble," Maxim muttered.

"Is that so? Either way, it would be annoying if another fool decided to imitate him. And so, I have a new request to make of you."

"What?"

"Banish all the residents of the noble district from this city," Erica stated simply.

"Wha…? I can't do such a thing! How would it even be possible?! Do you know how many residents there are?"

From Maxim's point of view, it was an absurd request.

"How many residents are there?"

"Over a thousand!"

"I see. But they'll leave if you order them to, no? Or do your retainers hate you just as much as your little brother?"

"What…?!"

"Order them to leave," Erica demanded mercilessly.

"I can't do that! That's what will make them really hate me!"

"I don't get it. If those thousand residents were from the slums instead, you wouldn't hesitate to obey me, would you?"

"…" Maxim didn't deny her words. Indeed, banishing the poorest people of the city wouldn't be much of a problem. The public order of the city would be unsettled for a while, but he would have overlooked it as a demerit of the current situation.

"You're fine with banishing the poor, but you can't banish your noble retainers. It really is a strange way of thinking."

"There's nothing strange about it! The nobles all serve the Gregory family. If I banish them, they'd all lose their faith in us."

"Yet you'd be fine with losing a thousand of the poorer residents of the territory? Both of them are your people, are they not?"

"They're not the same! Those filthy commoners could never compare to the retainers who work for our family!"

"That's where you're wrong."

"What...?"

"This is already my country," Erica said indifferently. "It is no longer the territory of Duke Gregory. I have no need for people with special statuses in my country. That is, of course, unless they're willing to give up those statuses."

"Father would never accept that. The kingdom won't remain silent either," Maxim muttered bitterly, expressing his utmost opposition.

"I see. Then perhaps I'll ask your brother instead. He becomes governor if I kill you, right? I didn't think I had a use for the third son with you around, but now I'm glad I didn't kill him right away."

Erica stood up and went over to the third son on the floor, removing his mouth gag.

"I-I'll do it! Let me do it, please! I'll convince all the retainers!" The third son immediately agreed. He nodded furiously, swearing to obey Erica.

"Fool! Fearing for your life doesn't mean you can discard your pride as a noble! You don't deserve to be called a member of the Gregory family—you don't even deserve to be called a noble!" Maxim yelled at his brother.

"P-Pride, you say? You must be kidding me! Just because I was born one year later than you, I've had to live an inferior life to you in every way! Father's also treated me as a lesser being my whole life! Perhaps I would have had that pride you speak of if I were the second son!" the third son yelled back.

"Wh-What did you say...?!" Maxim had noticed his little brother's rebellious attitude towards him, but he had never heard his true feelings expressed so clearly. He was taken aback by the sudden truth that was revealed to him.

"Goodness, the traditions of nobility are truly evil. Humans are born equal, yet you people somehow find value in the order of your birth. What fools you all are," she said, before turning to the third son. "You poor thing. I see you are just another victim of noble society."

They were the sweet, compassionate whispers of a witch.

"Th-That's right... The order of my birth was all it took for Father to ignore my abilities." But those whispers shook the heart of the third son.

"You'll cooperate with me, then? I will go with you, but you should be the ones to give the noble district residents the order. Tell them this is no longer their country, so they should leave. I will help with persuading anyone who refuses."

"Right..." the third son nodded.

"No one will accept such a thing..." Maxim mumbled to himself.

His words turned out to be in vain, as Erica's display of her military power sent the nobles scattering from the city that very day.

The sight of the nobles being banished from the city became a spectacle that was highly discussed amongst the commoners. The banished residents were taken in as refugees in the neighboring towns, and word of their banishment reached Francois's ears in the capital by the next morning.

Thus, in one way or another, the exclave of the Holy Democratic Republic of Erica was established successfully.

The next afternoon, at the bank of a lake about five kilometers from Greille, approximately one thousand troops dispatched from the capital of Galtuuk had set up an encampment.

Inside one of the tents, Rio was having a meeting with King Francois. Accompanying Rio were Aishia, Miharu, Celia, Latifa, Satsuki, Sara, Orphia, Alma, Gouki, and Kayoko. Charlotte, Duke Cretia, Liselotte, and Aria were also present.

"And you're sure you're willing to join the reconnaissance team, Haruto?" Francois asked.

"I'm the one who offered my assistance. If the Saint is truly alive, then Duke Gregory was right. It was my failure to finish her off that led to this situation."

"You are mistaken, Haruto. As an honorary knight, you have no duty to serve this kingdom. Yet you've lent us your strength numerous times until now. I appreciate your assistance greatly, but I must confirm this to be sure. Are you really okay with going?"

Francois gazed at Rio, assessing his resolution.

"What do you mean?"

"I believe in your strength. And I know just how reassuring it is to have it on our side. That is why I appreciate your volunteering yourself to the cause. However, this is a matter for the kingdom to resolve. Calling it a subjugation doesn't change the fact it is a dirty job to be doing. It's not the same as your mission to rescue Liselotte. It is not a burden someone with no duty to the kingdom needs to bear, and it is not a matter you need to be taking part in," Francois said, clearly seeking to gauge Rio's resolve.

"My decision was made with all these factors already in mind. If the Saint is truly alive, then in order to settle this as fast as possible… she must be killed. She is not someone that can be left to her own devices to roam."

It was rare for the warmhearted Rio to say something this extreme. He had even made this violent statement in front of Miharu and the others. The thought of their reaction was a little frightening, but he didn't intend on hiding himself from them at this point. He was a human capable of killing if he believed it to be necessary, and he was about to participate in an operation to kill someone. If he hid this from them, he would feel guilty for the rest of his life.

"It's true that I shouldn't be taking part in the matters of the Galarc Kingdom, but this is a personal matter to me. I do not wish to lose the people precious to me, and I don't want to leave their protection up to others."

That's why he was willing to do whatever dirty work necessary, Rio stated resolutely.

"I see… In that case, I gratefully accept your offer to assist. This isn't an order as the king, but a request: I am formally asking that you help subjugate Saint Erica. Do you accept this request?"

"Yes. I swear to do the best I can," Rio pledged firmly with his right hand over his chest.

"Thank you. Clement will be sending his private soldiers, but he doesn't have the best opinion of you. If his soldiers are uncooperative in the operation, you may act on your own judgment."

"Aishia will go and search for the Saint in her spirit form, so I plan on obeying the orders of the squad until an emergency arises. I don't know what will happen once the Saint is found, but I will follow your words if the need arises."

"Good. If any trouble arises with Clement after the operation, I vow to stand on your side. Do whatever you need to succeed."

"Yes, Your Majesty. But was it really okay for Your Majesty and Princess Charlotte to come here? If the beast of the land appears, you'd be in danger even at this distance…"

"We're here to subjugate a hero. This is an event that may impact the future of this kingdom. As the king, I have a duty to watch the outcome of this battle. And shouldn't you be asking that of your own companions?" Francois asked, looking around at Miharu and the others.

"I did tell them it was dangerous…" Rio's gaze was also redirected by the question.

"Everyone came here believing there's something we can do to help. We're all prepared for this, King. That's why I'm here as the hero of this kingdom as well," Satsuki said. This was something they had all discussed together. Aishia may be the only one who could fight the beast of the land with Rio, but they insisted there was a role that they could fulfill as well.

"They're all going to act as Your Majesty's guards here at this base. Sara's group will also bring out their spirits in case of an emergency."

"I see. Most of the military personnel will be leaving this base, so that is most reassuring," Francois agreed. As he said, most of the people remaining at the lake base would be noncombatants.

This was the breakdown of the one thousand troops that had been dispatched:

First, there was the reconnaissance squad that consisted of Rio and a select few. The role of this squad was to infiltrate the city and confirm Saint Erica's survival. Once they located her, they would consider subjugation.

Next, there was the capture squad led by the deputy commander of the First Order of the knights, William Lopes. Their role was to promptly take back the city once Saint Erica was confirmed either absent or subjugated. They would be on standby at the lake base until they received word from the reconnaissance team.

The final group was the base that set up the encampment. This group consisted of Francois and Charlotte, several important figures including Satsuki, and the rest of the noncombatants.

"Your Majesty."

Just then, the knight guarding the tent came inside.

"What is it?"

"Duke Gregory has arrived. He wishes to hold a strategy meeting regarding the reconnaissance team."

"Very well. Everyone besides Haruto may excuse themselves."

At Francois's order, everyone except Rio and Francois left the tent. They were replaced by Duke Gregory and his private soldiers that formed the reconnaissance team.

"Hmph. Bringing all those women to the battlefield... Hoping to get lucky, are we?"

Duke Gregory shot the girls a look of disdain as he walked past them on his way in, disregarding their strength completely. But no one heard his muttering.

"Welcome. Are those your people for the reconnaissance team?"

"Yes. I've selected the very best out of those directly under my command, Your Majesty."

At Francois's prompting, Duke Gregory introduced his soldiers proudly. There were a total of four people, and among them was Gilbert, who Rio fought the day before. When they met eyes, Gilbert gave Rio a silent nod in greeting.

Thus, the strategy meeting commenced.

"I believe the consulate is their headquarters! The refugees reported that the Saint took my son and shut herself inside the building. We should assassinate her right away!"

The first to speak was Duke Gregory, who immediately leaned forward and demanded Francois make a decision. Word of the residents of the noble district flooding the neighboring cities had arrived at the capital via the transmission artifacts this morning. That had probably increased his impatience.

However, Francois was only interested in proceeding carefully. "Calm down, Clement. Even if we go with subjugation, we must gather more information first. That is the purpose of the reconnaissance team, no?"

Duke Gregory frowned unhappily. "We already have all the information we need! My banished retainers reported seeing a woman that matched the description of the Saint. They also said she had shut herself away in the consulate. What more do you need?!"

"Even if the Saint is in the consulate, she would have naturally established her defenses. We also don't know anything about the forces she brought into the city. There's also the beast of the land to consider. In order to be absolutely prepared, we should do our due diligence," Francois said, admonishing Duke Gregory.

What beast of the land? As if she could summon a monster as big as a mountain. There's no sign of such a thing anywhere near the city right now.

Duke Gregory was extremely unsatisfied with the response. Perhaps that was why he gritted his teeth and opened his mouth. "Then what if we took a hostage to draw the Saint out? As a Saint, she values the people above all else, no? Oh, what a brilliant idea!" he said dramatically. It sounded like his emotions were causing him to speak out of desperation, but there was no telling how serious he was.

However, even if he had spoken out of desperation, Rio had a rare frown on his face. Although he saw the Saint as an enemy, he didn't want to participate in a plan that used innocent people as hostages.

"You would take your people hostage to regain your land? That makes it hard to tell which side is more justified."

Francois had a similar opinion to Rio. He expressed disapproval for Duke Gregory's plan.

What naivete! The greatest priority right now is to subjugate the Saint, is it not?!

Unable to criticize Francois directly, Duke Gregory used the last of his rationality to bite down on his lip in detestation and control his words. But he couldn't hold back the sarcasm from the question that came out next. "In that case, what would be a good plan? I would love to hear your thoughts, Your Majesty."

"I am thinking of splitting the team into two groups to scout the noble district and commoner district separately. I imagine the noble district will be heavily guarded due to the consulate within, but Haruto would be able to infiltrate from the skies with his enchanted sword."

"So you wish to send Amakawa to the noble district...?"

"Yes. Your subordinates are familiar with the land, so they should go question the commoners."

After a long pause, Duke Gregory nodded. "I understand."

There's no mistaking it... His Majesty wants to let Amakawa subjugate the Saint himself by splitting the team into two.

Although he had gained his position from his heritage, he wasn't a duke just for show. Duke Gregory wasn't foolish enough to miss Francois's true intentions. However, it was clear that any point he made would just be evaded.

I must do something... But what...?

What if Rio really subjugated the Saint like this? The resolution of this incident would be entirely credited to Rio, indebting Duke Gregory to him for the rest of his life. He wasn't willing to bear that humiliation.

It's my territory. I cannot let Amakawa resolve this incident...

If this was how Francois was going to be, then he had no choice but to convince him with the result. Just like how Haruto Amakawa once won over Francois's trust... That was the conclusion Duke Gregory came to, rivalry burning in his heart.

After that, the meeting concluded.

"We will excuse ourselves now. My men need to prepare for departure."

Duke Gregory led Gilbert and the other three men out of the tent, leaving Rio and Francois behind.

"Haruto. I'm sure you know already, but if you find the Saint in the consulate, you may engage her without contacting Clement. You may say that I ordered you to do so," Francois said to Rio.

At the same time, outside the tent...

"Follow me. I have something important to discuss," Duke Gregory said, leading his four men away.

✤ Chapter 8 ✤
Assassination

Roughly one hour after the strategy meeting, the five members of the reconnaissance team—including Rio and Gilbert—had successfully infiltrated the territory capital of Greille. Or rather, more aptly put, they had donned traveler outfits and walked straight through the gate.

"It was easier to get in than I expected..." Rio muttered in surprise, looking around at the street immediately past the gate.

There had been some armed laymen standing watch at the gate, but they merely asked them a few questions before letting them through. The city had been stolen by the enemy, so it wouldn't have been strange for the gates to be closed to all outsiders. It was rather anticlimactic.

"The gatekeepers weren't wearing the military uniforms of the duke's army. The city is most definitely being occupied. Although rather sloppily..."

"They looked like complete laymen to me. The abilities of the enemy cannot be much better," Duke Gregory's private soldiers said to Rio.

Out of the five of them, Rio was the youngest, but he also had the highest status. Duke Gregory considered him an enemy, but his subordinates had to treat him with respect.

Being able to walk in freely means the residents can walk out freely, right? Everyone's walking around so normally, it's hard to believe the city's been occupied...

It was almost like they had no intention of protecting the city they had captured. Even if the Saint could control the beast of the land, wasn't this a little too defenseless of them? It was almost like they were being lured in, giving Rio an eerie impression. At any rate—

"It may be obvious, but that's Duke Gregory's consulate, right?" Rio asked, pointing at the imposing fortress standing at the back of the city. It was the largest building in the city, and it appeared to be built very sturdily.

"Yes, that's right."

Aishia, can you check out the building first?

Got it.

At Rio's order, Aishia began moving alone in her spirit form. At the same time...

"If things continue like this, the plan should be easy to execute."

"Yeah."

Two of Duke Gregory's soldiers whispered between each other.

"How eerie..." Gilbert mumbled.

"What is?" Rio had been standing next to him, so he had overheard his mumbling.

"Nothing. It just feels like they're asking us to sneak in."

"Do you think it's a trap?"

"Yes, but that doesn't matter. We're not on some shopping errand, so we can't turn around either way. We can only fulfill our duty."

"Right." Gilbert had a similar opinion to Rio, but knowing it was a trap didn't mean they could cease their infiltration.

"Okay, we'll be moving separately from here. When the city bell rings twice, gather in the square at the end of this street. Sir Amakawa, please investigate the consulate in the noble district. We will go around the market and question the residents."

"Understood. Until then."

Rio split up from the other four. He headed towards a quiet alleyway to take to the skies and fly into the noble district.

"Let's go accomplish our mission as well."

Once Rio was completely out of sight, the four remaining men headed for the busy square.

Rio rose to the skies from the alleyway and flew straight towards the consulate. It took less than a minute for him to reach the noble district, where the streets were deserted.

With all the residents banished, this place is completely bare.

Duke Gregory's vassals who originally lived in the noble district had been banished from the city, so there was naturally no sign of anyone around.

But I didn't think there wouldn't be a single guard...

Rio checked the houses and streets of the noble district one by one, but there wasn't a soul to be seen. The gate connecting the noble and commoner districts was closed, but there was nothing stopping them from infiltrating on foot.

It's really as though they're inviting us in. Is it possible the Saint has left the city already?

The lack of a single guard was what made things truly suspicious. With things like this, it was more reasonable to assume they had deserted the city after capturing it.

Aishia, have you entered the building?

Rio made contact with Aishia, who had begun investigating in her spirit form already.

Yeah.

A reply came immediately.

There's no one on this side of town. What about you?

I haven't finished checking every room yet, but there's barely anyone here.

Barely...meaning there were some?

There was a family of five locked in a room guarded by two people. I think they might be the hostages, but I didn't see the Saint.

It seemed like the consulate was mostly deserted as well, but it was unlikely the Saint had left if the hostages were still being guarded.

The hostage is probably Duke Gregory's son... And if there are so few people in the building, I can probably sneak inside as well. I'll be there soon.

Okay. I'll finish checking the rest of the rooms first. Wait on the roof for me.

All right.

Thus, Rio descended for the consulate. He landed on the roof and waited for less than a minute.

"Haruto."

Aishia appeared less than a minute later.

"Did you find her?"

"No. There's no one in the building other than the hostages and their guards."

"I see..." Rio tapped a hand over his mouth, pondering what to do. Eventually, he came to a decision. "Then let's cast an illusion over the guards and question them."

"Okay. I'll cast it in my spirit form."

"Please."

Once the two agreed to a plan, they entered the building. Aishia led the way through the corridors in her material form, pausing at the corner before their destination. There, she returned to her spirit form.

Those two are the guards?

Yes.

They switched to communicating with each other telepathically.

The two guards in the corridor didn't seem to be expecting any infiltrators, as they were chatting to each other casually while lounging on the chairs they had brought outside of the room. It was clear they were relaxed.

I'm going to cast the illusion. Ready?

Whenever you are.

I'll call you over once I'm done.

With that, Aishia set off to commence the plan. Several seconds later, she materialized behind the two seated guards without any warning.

"Hmm...?"

She touched the two of them on the backs of their heads. The two guards soon had blank looks on their faces.

"Haruto, the illusion worked," Aishia called down the corridor.

"Thanks."

"They believe you're one of their allies that just returned from patrol."

"I see. Then... There's something I'd like to ask you," Rio said to the two guards.

"Oh, you're back already?"

"What's up?"

As Aishia said, the two believed Rio was one of their allies that had just returned. The two of them had been looking downwards, but they lifted their faces at the sound of Rio's voice.

Rio hesitated over what kind of tone he should use when addressing them, but he decided to go with a casual approach as allies. "Err, where did Saint Erica go again?"

"Saint Erica went out to observe the city."

"She went out to the city? Whereabouts?"

"I don't know that much. Probably the old commoner district."

"Right… So when will she be back?"

"Don't know that either. She said she'd be back by evening."

"I see…"

He had thought it was more likely for her to be inside the consulate, but it seemed his visit was for nothing.

"Who are the hostages inside?"

Since he was here already, he decided to gather some extra information.

"The family of the noble governing this city. I believe his name was Greg-something…"

"Duke Gregory."

"That's it."

So it's his son after all…

For a brief moment, he considered saving them right away. But if he did that, the guards would notice their disappearance as soon as the illusion wore off. His mobility would be lowered if he rescued the hostages now, preventing him from investigating properly.

"Did Saint Erica say what to do with the hostages?"

If they weren't in danger of being killed, he wouldn't have to save them immediately. With that in mind, Rio asked after the treatment of the hostages.

"The army of this kingdom could attack us, so we're leaving them alive for a while."

"I see…"

In which case, there was no need to rescue them immediately.

"I have another question. It's about the others that came with us..."

The lack of security was also bothering him, so Rio decided to question them more about the forces on their side and gather information.

Accompanied by seven of her companions, Erica was visiting the residential area of the commoner district roughly ten minutes earlier.

The purpose of her visit was to heal the sick and injured. She gathered people who had broken bones, bad backs, or other injuries, and treated them all for free. A long line extended from the vacant house she had turned into a temporary clinic.

"Ooh..."

Presently, inside the house, a man who had broken his leg after falling from the rooftop he had been working on was gazing at the divine light glowing from the end of the Divine Arms.

"That should do it. Can you stand?" Erica asked.

"Yes..." The man first stood up by putting his weight on his uninjured leg, then slowly lowered his previously broken leg and carefully put more weight on it.

"Wha...?!" The pain he had feared was nowhere to be found.

"I-It doesn't hurt! The pain is gone!"

The man stomped with the leg once, then twice. He then began walking around the room in joy.

"Oh, that's wonderful, dear!" a woman who appeared to be his wife exclaimed, hitting him on the back.

"Y-Yeah. But that hurts. You'll break my back next."

The woman slapped his back harder. "Don't be silly!"

"Oww! Jeez, I said that hurts…" the man chuckled in spite of his words.

"Go on, thank the Saint properly."

"Right. Thank you, Saint Erica!"

Erica turned to the man with a fake smile. "I'm glad to be of help."

"Are you sure you don't want payment?" the man asked worriedly.

"As I said earlier, I don't need it. I may take a few bronze coins as payment next time, but my objective today is to get to know the residents of this city. That is why it's free."

"I see. You've truly been a great help."

"The new lord of the territory is amazing, isn't she? I heard it normally costs a gold coin to receive magic healing."

"Yes, we were just despairing over how we'd survive until his leg healed."

There was no such thing as insurance in this world, so if anything happened to the breadwinner of a family, they were normally left without a means of sustenance.

"I've treated many people since this morning, but it seems there are many families struggling to make a living. I'm thinking of giving the residents an allowance in the near future, so please use that to pad your finances," Erica informed them.

"Hmm? Are you giving us something?"

"Yes. It will either be in the form of cash, or of something of high value you can sell yourselves."

"Why are we receiving something like that from you, the new lord?" While they had paid taxes many times in the past, they had never received any money from the lord before. The couple tilted their heads in confusion.

"It's my present to everyone, to celebrate my induction as the new ruler of this city. Think of it as part of the taxes you have paid until now being returned to you."

"Are you sure…?"

"Yes. I will discuss the details on a later day. I have to heal the next person now, so please leave."

"Right…" The couple made to leave the house, still bewildered. But just before they went out the front door, they exchanged glances with each other and turned back to wave happily.

"Thank you, Saint Erica!" they said.

Erica smiled cheerfully as she saw the couple off.

"Next person waiting, please," she called out the door. Just as the next patient was about to enter, a man ran inside, panting.

"Help! It's an emergency!"

He wasn't one of the subordinates Erica brought along from their homeland, so he was probably a resident of the city.

"What's the matter?"

"Nobles have gathered in the square! They're saying to bring the Saint!"

"So they've come," Erica muttered, smirking to herself. She then turned to the man. "Let's go. Show me the way quickly."

With that, she hurried towards the scene of the commotion, bringing her subordinates as guards. Some residents followed them curiously, making the residential area bustle with activity. There was a man who watched it all happen from the shadows.

That's the Saint?

It was Gilbert, the assassin hired by Duke Gregory. He had never seen her face before, but the woman who ran past matched the description he was given.

I thought she'd be in the consulate, but she was unexpectedly close by. How fortunate for Duke Gregory.

Blending in with the curious onlookers, he followed after Erica.

The square where the commotion was occurring was a few minutes away from Erica's temporary clinic.

Duke Gregory's three subordinates had taken a young mother and her daughter hostage. A crowd of residents from the city were watching on from afar. Eventually, the crowd in the square split to reveal the Saint.

"Hey…"

The attention of the three men was drawn towards Erica. When Erica saw the captured parent and child, she covered her mouth in horror.

"Oh, the inhumanity…"

"So you're the Saint!" one of Duke Gregory's men shouted.

"Yes, that is what everyone calls me. I beg of you, please release that family," Erica called out to the three men.

"Hmph. Listen, all of you! This woman is no saint! She's a witch!" the man yelled loudly for the square to hear. But there was no credibility to the words of a man who had taken a powerless mother and child hostage. To the onlookers, it was clear which side was the villain they should be glaring at.

However, for the men who had taken the family hostage, the antipathy of the civilians was inconsequential. As long as the Saint was killed, the people could be silenced later.

"The kingdom won't stay silent at the capture of this historical city. The army is marching towards the city right now, and they will seize back this city upon our order! You have invoked

Duke Gregory's rage. He laments the inaction of you foolish citizens—for your failure to take back this city, you will be shown no mercy!"

Duke Gregory's subordinate denounced Erica while threatening the residents in the square. The expressions of the residents stiffened.

The man noticed their fear and continued. "However, the benevolent duke has decided to give you all a chance! If you do not wish to be charged with treason, kill that woman immediately! Then you will all be pardoned!"

"..."

The gazes of the residents were drawn to Erica. Everyone looked nervous. The people that had accompanied Erica here from their homeland surrounded her to protect her.

"Am I really...a witch?" Erica said to the quiet square, her words seemingly directed to no one.

"That's right! You're a witch! That's why you must die! Kill her!" Duke Gregory's men demanded.

"..."

But no one leaped into action. They were afraid of the army, but they were similarly opposed to the idea of dirtying their own hands—either that, or this was a revolt.

What a farce... Gilbert thought, having watched the chain of events take place. He was currently located in the crowd behind Erica, prepared to assassinate her at any moment. In the current situation, it shouldn't be a difficult task.

As for why he had to go along with such a bothersome plan, Duke Gregory had promised rewards to whoever was able to complete the job, which the three men were all vying for. If Gilbert ignored their plans and killed Erica here, he could face some troublesome accusations later.

The plan was for someone else to hit Erica first so that Gilbert could blend in with the chaos and assassinate her. But the scene he was being made to watch was rather frustrating.

I assume this is their attempt to demonstrate the discord between the Saint and the people, but I don't see why they would make such an ugly show of themselves.

Humans were foul creatures. That was why Gilbert made a living of assassination, and after taking the lives of countless people, he could affirm that it was the truth. Nothing changed just because his target was a disciple of the Six Wise Gods. He had volunteered for the role of Satsuki's instructor out of the faint hope that heroes were special existences, but that Satsuki was just another human. She would eventually end up in the same place as the others, he had thought in disappointment.

Hurry up and show your true selves already, Gilbert thought, glaring around at the crowd coldly. If they didn't want to be trampled by the army, they had to murder Erica. That was what they were all thinking, yet no one moved. They were ashamed at the thought of dirtying their own hands. That was the mood that hung over the square, until…

"There's no need for everyone to dirty their hands!" Erica yelled to the crowd. She then turned to the three subordinates. "If I die, will you release that family?"

"Yeah."

"If I die, will the people of this city be spared from the army outside?"

"Yeah, they will! What, are you considering suicide? If you really want what's best for these fools, kill yourself!" the men taunted, believing she was incapable of doing so.

However…

"Very well."

Erica immediately materialized her bishop's staff, grabbing it with both hands. She then lifted it high enough to aim the end at her chest and pierced it through her heart without any hesitation.

"Wha—!"

"What in the world...?!"

Duke Gregory's three subordinates and the crowd of onlookers were all speechless. Even Gilbert had forgotten his mission and was merely watching on in shock.

"Heh heh," Erica giggled, gazing up at the sky with her hands grasped around the staff. She almost looked like a sculpture giving prayer to the gods.

"S-Saint Erica!" The escorts that had accompanied her from the Holy Democratic Republic of Erica rushed over to her in a panic.

"Ohh, what a tragedy…!"

"Help! Does anyone know healing magic?!"

"Someone, please! Please save the Saint!"

They truly believed Erica was dying. Their confusion was no act—to them, it was as though the world were ending.

But there was someone who was laughing in joy, having witnessed everything up close.

"Ha… Ha ha ha! Wonderful! What a masterpiece!"

It was Gilbert. He had always believed that humans were their ugliest when they were killed unfairly. But what about now?

How beautiful…! Has there ever been a more beautiful death than this? She is no witch! Yes, she is a saint! A true Saint!

She had taken her own life without hesitation, for the sake of some commoners who didn't even know her. She died gripping her staff in prayer, as though she believed in the beauty of mankind.

Gilbert grasped his own hands in prayer, holding his head up towards the skies.

Oh, Six Wise Gods! I give you my sincerest thanks for letting me witness this moment. I was wrong! I believed humans to be ugly creatures. That is why I dedicated my life to assassination. But humans are beautiful! She has taught me this! If she isn't a Saint, then who in this world is?!

He then walked over to Erica, who was still on her knees, and beckoned Duke Gregory's three subordinates over. "Now, come and confirm for yourself! She is most certainly dead!"

"…"

The three men exchanged looks with each other before approaching Erica, dragging the mother and daughter along.

"Did she really stab herself in the heart…?"

"No way…"

"Just what was she thinking?"

The men looked down at the kneeling Erica in disgust.

"People like you would never understand," Gilbert muttered loathingly. Then, at a speed faster than anyone around them could see, he flicked his right hand out.

"Huh…?"

A strange sensation immediately overcame the three men. Their vision blurred as they suddenly felt like they were falling. One beat later, pain ran through their heads. Three thunks could be heard in unison, and the world spun dizzily.

"What?!"

The men realized their heads were rolling along the ground. They looked up at Gilbert, who was glaring down at them in disdain. His hands were empty, but they could tell he was the one who had done this to them.

Why?!

They moved their mouths, but no sound came out. In place of their dead voices, the mother and daughter who were held hostage screamed.

Gilbert turned around to the crowd and held his arms up. "She—the Saint—taught me the beauty of mankind! She sacrificed herself for the lives of strangers…" he called out, loud enough for the square to hear.

"Th-That's right…!"

"The Saint was… Saint Erica was…!"

Those words stabbed deep into the hearts of the people who came from the Holy Democratic Republic of Erica. They clung to Erica's kneeling body and wailed in grief over her death.

"Can you all forgive something like this?!" Gilbert yelled like a changed person.

No, perhaps he really *was* changed.

"I cannot forgive my own disgraceful actions! That is why I will confess to my sins! I infiltrated this city as an assassin, hired by Duke Gregory! Yes, I was on the side of these three men who came here to kill the Saint!"

Still in a fevered craze from earlier, Gilbert revealed himself as an assassin.

"However, I have realized the truth! After seeing the Saint offer her own life to protect everyone here, I have realized it! I...was wrong...! I... I cannot forgive myself..."

He continued to blame himself in shame.

"No...!" a young man clinging to Erica shouted, getting to his feet. "It's not your fault! The true disgrace is the noble class! That's what happened here too... The ones who killed Saint Erica are the nobles who took the people they should have protected as hostages! Isn't that right?!"

He cried as he raised his voice, questioning every resident watching on.

"..."

No one said anything to confirm or deny him. But in their hearts, they probably agreed with the young man and Gilbert. They were all looking down in guilt.

"How can you all forgive them?! They've always suppressed us with their power! They threaten us into subordination! I cannot forgive that! Saint Erica came to this city to fight against such tyranny! Yet...!"

After yelling his heart out, the young man hung his head in silence.

"We have to avenge her…" someone eventually murmured.

"Yes, we must…!"

"Let's fight! Let's take on the army outside the city!"

The people from the Holy Democratic Republic of Erica began a call for a war of revenge. Their passionate belief in Erica seemed to transmit to the residents of the city, who began to adopt expressions of resolution.

"Yeah! Let us fight too!"

"Me too!"

"We can't forgive what they've done!"

"Grab your weapons!"

Once the dam broke, the residents began blurting out their pent-up emotions.

But there was a different voice among them.

"You must not…" Erica, who should have been dead, suddenly said.

"Wha—?!"

The people closest to her stirred at the sound of her voice. The next moment, the staff in her chest vanished into thin air.

Light wrapped around her body, rapidly closing the hole in her chest. The unrealistic scene was almost divine.

Everyone was speechless. Gilbert trembled as he witnessed Erica reviving before himself, letting out a noise of joy. "O-Ooh…"

"I will be the one to fight. This is a crusade. As a hero and the Saint, I must be the one to protect everyone. That's why…!"

Erica materialized her staff once more, holding it in her right hand. She stabbed the end into the ground and staggered to her feet. There wasn't a soul who wasn't moved by the sight of the weak Saint declaring to fight after a miraculous revival.

"I will fight in everyone's place! I was given this power to do that! I summon thee, beast of the land!" Erica yelled, raising her staff high.

Several seconds later...

"WROOOOOOH!"

The roar of a destructive monster echoed throughout Duke Gregory's territory.

✤ Chapter 9 ✤
Crusade

The beast of the land appeared on the outskirts of Greille. Its roar echoed through the air, reaching the Galarc army stationed on the plains away from the city, the base by the lake behind them, and even the neighboring cities and villages.

"That's the beast of the land that His Majesty described… I had my doubts, but…"

Leading the Galarc army was the deputy commander of the First Order of the Galarc Knights, William Lopes. With his enchanted spear in hand, he trembled at the presence of the beast. Even someone with as much experience as him was almost frozen to the core and paralyzed with fear.

"We must retreat immediately! All forces, retreat! Retreat! Fall back to the base at the lake! Change courses now!"

However, William was a brilliant commander. Having received orders from King Francois in advance, he yelled the retreat order to the troops.

The troops were all professional soldiers with training and expertise. It was also fortunate that Francois had limited the scale of the army so that they could be more mobile in an emergency. But the fact the army was only composed of cavalry—another decision made with mobility in mind—backfired. The horses and griffins that had been raised for the military were so frightened, they wouldn't move as ordered. Some people were thrown from their horses, and the army fell into disarray.

Inside the city, the residents were similarly trembling at the appearance of the beast of the land, which was the size of a small mountain.

"..."

It stood outside the city with its back to the residents—if it had been facing them, they probably would have panicked. No, it wouldn't be strange for them to panic anyway, if they continued to have no explanation regarding the beast. However...

"Everyone! That is a miracle created by Saint Erica!"

"It is the beast of the land, and it is our ally! Rest assured, it's on our side!"

"Saint Erica is both a saint and a hero!"

The people from the Holy Democratic Republic of Erica all knew about the beast of the land. They immediately called out to the residents, assuring them it was friendly.

"The beast of the land obeys my orders! As proof, you can see how it remains still as it waits for my command. I will now give the beast an order—the order to protect everyone and eliminate the Galarc army outside these walls!" Erica said, trying to emphasize the beast of the land's harmlessness.

"Can you forgive them all?! They declared you traitors without listening to what you had to say. They treat you like filth and throw you away. Can you forgive the noble class for that?!" she asked the people, stirring them up. "I cannot! The way nobility decides the value of others and places itself on top is an unforgivable evil of this world! Such people must be erased from this world! That is why I ask you all—can you truly forgive the royalty and nobility outside this city?!"

Her earnest words seemed to strike the hearts of those listening, as voices began to rise across the square.

"I can't forgive them!"

"That's right!"

The frustration from constantly being oppressed normally had nowhere to go. But now they were being told it was okay to release those feelings, which was why their emotions exploded.

"However, humans must not fight for hatred! Fighting for hatred is another evil—you must not attack others out of rage!" Erica preached her ideals. "Judging the evil in this world is a special duty bestowed upon the gods. You are not gods, so you must remain good through your actions!"

Erica continued calling to the people, advising them not to turn to evil.

"Vengeance is mine. I will reply. Your rage is my rage! That is why, as the hero and agent of god, I will execute judgment on everyone's behalf!" she declared grandly.

"Yeaaaaaah!"

"Great Hero!"

"Saint Erica!"

"We're not afraid of the duke! The army doesn't scare us!"

"We'll follow you and your beast of the land!"

"Those with the will to fight, rise!"

"Saint Erica will lead us to victory!"

"It's a crusade! Yes, this is a crusade!"

Voices called through the square one after another.

The spirits of the people had risen to the max. There were some parts of the Saint's speech they didn't understand, but her feelings had been conveyed.

Yet, for a brief instant, there was a cold look in Erica's eyes.

"The evil will receive the divine punishment they deserve! Everyone, this is a crusade! Now go, beast of the land!" she ordered.

However, on the head of the divine beast scowling outside the city like a guard dog was a young man in black, swinging down his sword. It was Rio. Immediately after he finished swinging, a slash of light was released, swallowing the giant head. The four-legged beast's huge body stumbled, sinking down.

"So he survived. I knew it."

Erica smirked, looking up at Rio above.

Rio and Aishia noticed the beast of the land's appearance just as they finished their interrogation and were about to leave the building.

"WROOOOOOOH!"

The monstrous roar could be heard through the thick walls.

"Oh no…" Rio mumbled bitterly.

He was inside the building so he couldn't see what had happened, but there was only one thing he knew that made such a noise. At the same time, the information he gained from the interrogation was rendered effectively useless.

I'll go check. Aishia immediately turned into her spirit form, slipping through the wall.

I'll be right behind you, Rio replied, already running. He flung open the balcony doors of the building and burst outside, rising straight to the skies.

"I knew it...!"

The monster was dozens of meters tall, making it extremely easy to spot.

It hasn't started rampaging yet.

Like Aishia reported, the beast of the land was still standing frozen for some reason. Far in the distance, William could be seen hurriedly getting the Galarc troops to turn back. The beast had its back turned to the city, so it was yet to notice Rio floating behind it.

The worst is yet to happen. I have to hurry.

Without waiting for Aishia's response, Rio approached the beast of the land.

Okay...

Aishia seemed to be bothered by something, her reply coming one beat late.

This was because her vision in spirit form was different to that of her materialized form. Right now, she was capable of visually seeing the waves of spiritual presences she normally couldn't detect.

What have I forgotten?

Once again, she was on the verge of remembering something. Every time she looked at the beast of the land, that feeling intensified. She just needed one last push.

Aishia?

Rio was unable to see Aishia in her spirit form, but he probably sensed something strange about her half-hearted response earlier. He called out her name worriedly.

...What?

There was a slight pause, but Aishia responded in her usual tone. In the time she had been absorbed in her thoughts, Rio had reached the skies above the square where Erica was located.

Erica was in the middle of giving her speech to the residents. Whether it was because she was mid-speech or because she was yet

413

to give an order, the beast of the land wasn't moving. Either way, Erica was most certainly in control of the beast.

The Saint is in the square. Three of the people we came with are dead. The man named Gilbert is still alive, but...

Did those men do something to the Saint?

Most likely. That's probably what incited the residents. I'll take this chance to make a preemptive strike on the beast. Please go and report this situation to His Majesty at the base. Tell them to leave us and run.

All right.

I'm going to start gathering magic essence.

Rio drew his sword. He wavered for a moment, wondering whether to attack Erica or the beast of the land first, but decided on the one that could do more damage. Besides, there was no guarantee the beast of the land would disappear if Erica was defeated first anyway.

I'll be right back.

Aishia began moving in her spirit form. She could travel faster if she materialized and accelerated herself with spirit arts, but she didn't want to risk being detected by the beast. That's why she planned on waiting for the moment Rio attacked before materializing.

"As the hero and agent of god, I will execute judgment on everyone's behalf!"

On the ground, Erica's speech was reaching its climax. The residents began roaring in excitement.

Okay...

Rio was able to refine the magic essence required. He condensed all the essence into his sword, not letting the slightest amount escape.

"The evil will receive the divine punishment they deserve! Everyone, this is a crusade! Now go, beast of the land!"

As Erica was saying those words, Rio closed in on the beast of the land from several hundred meters away, aiming straight for its head.

"Hah!" He slammed a powerful strike into its vital point. The beast's head was enveloped in light, stumbling forward as its four legs were shaken off-balance.

That wasn't enough!

Rio readied his sword once again, promptly changing course midair and aiming for the beast's rear. The snake heads at the end of its three tails had their mouths open, ready to fire a blast of light—until Rio slashed at them with a similar blade of light.

After that, he continued refining magic essence to create giant blasts of light aimed at the base of the tail and the body of the beast.

"GRAAAAAAH!"

The beast of the land suddenly leaped upwards, attempting to blow away Rio floating above its back.

"Huh?!" Rio used the wind to move like a leaf, evading the beast. The beast of the land was still full of life, baring its full hostility towards Rio. It had been damaged by the attacks Rio landed, but the wounds were healing before his eyes.

As I suspected... It was pretending to be dead last time I cut its neck.

He still had no idea how much damage it would take to defeat this beast. But he had to try anyway.

Meanwhile, in the skies away from the city, Aishia materialized.

"RAH!"

The beast of the land whipped around in her direction with a start. It glared at Aishia with clear hostility, and the three snake heads at the end of its tail opened their mouths at her. Magic essence gathered so that it could fire a blast.

415

"RRAAAGH?!"

However, Rio landed a slash of wind at the beast's abdomen. The hundred-meter-long torso of the beast shook violently in the air.

"Your opponent is over here." He didn't believe it could understand words, but he spoke to it anyway.

"GRAAAAAAH!"

The beast of the land glared at Rio in annoyance and roared. Thus, the battle between Rio and the beast of the land resumed.

In her materialized form, Aishia made the last five kilometers of the distance to the lake in half a minute. She spotted Miharu and the others outside a tent and landed beside them.

Celia, Satsuki, Francois, and everyone else were all watching the beast of the land with pained expressions.

"Ai-chan!" Among them, Miharu called out, running up to Aishia first.

"Spirit girl—Aishia. Is that the beast of the land? It seems like it is fighting someone…" Francois asked with a tense look.

"Yes. Haruto is keeping it from running wild. The army is pulling back to this base right now, so flee on the enchanted airships immediately once they get here."

"I see… All right, I understand."

"Also…"

Aishia was about to continue speaking, when—

"Is that the beast of the land?! Amakawa is fighting that thing?!" Duke Gregory shouted from beside Francois.

"That's what she just said."

"No, I just didn't think it would be a monster like that…!"

"Hmm. That's because you didn't believe the beast of the land existed to begin with. But there's no time to be dealing with you right now. Wait, Clement," Francois said, dismissing Duke Gregory in annoyance.

"I'm going to fight with him. Don't worry about us when you flee."

"All right. Sorry about that."

But Duke Gregory ignored the situation at hand. "Wait! Is Amakawa fighting that monster?! What happened to eliminating the Saint?! Did he fail?!" he continued, hounding Aishia with questions.

"That's not what happened. Haruto and I were inside the consulate when it woke up. We saw three of your subordinates dead in the square. They probably started something."

Aishia explained what happened, then gave her own guess as to why.

Francois immediately regarded Duke Gregory with suspicion. "Clement. What did you order your men to do?"

"Wha...? I-I know nothing! That woman is rambling pure nonsense! Why did you even infiltrate the consulate? And why were you even with the reconnaissance team in the first place?!" Duke Gregory wailed in a panic.

"Enough of this, Clement! Are you really going to make a bigger mess of this situation and risk my rage?"

"Ah..."

Duke Gregory paled, snapping his mouth shut at Francois's uncharacteristic explosion of anger.

"This is an emergency situation. You should prepare for evacuation. Your reply?"

"U-Understood. I apologize for making a fuss..."

Gritting his teeth down on the mix of panic, uncertainty, anger, and fear, Duke Gregory left them.

"I'm going to go back, then. The Saint is alive, so we have to defeat her too," Aishia said, showing no interest in Duke Gregory as she turned around. But just as she was about to fly off again, Gouki called out to her.

"One moment please, Lady Aishia."

"Yes?"

"Leave the subjugation of the Saint to Kayoko and me. You two focus on defeating the beast of the land. We will depart right after you."

"Okay. Thank you. The Saint was in the square in the city. But she might have moved by now."

"All right."

"See you, then."

With that, Aishia flew off.

"You heard her. Let's go, Kayoko."

"Yes, dear."

It was only natural for them to assist their master. Kayoko expressed no objections as she nodded quietly.

"In that case, please ride on Ariel. I will accompany you," Orphia said, offering Ariel as a means of transport.

"We'd appreciate that," Gouki accepted, bowing his head. "Let's leave right away. We should head for an open space for our departure."

Then, he started to walk away, heading for an open space where Ariel could materialize, when...

"Hold on!" Celia and Liselotte stood together. Aria, who was behind them, was the one who had stopped Gouki.

"The two of you don't know what the Saint looks like. Would you consider taking me along?" Aria asked, seeking Gouki and Kayoko's permission to accompany them. She then turned to her master, Liselotte, to do the same. "Lady Liselotte, I owe a great debt to Sir Amakawa. I also have a score to settle with Saint Erica. You are my appointed lord and master, so please grant me permission to go."

"You may go, but you have to return," Liselotte agreed, respecting Aria's intentions. She then turned to Gouki and Kayoko. "She's my most skilled subordinate, so I believe she will be of help to you. Is it all right if she accompanies you?"

"We would be glad to have her. Let's get going."

Gouki left, taking Kayoko, Aria, and Orphia with him.

"We'll focus on protecting the base. The beast of the land's attacks may fly this way," Sara suggested.

"Hel and Ifritah might need to help out too," Alma agreed.

Hearing that, Miharu offered to supply her magic essence. "In that case, I'll provide the essence they need to materialize. You two should save your essence."

Meanwhile, Rio was engaged with the beast of the land in a close-range battle.

"GRAAAGH!"

The beast swatted at Rio as though he were an annoying fly buzzing around its body. It wouldn't have been surprising for a creature of its size to create earthquakes with every leap, but Erica must have ordered it not to damage the city, as its landings were surprisingly light-footed.

"RAH?!"

Each time Rio spotted an opening, he would envelop his blade in wind and light and create a slashing attack that was twenty meters in length, aiming it at the beast's body.

At a glance, fighting at such a close distance seemed dangerous—but the most troublesome attack the beast of the land possessed was the breath attack it released from its mouth and tails. By sticking close to its body, Rio succeeded in sealing those moves. In that sense, he seemed to have the advantage. However...

It heals rapidly every time I damage it.

His attacks themselves seemed to be effective, but there was no way of telling how much so. Was there no limit to the beast's recovery? How much damage was required for a fatal wound? Would it eventually fall if he continued attacking it? There was no way of knowing.

I can at least buy some time, he thought.

"GRRR..."

The beast of the land halted its swinging at Rio and stopped moving.

What is it thinking?

He had a bad feeling about it, but Rio continued his attacks.

"RRRGH!" The beast of the land motionlessly endured it; in fact, it seemed like it wasn't affected at all.

What?! Just as Rio released another slash, the beast twisted its body. The next moment, it used Rio's attack to sever its own tails.

"RAAAGH!"

The three tails started flying of their own will, accelerating towards the Galarc army that was still retreating—and the base with Miharu and the others past them.

"No!" Rio tried to pursue the tails in a fluster.

"GRAAAH!"

But the moment he turned his back, the beast of the land let out a breath from its mouth.

From the square where Erica was located, it appeared as though Rio had been swallowed by the beast's breath.

"WHOOO!"

Cheers erupted from the residents. They were worried when Rio first appeared out of nowhere and put up an even fight with the beast, so they were clearly relieved at this turn of events.

"Ha! Ha ha!"

"He got blown away!"

"There'll be nothing left of him!"

They all rejoiced.

"Did you see that? His attacks are powerless before the beast of the land! But the reverse does not apply! He was the strongest warrior of the enemy, and he is now defeated! This is the moment to march forward! Let us go!"

Erica chose this moment to start running for the gate of the city.

"Follow Saint Erica's lead!"

"Victory will be ours with Saint Erica's guidance!"

"The kingdom's army won't stand a chance either!"

"Chaaarge!"

"Raaah!"

The residents were completely swept away by their elation. Most of the people in the square hadn't been carrying weapons on them, yet they rushed out the gate completely unarmed.

Meanwhile, Rio had just accelerated to the side, escaping the attack range of the breath aimed at his back. However, doing so caused him to fall far behind the tails flying ahead. Rio chased after them as fast as he could.

"GRAAAH!"

The beast of the land used another breath to obstruct Rio from pursuing. "Ngh!"

Aishia would protect the base by the lake even if Rio didn't take chase, but there was a chance the retreating army could suffer damages.

Just then, a thick beam of light fired over from the direction of the lake. It struck all three of the snake-headed tails in succession, repelling them midair.

Aishia!

Rio could see it was Aishia who had cast the art. She proceeded to create huge orbs of light and fired them with rapid succession and precision. An intense explosion occurred with each impact, swallowing the helpless tails.

"Hssshah!" the tails hissed.

"GRRRAH!" roared the beast; it tried to interrupt Aishia with a breath.

"I won't let you!" Rio shouted, immediately cutting deeply into the beast's neck to throw off its aim. The tails suffered a barrage of Aishia's attacks in that time, eventually becoming unable to maintain their shape. They dispersed into the air like a spirit leaving its material form, disappearing completely.

"Sorry I'm late," Aishia said, appearing right beside Rio.

"No, you came just in time. Thank you."

You really saved me, Rio was about to say, when—

"GRUUUH!"

The beast of the land opened its mouth wide, accumulating magic essence for its next attack.

"Hah!"

"Out of the way."

Rio and Aishia both activated their spirit arts before it could attack. They both created huge fireballs in the same breath, firing them into the beast's mouth.

"RAH...!"

The explosion in its mouth shut the beast up all at once. Aishia took that chance to give Rio an update on what happened.

"Gouki and the others said to leave the Saint to them. They asked that we focus on taking down the beast of the land," she said.

For a brief moment, Rio looked opposed to the idea of Gouki bringing more people into this dangerous area. But he didn't have the leisure to handle both when the beast kept regenerating on the spot, so he resolved himself to his only option.

"I see. In that case..."

"Yup. We'll defeat this thing."

Even if they couldn't defeat it, they had to suppress it to prevent it from causing any damage to the others. Rio and Aishia immediately turned to attack the beast of the land together. By then, the beast had almost completely regenerated the tails on its body. "UUURH!"

Rio and Aishia fired large orbs of light to prevent its full regeneration. It was hard for Rio to reach the body and three tails in a single attack, but he was fighting together with Aishia right now.

I'll focus my attacks on the front half of its body.

Then I'll take care of the rear half and tails.

Thanks. Not having to worry about the tail attacks will be a great help.

They communicated telepathically while flying at high speed, planning their strategy. Not having to allocate as much brainpower to evasion made it much easier for Rio to fight.

There may be a limit to its regenerative ability. Let's suppress it by sticking close to its body and attacking in waves!

423

Got it.

The two of them had the best coordination and support for each other. The beast of the land attempted to ward them off by swinging its tails and expelling its breath, but...

"GRAAAH!"

None of its attacks made contact. In no time at all, the two of them had begun to overpower the beast of the land.

At the same time, Ariel was flying high in the skies above. Riding on its back were Gouki, Kayoko, Aria, and Orphia. They had a clear view of Rio and Aishia suppressing the beast of the land below.

"Wow, watching those two fight together is something else," Gouki murmured. The beast of the land in the distance almost seemed pitiful. But despite that thought, he observed the battlefront carefully.

"Hmm. There's a crowd rushing out of the city," he said, spotting the running group with his spirit arts-enhanced eyesight.

"The person leading the group at the front is Saint Erica."

Aria identified the Saint to Gouki and Kayoko.

"Excellent. That makes things easy." Gouki grinned.

"Let us go, dear."

"Indeed!"

The couple leaped from Ariel's back as though they were merely stepping off a small platform. But instead of falling through the air, they started running across invisible footholds in the air.

"Amazing..." Aria mumbled as she watched them descend. Their current altitude was nearly three hundred meters. Even if she enhanced her physical body with her sword, she'd die falling from this height.

Seeing Aria left behind, Orphia smiled wryly.

"Ha ha. I'll lower us so that you can get off the normal way."

Erica was running at the front of the pack when Gouki and Kayoko descended before her. "Halt."

"Oh? Who might you people be?" Erica looked at the middle-aged couple with black hair curiously. She must have found them similar to the Japanese people on Earth. But encountering them here didn't change anything.

"Well, whatever. What do you want?" She didn't care.

"It doesn't matter who we are. On behalf of our master, we have come to stop the person in control of that monster," Gouki declared, drawing his prized sword Kamaitachi.

Kayoko similarly drew her kodachi. "We cannot let you pass us."

"Why, you're like a samurai and a ninja! How fascinating."

In contrast to Erica's words, her tone and smile were completely devoid of emotion.

"I see… You have such an empty look in your eyes," Gouki observed.

"The eyes of a troubled woman," Kayoko agreed.

"Saint Erica!"

Just then, Aria arrived belatedly, dropping from the sky. Ariel passed over at an altitude of ten meters, flying away once again.

"Oh, you're here as well." It seemed Erica still remembered Aria.

"I heard you survived being stabbed in the heart. So I came to finish you off." Aria also drew her sword and readied herself.

425

"Heh heh. Are you capable of such a thing?" Erica smirked boldly, readying her staff.

"Unfortunately for you, I have no intention of facing you alone."

"Oh? Three against one sounds terribly cowardly."

"Can you blame us? This is a battlefield. The enemy that invaded without warning is right before us."

As a seasoned veteran, Gouki brushed off Erica's taunting remark easily. Her ability gave her the strength of an army. There was nothing wrong with teaming up in a group of three to defeat her—or rather, kill her. Merciless as it may have been, that was their goal.

"You have plenty of comrades behind you, anyway," Kayoko said, looking at the crowd of people that had followed Erica out of the city.

"I won't let anyone approach, so fight to your heart's content!" Orphia called from Ariel's back, firing a warning arrow with her bow. The ray of light that shot down split into countless branches, raining before the crowd.

"Whoa!"

"Eek…!"

The crowd screeched to a halt.

A militia… No, they're not even wielding proper weapons.

In short, Erica had brought unarmed humans onto the battlefield. Gouki was shocked at their appearances up close.

"You cannot be sane… You brought the residents out without even arming them. What were you thinking?"

Erica cocked her head curiously. "I don't remember bringing them anywhere, though? They stepped onto the battlefield of their own will."

"This is a result of you deceiving them with your words," Aria stated as if it was obvious.

"No, my words had no effect on them. If they did, they wouldn't have come after me."

"What are you saying…?"

"I told them about how humans are foolish and evil. It seems they won't understand even if it kills them." Erica sneered scornfully.

"Hmm. Either way, everything will be resolved if we defeat you. Both the troops behind you and that monster will lose the will to fight," Gouki pointed out. The crowd was clearly losing their will to fight already, seeing the barrage of arrows Orphia had released.

"Yes, that is true."

"In which case, we should get started." Gouki took half a step forward, ready to face Erica. "Hmph."

Just then, a knife came flying from within the crowd. It was aimed precisely for Gouki's heart, shooting at a terrifyingly fast speed. But Gouki merely flicked his sword, knocking the knife away.

"Lady Saint…"

One man rushed forward from the crowd. He was surprisingly fast to approach Erica, immediately bowing his head in a fluid motion.

"Oh? You are…"

"My name is Gilbert."

"Yes, I remember," Erica said, looking at his face. "The one who had a change of heart."

"You are too kind, Great Saint. Earlier, you said that one should not fight out of hatred. That only the gods are allowed to bestow punishment upon others. In which case, I wish to fight to protect you. I know I originally came here to kill you, but will you allow me to fight to protect you?" Gilbert drooped his head as though he was completely enraptured by her.

"Isn't that one of the men that infiltrated the city with Sir Haruto?"

427

"He seems to have switched sides." Gouki and Kayoko looked on in annoyance.

"I am grateful for your devotion, Gilbert. Please give me your assistance."

"I am but a lowly human only capable of killing others. I have committed many sins throughout my life. But that is why I may be of use in this situation. Allow me to join you on your journey."

"In that case, please take care of one of these three. I will take on the remaining two."

"As you wish." And so, Gilbert joined Erica's battle.

At that, Kayoko turned to Gouki and Aria. "I will handle that man... You two focus on the Saint."

"Heh heh. Now it's three against two." Erica smiled fearlessly.

"Your destiny to die here will not change," Aria said coldly.

"Will you people be able to kill me? I shall look forward to it. Truly," Erica replied, almost as though she desired that. "Let's begin."

She then raised her staff and slammed it into the ground. Countless spears of dirt immediately attacked Gouki, Kayoko, and Aria.

"..."

The three reacted instinctively, leaping back. The spears became obstacles hiding Erica and Gilbert from view.

However, Aria and Kayoko immediately dashed around the spears from each side. This left Gouki behind the dirt spears.

These two are fast. They must have enchanted swords.

As a fellow enchanted sword wielder, Gilbert immediately sensed that they were formidable opponents.

"So you're the one facing me," he said to the approaching Kayoko, taking out a throwing knife hidden under his coat and flinging it with his right hand. He then took out another knife with his left hand and closed the distance with Kayoko.

Kayoko swung the kodachi in her left hand, deflecting the throwing knife. Her speed didn't falter at all as she drew closer to Gilbert.

Once the two were within reach of each other, their left hands swung at a speed faster than the eye could see. The screech of metal clashing with metal echoed.

"Splendid," Gilbert grinned. A knife had suddenly appeared in the right hand he had held lowered. The knife was soon released, flying towards Kayoko's throat.

"..." Kayoko swung the kodachi in her right hand, knocking away the flying knife without even looking.

Gilbert backed away, eyes widening faintly. "I'm shocked. Most of my opponents die from that right away."

"I learned from your match with Sir Haruto that you excel in targeting people's blind spots. And I know how to deal with the devious techniques of assassins."

"Oh? You don't seem to be from the same profession. Were you a bodyguard of someone important?"

As Gilbert guessed, Kayoko was once the royal guard of Rio's mother, Ayame. She had learned various assassination techniques and how to counter them in order to protect her charge.

"You're very talkative for an assassin."

"I've already washed my hands of the profession."

"Your hands seem to be contradicting your words."

Another throwing knife had gone flying as they spoke, weaving through the gaps of awareness. Kayoko knocked it away in annoyance.

"Alas. It seems the best way to kill you is from up close."

No sooner had Gilbert said those words than he started running, holding the knife in his left hand ready as he took another throwing knife out with his right hand. At the same time, he glanced over at the Saint fighting Aria beside him.

"Ooh, Lady Saint!" At the shocking scene beside him, Gilbert came to a screeching halt.

A bit earlier, having just evaded the rising spears of dirt, Aria charged in the opposite direction to Kayoko, rushing straight for Erica.

Erica exceeded her in physical strength, but Aria's technical skills balanced the scales. If she faced her in her best condition in a direct battle, it would only be a matter of time before she won. However, there was one way for an amateur at combat to win against a seasoned fighter.

This woman is prepared to take damage in exchange for the chance to counterattack.

And that was to place one's life on the line, attacking with the intent of getting attacked in the process. But it was a much harder method of fighting than it sounded, and not an option for the average person.

There was no way for someone to truly put their life on the line unless they had no fear of being hurt and absolute confidence in their ability to endure any attack. And there was no human that fulfilled such criteria. Yet, Erica probably fulfilled both.

"Heh heh. You seem rather wary of me, even though you're stronger." Erica smirked tauntingly.

"Now that I know you can survive a sword through your heart, it's only natural. But..." If she knew Erica's goal, she could plan how to deal with it. "I don't know how your abnormal vitality works, but you put too much trust in it. You're completely defenseless," Aria stated. She then rushed right at Erica.

"Oh?" Surprised by the choice to charge forward after being so wary of a counterattack, Erica lifted her staff curiously.

"...Oh?" Erica looked around. At some point, Gouki had rounded behind her, where he stood now, posing at the end of swinging his sword. With allies on their side, there was no need for them to take a one-on-one approach with fear of counterattacks. They could just send someone to make a surprise attack from behind.

"It's just as the young ones described. You're truly an amateur at combat, completely open to attack. It doesn't leave a good taste in the mouth, but..."

With a whoosh of wind, Gouki flicked the blood off his sword. Erica's head rolled across the ground.

"You said it was two against one yourself, no?" Aria said, stabbing her sword through Erica's heart from the front. If their opponent didn't die to a sword in the heart, they'd just behead her. Then stab her through the heart on top of that.

"Ooh, Lady Saint!" Just as Aria withdrew her sword, Gilbert witnessed the terrible sight and yelled. He tried to run over to Erica in a hurry.

"Your opponent is over here," Kayoko intervened, stopping him.

"Ngh! Move it, you hag!" Gilbert yelled in fury.

In contrast, all the warmth drained from Kayoko's expression.

"..."

"It's fine, Gilbert." Erica's detached head disappeared. In the next moment, it was reattached to the body it should have been separated from. Erica had called out to Gilbert with a hole in her chest.

"Wha?!" Aria immediately backed away from Erica.

"How mysterious…" Gouki also leaped back.

Was she really human? They stared at Erica in wonder.

"That wasn't enough to kill her…?" Aria muttered in shock.

"Strange, isn't it? I've tried it myself, you know. If you cut off my head and take it away from my body, one will disappear and reattach itself to the other. In the beginning, I lost consciousness when I died, but even that stopped happening." Erica cracked her neck as though to test the strength of the reattachment.

"Are you truly a human?"

"I wonder that myself." Erica casually agreed with Aria's sentiments.

"Ooh, Lady Saint! Great Hero! You truly are an agent of the gods! I am convinced of that even more now!" Gilbert yelled, rejoicing Erica's revival.

"That's right—I am an agent of the gods. That is why it is my duty to present the answer only the gods know to everyone. Until my duty is over, I cannot die."

Whether she truly thought that or was just playing into her role of the Saint, Erica made her declaration dramatically.

"That's impossible!"

"Hmm…"

At the realization they were facing an inhuman existence, Aria and Gouki both let out anxious noises.

"Foolish humans. Let me ask you once again. Will you really be the ones to kill me? Are you capable of such a thing?"

"…"

Neither Gouki nor Aria could answer.

"Please kill me. If you can, that is." The magic essence flowing out of Erica's body surged suddenly.

Good heavens... She still had this much magic essence hidden?

Gouki was taken aback by her overwhelming power. But for the sake of his master, he couldn't back down. He had absolutely no intention of losing.

Thus, the battle with the Saint resumed.

Kayoko and Gilbert's battle also resumed.

"Bwa ha ha ha!" Gilbert was cackling louder than he had ever laughed in his life. He was grateful for her two resurrections and the fact he had met her sublime existence today.

Kayoko swung her two kodachi with a disgusted look on her face. Facing her, Gilbert had a long-handled knife in his left hand and a short-handled throwing knife in his right. The strength of their physical body enhancements appeared to be equal as they exchanged blows with each other.

In the midst of one such exchange, Gilbert threw another throwing knife with his right hand relaxed at his side. He flung it with the snap of his wrist, resulting in nearly no warning motion.

It would have been impossible to react without watching his hands. But he had used the same type of attack on Kayoko already.

"..." Kayoko deflected the knife with a bored look.

"Heh."

Gilbert smirked as he moved to release the knife in his left hand at Kayoko's body. He twisted his arm like a snake to alter the trajectory of the knife, but Kayoko used the kodachi in her right hand to knock the edge of the knife before it could change course.

"Impressive, but…!" Gilbert stumbled backwards, left hand recoiling from the deflection. His right hand had lost the throwing knife, so he was full of openings in his current posture. At least that's what it looked like.

Kayoko stepped forward to pursue him. Gilbert used the momentum of the recoil to swing his left knife and stop her. But the kodachi in Kayoko's right hand parried the knife, allowing her to strike the kodachi in her left hand at his unguarded solar plexus.

"Guh!" Gilbert grunted as he thrust his right shoulder forward to evade the strike. This inevitably caused his left hand with the knife to pull backwards. The kodachi in Kayoko's left hand swiped through empty space.

"Hmm…?" Gilbert's mouth was twisted in a smirk. But when he heard the screech of clashing metal before him, his eyes widened. He immediately looked down.

"Your techniques are truly devious."

The kodachi in Kayoko's right hand was held up against something Gilbert held in his right hand. "Something," because the object couldn't be seen. The invisible object was actually Gilbert's knife-shaped enchanted sword.

"Could you see it…?" Gilbert asked in astonishment.

"No. The invisible weapon was beyond my expectations. But I assumed you were doing something with your right hand, so I was able to deal with it. I said I was experienced in dealing with the tricks of assassins, did I not?"

Kayoko made it sound simple, but it was an invisible knife—the perfect weapon to catch someone unawares. If anything, *she* was the strange one for blocking it so naturally.

"Ha ha, how formidable. It's the first time someone's ever blocked this enchanted sword's attack, you know. And for me to be beaten at my own game..."

Using the kodachi in her left hand, Kayoko pierced Gilbert through the heart. She then withdrew her sword and quickly backed away.

"Oh, Lady Saint..." Gilbert called for Erica, then collapsed.

"Finally, some quiet." Kayoko sighed in annoyance and turned her gaze towards Gouki's fight.

Erica caught sight of the fatally wounded Gilbert. She paused midbattle, ignoring Gouki and Aria to run over to him.

"Thank you for your sacrifice, Gilbert," she said to him.

"I am...unworthy...of such words..." Gilbert closed his eyes with a satisfied expression.

"May you rest in peace." Erica stabbed the end of her staff into the ground in a silent prayer. Several seconds later, the ground folded up to swallow Gilbert's body.

"You may not die to a sword through the heart, but aren't you ignoring us a little too much?" Kayoko's voice said from behind her.

The next moment, a blade of water stabbed through Erica's heart from behind. The one who had attacked her was Kayoko. The kodachi in her hand had extended through spirit arts, creating a blade to pierce Erica's chest.

"You won't even allow me to give a proper burial... How saddening," Erica sighed sadly, her heart still in a skewered state. Blood poured out of the wound, staining the ground where Gilbert was buried.

"I heard you ordered the beast of the land to attack your own comrades. And now you're burying allies in the middle of battle? That's quite the dramatic change of heart," Kayoko said, glaring at her back coldly.

"He had only just met me, yet he believed in my words faithfully. I believed he was worthy of my compassion. However…"

Erica had been standing with the end of her staff stabbed into the ground, but the next moment, dirt spears shot up from the ground at Gouki, Aria, and Kayoko's feet.

"Huh?!" They all jumped aside at once.

"I won't have any compassion for you." Erica stared at them with vacant eyes.

"Goodness. Fighting an opponent that doesn't die from stabs and cuts is rather unpleasant, isn't it?" The battle seemed to have left a bitter aftertaste in Gouki's mouth, as he frowned in shame.

"But we have no choice but to keep killing her. As many times as it takes, no matter how many times she revives," Kayoko stated flatly.

"Fortunately, this woman is an amateur at combat. We have all the opportunities we need," Aria agreed, readying her sword.

"Heh heh heh. Go on, come at me then." Erica readied her staff leisurely.

"Hmph." Gouki disappeared. He approached her with the movement spell Rio used—coined Shukuchi by Satsuki—and swung his sword as he passed.

"Oh my…" Erica's body was split into two. But the two pieces were being drawn together as though time was rewinding. In order to prevent that, Kayoko landed a knee kick to Erica's upper body, sending her flying.

"*Magicae Displodo.*" Aria pursued Erica's upper body while chanting a spell. A magic circle appeared before the left hand she had extended. In the time it took the spell to activate, Aria leaped, catching up to Erica's body, and slammed the essence cannon into her from point-blank range.

"Haaah!"

The thick beam of light swallowed Erica's body. However...

"So you can withstand an intermediate-class attack spell from up close too," Aria muttered, furrowing her brow in contempt.

"Are you satisfied now?" Erica's voice called from where her lower half was lying. At some point, she had returned to her unharmed state and got back to her feet.

"Hmph!"

But Gouki and Kayoko immediately struck, piercing her heart and throat respectively.

"This is the most I've ever died in such a short span of time."

As she said those words, Erica swung her staff. Gouki and Kayoko immediately leaped away to avoid the attack. Once Erica finished swinging, Aria cut off her arms, which were holding the staff. Using the momentum of her motion, she turned her blade and slashed Erica's body with a return swing.

"When will you people learn?" Erica muttered tiredly. "No one can stop me." She lifted her staff.

Meanwhile, Rio and Aishia were both under attack.

"RAAAH!"

The beast of the land opened its mouth. Light gathered rapidly, aiming at the spot where Erica and the others were.

"No!" Rio had experienced the attack before, so he knew that the beast of the land was about to fire at everyone where Erica was located. This allowed him—and Aishia—to react rapidly. They locked onto the beast's face, which had stopped to take aim.

"I won't let you!" Rio released a blast of magic essence. Aishia created three orbs of light, firing them at the three snake heads.

"RAH?!"

A total of four explosions occurred at once. For a brief instant, the world turned white as a tremendous noise thundered through the area. The force of the explosion blew up the beast's head, causing pieces of its skull to go flying. But Rio and Aishia knew that this wasn't enough to defeat it—they had already damaged it to this extent countless times.

This much was nothing for the beast of the land's superregenerative abilities. Rio and Aishia braced themselves, watching for the beast's next move carefully. The pieces of its head were rapidly regenerating already.

"Ruuuh…"

It was strangely quiet. Just a short while ago, it had been rampaging violently in a mad rage, but now there was a strange clarity in its eyes.

"What? It suddenly calmed down…" Rio said, confused as he noticed the abnormality.

"Did it fight wildly enough to settle down?"

"No, I don't think that's it…"

That didn't sound possible, but it was true it had calmed.

What to do…?

They could use this chance to attack it, but it would just be a waste of energy if they couldn't defeat it. It didn't seem like the beast was about to make an attack, so they decided to observe it for a little longer.

"Grrr…"

The beast of the land stood still as it stared down at Erica. Then, for some reason, it glanced over at Aishia. Finally, it gazed over at the lake. The beast looked between those three points once more.

"It disappeared...?"

Like a spirit returning to its spirit form, the beast of the land vanished.

Meanwhile, just before the beast of the land disappeared...

"Bwa ha ha! Sir Haruto saved our lives."

Gouki had noticed the beast of the land aiming at them, but Rio and Aishia had stopped it immediately. That realization made him burst into hearty laughter.

"Goodness. If only he had died back then," Erica sighed, looking up at Rio in annoyance.

"Kayoko, have you noticed? The more we kill her, the faster she heals from her wounds," Gouki said to Kayoko, who was standing beside him, without taking his eyes off of Erica.

"Yes, and her movements are getting faster. Things may get a little tricky if she gets any faster than this."

"At this rate, I'm going to run out of magic essence..." mumbled Aria.

"Hmm. How should we deal with this...?"

In their current state, they hadn't succeeded at anything more than buying time. And at this rate, even their ability to do that seemed limited. Gouki hummed in thought, considering their options to break through this situation.

"Heh heh heh. I'm still brimming with power. At this rate, I won't even need the beast of the land to—" Erica cut off midsentence. "Why...? Why has the beast of the land...?"

The beast had disappeared. Erica's eyes widened in surprise, even though she should have been the one in control of it.

"Aaaaaah!"

Suddenly, despite having endured numerous attacks without so much as a flinch until now, Erica suddenly clutched her head and screamed.

⁘ Chapter 10 ⁘
For Whom Is the Crusade

"Aaaaaah!" Erica screamed, clutching her head in distress.

Everyone was taken aback by the sudden change in her.

"Wha?!" Gouki shouted, leaping back.

Spears of dirt rose from the ground, creating a circle protecting Erica. They spread at a tremendous speed, filling a hundred-meter radius around her. Everyone, including Gouki, managed to evade the attack.

"Get on." Orphia descended with Ariel.

"Many thanks!"

Gouki, Kayoko, and Aria all jumped onto Ariel's back. Meanwhile, the crowd that Orphia had been keeping back saw what had happened on the battlefield and scattered back towards the city.

"Are you okay?!"

Rio and Aishia also descended from the sky.

"Yes, all present and accounted for!" Gouki replied stiffly.

"What in the world happened here?" Rio asked, looking down at Erica as she screamed.

"She suddenly started screaming... Even though she was fine when we killed her all those times..." Confused, Gouki followed Rio's gaze down to Erica.

Then, it happened.

Erica's screams came to a sudden stop. She slowly raised the head she had clutched in her hands.

The dirt spears surrounding Erica separated from the ground, shooting up towards them. Each one only had the force of a lower-grade attack spell, but there were enough to cover the whole sky. Controlling this many spears of dirt was no easy task. It was clearly Erica's doing.

Rio and Aishia lowered their altitude to protect Ariel. But it seemed like most of the dirt spears were aimed at Aishia.

"Orphia, get everyone away immediately!"

"Right!" At Rio's order, Orphia immediately rose higher into the sky with Ariel. Meanwhile…

"…" Seeing the trajectory of the spears aimed at her, Aishia deduced that Erica was able to freely control them. She flew to lure the spears away from everyone.

"Aishia!" Rio sent magic essence into his sword, slashing away some of the spears. There were too many to cut down in one swing, so he repeated his slashes again and again.

"I'm going to fight with Aishia! Retreat to the base!" Rio shouted at Orphia, intuitively sensing something was wrong. Orphia did as she was told and flew away with Ariel, leaving Rio and Aishia in the sky alone. Saint Erica was still on the ground. She had been watching the spears fly about without any emotion, until…

"Heh… Heh heh heh…"

"Ha! Bwa ha ha!"

Two laughs overlapped with each other; the voices had both come from Erica. The same person was speaking, yet the two voices were different. One was clearly feminine, while the other was masculine. The feminine voice indisputably belonged to Erica, but the masculine voice was unfamiliar.

What…?! Rio cut down more spears as he watched the ground in disbelief.

"…" Aishia had been preparing her magic essence while luring the dirt spears after herself. She cast several hundred orbs of light around herself, sending them hurtling towards Erica on the ground.

"Hmph." Erica swung her empty-handed arm. All the orbs Aishia had released disappeared.

"Wha…?" Rio was speechless.

"Hah!" Erica immediately leaped at Aishia at a tremendous speed. Her physical abilities were far greater than anything Rio had seen from her up until now. She closed the distance to Aishia instantly.

"I won't let you…!" Rio wedged his body between them.

"Out of my way!" The voice of an annoyed man left Erica's mouth. She swung her fist to shake Rio off. Rio brought down his sword with the intention to sever her arm, but he couldn't cut it.

That can't be…

Rio's sword and Erica's arm clashed midair, but Erica had far more physical strength and was overpowering him easily. Rio used his wind spirit arts to push back with all his might.

"Why do you hinder me, Dragon King?!" Erica yelled in a man's voice, glaring at Rio.

"What are you saying…?!"

"That woman betrayed us both!"

"I said what—"

What was she going on about?! Rio couldn't make any sense of it. He was confused beyond belief.

"We must kill that woman!"

"I won't let you!" Rio raised his voice, desperately protecting Aishia.

"Why?!" Erica raged, her power increasing explosively in a single instant.

"Guh!" Rio finally lost to her strength and was blown backwards. Fortunately, they were in the air. He used his wind spirit arts to immediately decelerate, minimizing the distance he was sent back. He quickly came up beside Aishia once again.

Aishia was clutching her head and groaning in pain. "Urgh…"

"A-Aishia?!" Rio called out in a panic.

"Damn it, I can't use my full power while possessing another. And my memory has been affected by that one…!" Erica muttered hatefully. She also seemed to be experiencing pain, as she was pressing her forehead while glaring at Aishia.

Rio took that chance to send a slash of wind her way.

"Dragon King. Why has your power declined even more than mine? Have you also possessed that creature because of them?"

Erica sent a tremendous amount of magic essence into her arm, catching Rio's sword.

"I have no idea what you're saying," Rio said, sweating profusely. He didn't know what was going on, but Erica was even stronger than the beast of the land right now. That was the only thing he knew.

"Have you lost even more memories than me? No… That woman resides within you? And that woman's soul is… What is the meaning of this?"

Erica looked between Rio and Aishia questioningly.

"I… I…" Aishia seemed to be in terrible pain.

"Does that woman have two souls? No… This woman is an empty shell. The soul I sense over there has a far stronger aura to it."

Erica suddenly looked over at the lake. She then glared at Rio in suspicion. "Dragon King. You haven't betrayed me as well, have you…?"

"I said I have no idea! Who are you?! What happened to Saint Erica?!" Rio yelled.

Just then, Erica yelled in Erica's voice. "Stop! Stop it! Who are you?"

Her voice changed to the man's voice. "Me? I'm the Saint. Saint Erica. No, I'm…!"

Erica started groaning in pain again.

"This is my fight!" she yelled in her own voice. "Don't get in my way!"

There appeared to be someone else within Erica—someone who was a man.

"Fool. You're nothing more than a mere puppet. This is not your war," the man inside Erica said to her.

"No!" she yelled in desperation. "This is my crusade! No one has the right to stop me!"

"You are irrelevant! I... I...!" The man inside Erica appeared to be just as confused. "You are no agent of god! There are no gods in this world—they have all left! The only fools that haven't accepted that are the demigods!"

"That's right, there are no gods in this world! That's why I was trying to become god! I wanted to exact divine punishment!"

"You are an imitation of a god! No, you are a mere puppet!"

Erica and the man's voice argued loudly with each other.

"Damn it... I can't remain as myself for that long, yet... Argh, forget it! It's annoying enough having the Dragon King's interference. In that case..."

The man within Erica seemed to be in a hurry. She glared in the direction of the lake.

"Wha..." She accelerated rapidly, leaving them all behind.

"No! Aishia...!" Rio yelled, about to chase after Erica. But he paused upon seeing Aishia curled up in pain.

"Sorry... Go on ahead..." Aishia groaned.

"All right...!" Rio moved faster as he flew after Erica.

At the lake located five kilometers from the territory capital of Greille, the army led by William Lopes had just returned to the base.

"It's been a few minutes since the beast of the land disappeared..." Francois murmured, gazing in the direction of Greille from aboard the enchanted airship.

Just then, one of the ship's crew came running over. "Your Majesty, almost all personnel have finished boarding."

"I see..."

With the beast of the land gone, there was a possibility the fight was over. However, with no way of knowing the victor, they could only send a scout or wait for Rio or someone else to come back. Francois hesitated over whether he should give the order to depart for some moments.

"Inform me when all boarding is completed," he decided eventually. If the battle was over, someone may still return to them. He wanted to delay his decision until everyone was on board.

"Yes, Your Majesty!"

The crew member who came to make the report quickly departed. Then—

"They've returned! Over there!" Miharu shouted from the deck, pointing at Orphia and Ariel, who was carrying Gouki's group.

They're all safe. That means...

Did they win? He couldn't see Rio and Aishia anywhere. For now, he'd have to hear what happened from Gouki. However, someone suddenly appeared, passing by Ariel.

"What? Saint Erica...?!"

Indeed, it was Erica, flying through the air. Her arrival out of the blue left everyone looking up, lost for words.

"I've found you, accomplice to the traitor. I see you've also possessed a human soul like the Dragon King, though I cannot fathom why..."

The person who looked just like Erica glared down at a girl on the deck. At the end of her gaze was Miharu.

"Huh…?" She looked confused as to why she was being glared at.

"It would be easy to kill you right now…" Erica held a hand out at Miharu. A beam of destructive light extended towards Miharu. She was standing beside Celia and Latifa, who would inevitably be caught in the attack.

In the last moment before the beam hit—

"Haaah!"

Rio appeared before them. He poured all his magic essence into his sword to deflect the destructive beam in another direction.

"Why do you interfere, Dragon King?"

The person inside Erica looked down upon Rio.

"Why do you want to kill them?"

With Miharu, Celia, and Latifa behind him, Rio shot Erica a deathly cold glare.

"If I answer that, I will no longer remain me. That woman over there forced that limitation on me. Fortunately, it seems there are no demons around…"

"Limitation? Demons? What are you…?"

"Either way, there's no time. Which is also that wicked woman's fault." Erica tried to fire another destructive beam at Miharu.

However, using flying spirit arts, Rio stopped the spell right before it reached him. He used a wind-clad slash to drive Erica away from the airship. In fact, he slammed the attack into her—a regular human would have been crushed by the destructive force of his swing, but…

"…"

Erica caught the blow with a cool expression. The impact only knocked her back a little.

In which case…

"I'll distract her! Run away!" Rio yelled, beginning a fierce attack on Erica.

"Take off now!" Francois immediately ordered. But no matter how much they hurried, it would take a few minutes before they could depart.

"Did you think I'd let you run?" Erica said coolly, blocking Rio's slashing attack with both arms. In the next moment, she disappeared from before him, moving rapidly to the side.

She silently held her right hand towards the airship, preparing to fire a destructive burst of energy. She seemed to be intent on aiming at Miharu aboard the ship. But Rio kept up with her speed using wind spirit arts, swinging his sword to interrupt her.

"It seems you have the speed, at least. In that case…"

Erica frowned in annoyance, sweeping her arm to the side powerfully. The next instant, the sword that had accompanied Rio through countless battles…

"Wh—"

…shattered into pieces.

"Hah!" Rio immediately abandoned his bladeless sword handle and closed in on Erica empty-handed. He used his punches and kicks to slam spirit arts into her.

"How irksome."

Erica tried to brush him off, but he saw through her movements and evaded her accordingly.

Rio's attacks were fearsome; he obviously surpassed the realm of being simply a human in combat. Those who were watching their fierce battle from below were overwhelmed by the sight.

However, Erica was unfazed. "You've truly weakened, Dragon King."

"Ugh! Hhaaah!"

With a one-armed shoulder throw, Rio hurled Erica at the ground. He accelerated his own speed to descend with her, stomping down on her abdomen as she fell. A small crater formed at the point of impact, but...

"Hmph."

With her back to the ground, Erica held her hand up and fired a bullet of light at Rio. It was only twenty or so centimeters in length, but it was too fast to evade. On top of that, it contained extremely condensed magic essence.

"Wha?!" Rio barely managed to raise his arms and create a barrier of essence to guard himself. When the bullet made its direct hit against it...

"Guh...!" The fierce knock back sent him flying.

Erica fired several additional bullets after Rio's retreating form, and they all found their mark. The explosion swallowed Rio, blowing him back even farther.

"Haruto!" Several girls screamed at the chain of attacks Rio had taken.

Meanwhile, Erica looked away from Rio and towards the airship with Miharu on board. While she was distracted, Gouki, Kayoko, and Aria all made a move, swinging at her with all their strength. But with her pale, thin limbs, Erica caught all of their attacks. She then brushed them away like flies.

"Wugh..."

Gouki and the others easily went flying.

"..."

Orphia fired a rain of arrows at Erica. Several made a direct hit, but they bounced off of Erica's body as though it were made of rock.

"Alma!"

"Right!"

Sara and Alma placed their hands on the ground and activated a spirit art together. One side used ice while the other used dirt to bury Erica alive.

"Oh no!"

"The art is…!"

The formation was obstructed as though the activation of their art had been denied.

"Infants of the species that inherited our blessings. Did you really think that such child's play could seal the upper high class spirit of earth?" Erica said to them.

"The upper high class spirit of earth…? Are you saying…?"

Sara and the others were dumbfounded.

"…" Erica didn't answer them. Just then, the kingdom's army started attacking as well. But Erica paid them no mind as she held her hand out towards the airship once again. Then, Miharu came running out of the airship.

"Wait! Don't go, Miharu!" Satsuki was following her in a fluster. Erica aimed her hand at Miharu as soon as she was off the ship.

"She's definitely aiming at me! That's why I have to leave the ship! You can't come after me!" Miharu was yelling as she tried to move to somewhere with no one around, but…

"There's no way you can do that!"

Naturally, Satsuki won in physical ability. She caught up to Miharu quickly, holding her spear-shaped Divine Arms ready to protect Miharu.

"…" Erica released a destructive light without thinking twice.

"I won't let you! Ugh…!" Aishia said, cutting in. She stood before Miharu and Satsuki, casting a barrier of magic essence to block the light.

"Ai-chan!"

"Fall back! This man is after you, Miharu!"

Erica was clearly a woman, yet for some reason, Aishia had called her a man. At that moment, the headache seemed to strike once again, as Aishia grimaced in pain.

"Perfect. You can all die together." The destructive light Erica released expanded.

"Ugh…!" The barrier Aishia had created was unable to withstand its strength and began creaking.

"Ai-chan! If you don't have enough magic essence, take mine…!"

Miharu clung to Aishia's back, pouring all the magic essence she had into her. At that, Aishia seemed to realize something; her eyes widened in shock. For a moment, Aishia froze, staring into space as though time had stopped.

"I'll help!" Satsuki put up a barrier of wind to reinforce Aishia's essence barrier.

"Miharu, this man has a grudge against you and me..." Aishia suddenly said, as though she had remembered something.

"A grudge against us...?"

Whatever for? Miharu was bewildered, unable to think of a reason why. As she was thinking that, Aishia's barrier was on the verge of breaking.

"Haaaaaah!" Suddenly, Rio returned from being blown away by the earlier attack. He came up beside Aishia and held out both hands to support the barrier with her.

"Ugh..."

Even then, pushed by the destructive light, Rio and the others inched backwards.

"*Ignis Iecit!*" A ball of fire came flying from the airship. The sorcerers of the kingdom had made an attack. Liselotte and Charlotte were among them. Fireballs struck Erica's body in succession, enveloping her flesh in flames. But those flames were also extinguished instantly.

"Pesky things..." Erica clicked her tongue in slight annoyance. Then, she started walking forward while still releasing her destructive light.

"Gah, it's no good. At this rate..." He wouldn't be able to protect everyone. But he absolutely didn't want that. Rio desperately resisted the force pushing against him, maintaining the barrier.

"..." Aishia watched Rio's profile, her heart feeling like it would burst from her chest.

"Give it up, Dragon King. That is the limit of a human vessel. My vessel is also a human, but her body ceased to be human the moment she became a hero. She is far different from you," Erica said to Rio.

"Huh…?" Satsuki looked perplexed. As a hero, it was a sentence she couldn't overlook. If what Erica just said was true, heroes were no longer humans. Did that mean she wasn't human either?

Just then, a slash of intense light came falling down.

"*Durandal*!" Latifa came rushing over, carrying Celia. She must have been preparing her magic while everyone was fighting. The range had been adjusted a lot compared to the fight with the Hero Killer Draugul, but the strongest attack magic in Celia's arsenal struck Erica directly.

The surprise attack from behind caught Erica with her guard down, successfully dealing more damage than any other attack until now. The half of Erica's body that touched the slash was completely disintegrated. As a result, the attack Erica was using against Rio's essence barrier also vanished.

"To think a human could use transcendent magic… Did that woman teach you?" The disintegrated half of Erica's body rapidly restored itself. She looked away from Miharu to glare at Celia for a brief moment.

"No way…" Celia was dumbfounded. Erica swung her arm at Celia and Latifa in annoyance. However…

"I won't let you!" Rio flew in between them, taking the blow from her arm in their stead. Of course, his physical body was enhanced.

"Gah!" A terrible cracking sound could be heard from the right arm and rib cage that Rio used to guard them.

"Onii-chan!" Latifa screamed in fear.

"I'll be fine! You stay back. No—you should all flee!" Rio shouted, tackling Erica back two meters.

"How annoying… I see. So this is the strength of humans. Each of you may be insignificant alone, but you can support each other by flocking together. I was able to surface today through a stroke of luck, but it seems I'm out of time... Very well. Let's see if you can protect yourselves to the end," Erica said with a sigh, then vanished.

"Did she leave...?" Satsuki murmured. But that wasn't possible; Rio immediately looked at the tsunami of magic essence rising on the other side of the plains.

"Wha...?" He fell speechless. It wasn't an amount of essence that could be handled by a human—or any other living creature in this world, for that matter. Even if someone could hold this much essence in their body, there had to be a reasonable limit for any living creature, and this amount clearly surpassed that. It surpassed it by so much, he didn't know what to do.

"No...!" Rio yelled hoarsely. "She hasn't merely departed! She changed locations so that no one would get in her way! Get the airship away right...!"

Right now, was what he wanted to say, but where would they go?

There was so much magic essence, it was impossible to imagine what would happen. The range of its effect could be unfathomable. There was no way the airship could flee high enough in time.

It was impossible for all of them to run. He could only save a few of them at most. He'd have to make a choice on who to save.

"..."

Rio didn't know what to say.

"Haruto..." Just then, Aishia stood next to Rio.

"Aishia..."

"I'm sorry..." she apologized.

"What for...?"

She suddenly started speaking. "I remembered... Not everything, but the reason why I don't have memories. And what my role is..."

"What are you saying…?" Everything that had happened today was so bewildering.

Aishia continued. "I was an empty shell. A temporary container to store power. That's why I was meant to return that power to you with an explanation."

"Is this the time for that, Aishia?" In this situation that resembled the end of the world.

"But because of you, Haruto, I stopped being an empty shell."

It was almost as if…

"You gave me my name. A precious name, warm like the spring."

Almost as if she was saying goodbye…?

"I was so happy," Aishia said earnestly. "Thank you." She touched Rio on the cheek, thanking him as though it was the end.

"I know I should return this power to you. But…" It was at this moment that Aishia looked a little hesitant.

"But I can't do it," she said, shaking her head.

"Why not…?"

"You already have everyone," Aishia said, looking around at everyone. They were all watching her anxiously.

"The lonely child named Rio grew up into you, Haruto. I cannot steal your precious bonds with everyone."

Aishia stared at everyone's faces closely. She then turned around to face the wave of essence across the plains with a look of determination. "The only person that needs to be forgotten is me. That's why…"

Rio couldn't comprehend what she was saying at all. No, he didn't want to.

"This is our final farewell. I will defeat the Saint—no, that man—myself…" Aishia left. But just before she flew off, she glanced back at Rio.

"Bye-bye, Haruto."

She smiled gently and chuckled cutely. She wasn't her usually emotionally detached self, but a young woman with a vivid range of emotions.

Thus, Aishia left Rio's side.

⸙ Epilogue ⸙
The Transcendent Ones

"No!" Rio yelled desperately, ignoring the pain in his cracked ribs and arm.

"Aishia!"

He called for Aishia frantically; he had a bad feeling about this.

If Aishia left here… He had a feeling something very, very bad would happen.

Horrified, he used his wind spirit arts to accelerate after her.

"You said it yourself!" he yelled. "You said we'd always be together!"

Because he had everyone else? What was she saying?

"Everyone…"

That's right, everyone…

"Everyone includes you, Aishia!" Rio roared.

He reached for Aishia, who was already far ahead.

"So don't go alone!"

As though extending his hand towards the unreachable sky…

"AISHIA!" Rio called her name.

Erica stood far in the distance. Aishia released her power—the power that didn't originally belong to her.

I don't want Haruto to be lonely anymore. That's why I'll…!

She would be his substitute. Aishia was trying to use that power with determination in order to remove the towering threat before them, protecting Rio and Haruto's precious bonds...

"Why are you trying to use the Dragon King's power, you creepy little puppet? Did you deceive him and steal it? Just like how you did to me."

Erica glared at Aishia, enraged. The mountain of magic essence flowing from Erica responded to her fury, swelling in size.

Thus, the power of the two sides increased more and more.

Haruto...?

Aishia whipped around in a panic. She could tell the power she had released was being drawn in towards its original owner—Rio.

"No! Don't come near me!" she screamed in a fluster. She desperately fought against Rio's pulling power, resisting the draw.

"So that's what it is, Dragon King." Erica's eyes were locked on the power flowing between Rio and Aishia. She seemed to comprehend something from that.

"You..." She glared at Rio. "You betrayed me too!"

Her rage had reached its peak. She yielded the last of the rationality she had been maintaining in the little time she had left. Immediately after, a tsunami of dirt rose from the ground, reversing the heavens and earth.

Or so it seemed.

It wasn't a sight that was of this world.

The ground shook—the world shook.

"What...is that...?" The Galarc Kingdom army beside the lake looked up in horror.

The shape was similar to the beast of the land. However, the beast of the land couldn't compare to this. It would have looked tiny in comparison. The creature was enormous in size.

There was no doubt this creature was the cause of the earthquake. It was undeniably a symbol of catastrophe.

"WROOOOOOH!"

With eyes that had lost all rationality, it roared up at the skies. This time, the earth flipped over.

"Wha…?!" Everyone standing on the bank of the lake was frozen in fear.

A volcano erupted, sending debris flying.

No, calling it that wasn't enough. The earth had flipped over, literally. A tsunami of dirt tall enough to swallow everything spread before them, advancing towards the lake.

"So this is the power of a hero…" Galarc King Francois mumbled, as though he had given up on everything. The legends of the heroes were no exaggeration after all. No, the legends seemed trivial in the face of this. At the very least, there were no records of monsters like this in the legends.

"What are the heroes? No, that no longer matters…"

There was no need to question it anymore since they were dead anyway. There was no way for mankind to survive such an enormous natural disaster.

In a dozen or so seconds, Francois and everyone else would be swallowed along with the lake. Even the bravest soldier was no more than a mere human—there was no way for them to defy nature. The soldiers of the Galarc Kingdom army all had expressions of resignation at their imminent deaths. There were some like Duke Gregory among them, who were wailing shamefully, unable to accept that.

"It's not over yet!" Celia yelled.

"That's right!" Latifa yelled too.

"The two of them haven't given up yet!"

"We can't give up either!"

"Let's all put up a barrier together!"

Sara, Alma, and Orphia also yelled frantically, encouraging themselves.

"Use my essence! Take all of it!"

"Everyone gather together, quickly!"

"Let me help out too!"

Miharu, Satsuki, and Liselotte also yelled.

"..." Seeing the girls' faith in Rio and Aishia under such a situation rendered Francois speechless. No matter how strong the magic essence barrier was, there was a limit to the area it could cover. There was no way it could withstand the overwhelming mass of the flying debris. Their greatest hope, Rio, was helpless before Erica earlier. Yet the girls were still optimistic.

"We'll have to entrust this to them, Father. Our fate is in the hands of Sir Haruto and Lady Aishia. If they fall, then we'll graciously fall with them," Charlotte said to Francois, giggling as she looked around at the girls that were working hard. That seemed to strengthen Francois's resolve, as...

"All forces that can create essence barriers, prepare for impact!"

He gave the order to resist death.

The earth flipped over, and the end of the world approached.

"Why did you come, Haruto?" Aishia stood facing Rio, who had arrived belatedly.

"I don't want to lose anyone important to me anymore. That includes you, Aishia. I want to be with everyone."

Perhaps it was greedy of him. Perhaps he sounded like a spoiled child. Even so, he didn't want to lose his most important bonds.

That was why Rio expressed his feelings with determination.

"But you can't stay with everyone anymore, Haruto. You'll lose everyone precious to you. You should have just let me go. I could have become your substitute…"

Now it was too late. Aishia was nothing more than the safe-keeper—she could no longer use the power. Sensing that, Aishia had an extremely flustered and saddened expression on her face. She hung her head in deep regret.

Rio began to speak about himself. "I was always afraid of losing the people important to me… No, I'm still afraid now. That's why I tried to distance myself from them. But…"

He continued.

"You're the one who taught me that was unnecessary. Aishia, you saved me from solitude. That's why…"

He faced himself as a person.

"That's why there's no way I'll leave you alone. I won't let you go alone if I know you're not coming back." Rio grabbed Aishia by the shoulder, staring straight into her face as he made his point.

"Haruto…" Tears flowed from Aishia's eyes.

Rio wiped them away. "It's fine. You said I can't be together with everyone anymore. I don't know what you mean by that, but it's fine. This is my decision." He smiled at Aishia gently.

"No matter what happens, I won't regret anything."

Rio looked away from Aishia, turning his back to the lake where the people precious to him waited. He faced the looming despair approaching them.

The overwhelming mass covered the entire sky. If they continued standing here, they would be swallowed in a matter of seconds.

"That's why...!"

Rio released his power.

He still had no idea what this power was, but for some strange reason, he understood how to use it.

Oddly enough, it felt familiar in his hands.

Why was that?

Make a sword.

Rio imagined the power as a sword.

This was the easiest way for him to use this power right now.

His instinctual understanding told him that.

Aishia came to stand beside him.

"That power is too much for a human body to handle... If you force yourself to use it, your body will fall apart. But that's why I'm here," she said, gently touching Rio's hand that was holding the sword. As soon as she did so, she disappeared as though she had turned into her spirit form. But immediately afterwards...

"..."

Rio gasped, his eyes widening.

He could tell the power was flowing from his body.

No, he could tell his body was being rebuilt.

In order to make the power easier to use, his existence was ascending to something beyond that of a human.

Now it'll be fine. Go on, Haruto, Aishia's voice echoed.

"Haaah!"

Rio slashed his sword horizontally with all his might. A blinding light that could erase everything was released from his blade. "Wha..." Those standing beside the lake were speechless.

The tsunami of dirt that was tall enough to cover the skies had been swallowed by a blinding light.

And when that blinding light eventually faded, the tsunami of dirt had vanished without a trace.

Immediately after, Saint Erica stood where the enormous creature had towered before. There had been nearly a kilometer of distance between them before, but Rio had closed that gap in an instant…

"Ghh…"

…and embedded his sword in Erica's heart.

"Heh… Heh heh…"

Erica was smiling. The voice coming from her mouth wasn't the man's, but the original Erica's.

"I'm sorry. I had no other choice," Rio said to Erica. This time, he would kill her. He was able to actually kill her in his current state.

"You're so kind. There's no need to apologize," Erica mumbled with a vacant look in her eyes. "Even if you didn't deal the final blow, I would have died anyway. I can tell. I used more power than I can handle. The price of that is death. But thanks to you, I can die. I'm so, so happy—I'm overjoyed. I've always, always wanted to die… So thank you for killing me." Erica smiled from the bottom of her heart.

"You…" Rio was at a loss for words.

You never wanted to do this in the first place, did you?

"Humans are extremely foolish and ugly creatures. That's why I don't regret what I've done. I still think those fools should die. But there are kind people out there. Foolishly kind people. You must be one of them. So I have a favor to ask of you, kind one. Whether you listen is up to you," Erica said eloquently, even as the light in her eyes dimmed. She really didn't seem to have long left. Rio realized that.

"What is it?"

"There's a remote village in the nation that I established, fifty kilometers east of the capital. The worst village with the worst people living in it. But deep in the mountains past the village, there's a waterfall, where his grave is… If possible…I'd like to be…"

Erica's consciousness was beginning to fade. Honestly speaking, her explanation was rather insufficient, but…

"I understand. I will search for it." Rio got the gist of it and agreed.

"Thank you. Please apologize to Rikka for me. She was a very good girl…"

"I will."

"Thank you… Goodbye, true hero. I'm sure you know this already, but be very careful of the other heroes…"

With those final words, spoken with satisfaction, the light finally disappeared from Erica's eyes.

Once upon a time, there were fourteen transcendent ones in the world. The one and only god of that world created a handful of absolute rules.

Not even the fourteen transcendent ones could escape those rules.

And now, over a thousand years later, one of those rules had been triggered.

Beside the lake, Miharu, Celia, Latifa, the other girls, and the people of the Galarc Kingdom were all standing, stunned. Not a single person could even begin to comprehend what had just happened.

They had witnessed a cataclysm before their very eyes, and then that cataclysm had vanished completely. Their utter confusion was very much justified.

Then, someone spoke up.

"Wait…" they said in a very panicked voice.

"Who's that fighting over there?"

Afterword

Hello, everyone—this is Yuri Kitayama. Thank you for picking up *Seirei Gensouki: Spirit Chronicles Volume 20 - Her Crusade.*

It was over seven and a half years ago that I first planned the overview of this series, and as of volume 20, I'm finally able to write one of the scenes I thought of at that time. I am blessed as an author to have readers that follow my series with bated breath. The story will get even more exciting from here, so I hope you'll look forward to it.

The anime for this series is also on air right now! Seeing Rio and all the characters move about is so thrilling. The Blu-ray and DVD are also on sale right now, featuring a short story from me and an illustration card from Riv, so please check it out!

Yuri Kitayama
August 2021

Yuri Kitayama
Illustrator • Riv

Seirei Gensouki: Spirit Chronicles

NOVEL
Omnibus 11
On Sale 2024!

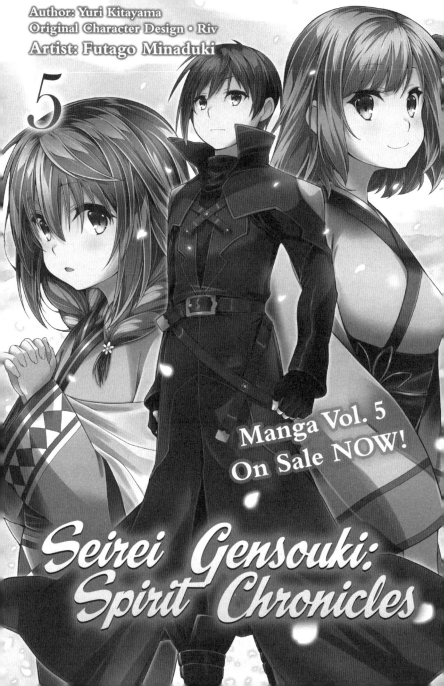

Tamamaru

Illustrator **Kinta**

My Quiet
BLACKSMITH
Life in Another World

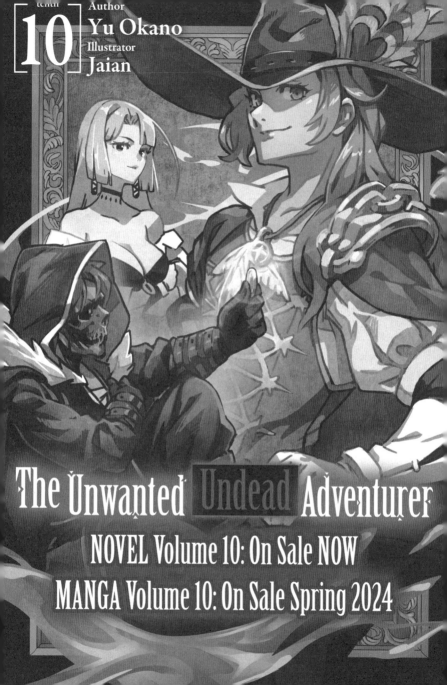

tenth
10
Author
Yu Okano
Illustrator
Jaian

The Unwanted Undead Adventurer

NOVEL Volume 10: On Sale NOW
MANGA Volume 10: On Sale Spring 2024

In Another World With My Smartphone

26

Patora Fuyuhara

illustration・Eiji Usatsuka

VOLUME 26
ON SALE NOW!

BLADE & BASTARD

—Warm ash, Dusky dungeon—

Kumo Kagyu

Illustrations by so-bin

Light Novel
Available Digitally!

Wizardry

HEY///////

▶ **HAVE YOU HEARD OF**
J-Novel Club?

It's the digital publishing company that brings you the latest novels from Japan!

Subscribe today at

▶ ▶ ▶**j-novel.club**◀ ◀ ◀

and read the latest volumes as they're translated, or become a premium member to get a *FREE* ebook every month!

─── Check Out The Latest Volume Of ───

Seirei Gensouki: Spirit Chronicles

Plus Our Other Hit Series Like:

- ▶ In Another World With My Smartphone
- ▶ Rebuild World
- ▶ Infinite Dendrogram
- ▶ Slayers
- ▶ Black Summoner
- ▶ Reincarnated as an Apple: This Forbidden Fruit Is Forever Unblemished!

- ▶ Tearmoon Empire
- ▶ Isekai Tensei: Recruited to Another World
- ▶ By the Grace of the Gods
- ▶ How a Realist Hero Rebuilt the Kingdom
- ▶ The World's Least Interesting Master Swordsman
- ▶ The Conqueror from a Dying Kingdom
- ▶ An Archdemon's Dilemma: How to Love Your Elf Bride

...and many more!

In Another World With My Smartphone, Illustration © Eiji Usatsuka   *Arifureta: From Commonplace to World's Strongest,* Illustration © Takayaki

J-Novel Club Lineup

Latest Ebook Releases Series List